GENERATIONAL USE OF NEW MEDIA

Generational Use of New Media

Edited by

EUGÈNE LOOS
University of Amsterdam, The Netherlands

LESLIE HADDON
London School of Economics and Political Sciences, UK

ENID MANTE-MEIJER
Utrecht University, The Netherlands

ASHGATE

Published by
Ashgate Publishing Limited
Wey Court East
Union Road
Farnham
Surrey, GU9 7PT
England

Ashgate Publishing Company
Suite 420
101 Cherry Street
Burlington
VT 05401-4405
USA

www.ashgate.com

British Library Cataloguing in Publication Data
Generational use of new media.
1. Information technology–Social aspects. 2. Internet and youth. 3. Internet and older people. 4. Technology and older people.
I. Loos, Eugene, 1963– II. Haddon, Leslie.
III. Mante-Meijer, E. A., 1939–
306.4'6–dc23

Library of Congress Cataloging-in-Publication Data
Loos, Eugene, 1963–
Generational use of new media / by Eugene Loos, Leslie Haddon, and Enid Mante-Meijer.
p. cm.
Includes bibliographical references and index.
ISBN 978-1-4094-2657-8 (hardback : alk. paper)—ISBN 978-1-4094-2658-5 (ebook) 1. Information technology—Social aspects. 2. Ability, Influence of age on. 3. Intergenerational relations. I. Haddon, Leslie. II. Mante-Meijer, E. A., 1939– III. Title.
HM851.L664 2012
303.48'33—dc23
2012000446

ISBN 9781409426578 (hbk)
ISBN 9781409426585 (ebk)

MIX
Paper from responsible sources
FSC www.fsc.org FSC® C018575

Printed and bound in Great Britain by the MPG Books Group, UK.

Contents

PART III YOUNGER AND OLDER PEOPLE USING NEW MEDIA: A CONTRASTIVE ANALYSIS

List of Figures

List of Plates

The plates are located between pages 110–111

List of Tables

Notes on Editors and Contributors

Editors

Eugène Loos is currently a Professor of Old and New Media in an Ageing Society in the Department of Communication Science at the University of Amsterdam and Associate Professor at the Utrecht School of Governance, Utrecht University. He is also a member of the research schools ASCoR (Amsterdam School of Communication Research) and the Netherlands Institute of Government (NIG). As a linguist, he has conducted research and written several books, book chapters and journal articles in the field of organisational (intercultural) organisation and the use of new media. Currently his research focuses on the role of new media related to accessible information for older people. He was part of the European network COST 298. He is a reviewer for Ashgate, a member of the Evaluation Board of the European research project "Third Age Online (TAO) Community & Collaboration", associated editor of the international peer-reviewed Observatorio (OBS*) Journal, a quarterly academic publication in the field of Communication Studies (http://obs.obercom.pt) and a member of the Editorial Board of the Journal of Communication and Media Technologies (www.ojcmt.net). His international books include *The Social Dynamics of Information and Communication Technology* (Ashgate 2008, co-edited by Haddon and Mante-Meijer), *Innovating for and by Users* (Office for Official Publications of the European Communities 2008, co-edited by Pierson, Mante-Meijer and Sapio) and *New Media Technologies and User Empowerment* (Peter Lang 2011, co-edited by Pierson and Mante-Meijer). In 2010, Eugène Loos published his inaugural lecture *De oudere: een digitale immigrant in eigen land? Een verkenning naar toegankelijke informatievoorziening* [*Senior citizens: Digital immigrants in their own country? An exploration of information accessibility*] (Boom/Lemma 2010), which questions the gap between "digital immigrants" and "digital natives".
More at http://www.uu.nl/leg/staff/EFLoos/0

Leslie Haddon teaches part-time at the London School of Economics, where he is currently helping to coordinate the EU Kids Online research project. For over two decades he has worked chiefly on the social shaping and consumption of information and communication technologies. This has covered computers, games, telecoms, telework, intelligent homes, cable TV and mobile telephony and internet use. He was part of the European networks COST 248, 269 and 298. Leslie Haddon has published numerous journal publications, book chapters and has authored, co-authored and co-edited several books including *Information and Communication Technologies in Everyday Life: A Concise Introduction and*

Research Guide (Berg 2004), *Everyday Innovators, Researching the Role of Users in Shaping ICTs* (Springer 2005, co-edited by Mante-Meijer, Sapio, Kommonen, Fortunati and Kant), *The Social Dynamics of Information and Communication Technology* (Ashgate 2008, co-edited by Loos and Mante-Meijer), *Kids Online. Opportunities and Risks for Children* (Policy Press 2009, co-edited by Livingstone), *Mobile Communications. An Introduction to New Media* (Berg 2009, co-edited by Green) and *The Contemporary Internet: National and Cross-National Comparative European Studies* (Peter Lang 2011).

Enid Mante-Meijer is currently an emeritus Professor in the Utrecht School of Governance at Utrecht University in the Netherlands. As an (organisational) sociologist, she taught methods and techniques of social research at Leiden University, and was, up till March 2002, senior researcher at the Dutch Telecom research department, KPN Research. She was part of the European network COST 248, 269 and 298. In 1999-2002 she was project leader of a large European research project, sponsored by Eurescom, on information and communication technology and users. Since 2005, her main field of research has been consumers of ICT, both in an individual and institutional context. Enid Mante's most recent international books include *The Social Dynamics of Information and Communication Technology* (Ashgate 2008, co-edited by Haddon and Loos), *Innovating for and by Users* (Office for Official Publications of the European Communities 2008, co-edited by Pierson, Loos and Sapio) and *New Media Technologies and User Empowerment* (Peter Lang 2011, co-edited by Pierson and Loos).

Contributors

Joke Bauwens is Professor Media Sociology at the Department of Media and Communication Studies, Free University of Brussels (Dutch speaking part). Her research activities, situated in the research group Studies on Media, Information and Telecommunication (SMIT), involve three distinct areas: young people's media use, the virtualisation of social and cultural life, and the digital television transition. In particular she focuses on the social and moral dimensions of these developments within an interdisciplinary theoretical framework (e.g. sociology, media-theory, anthropology). In Belgium she coordinated research on teenagers' ICT usage and the risks and opportunities entailed (*Cyberteens, Cyberrisks, Cybertools*, Academia Press 2009). She is also one of the Belgian team members of the EU Kids Online research network, co-ordinated by Sonia Livingstone and Leslie Haddon of the London School of Economics. In this particular context she published on public discourses and policy issues related to young people and the internet.

Gustavo Cardoso is an associate researcher at CIES-IUL and Professor of Media, Technology and Society at IUL – Lisbon University Institute. He also works with the Department of Communications and Performance Studies of the University of

Milan and with the ESCS, School of Communications in Lisbon. His international cooperation in European research networks brought him to work with IN3 (Internet Interdisciplinary Institute) in Barcelona, WIP (the World Internet Project) at USC Annenberg, COST A20 "The Impact of the Internet in Mass Media" and COST 298 "Broadband Society". Between 1996 and 2006 he was adviser on the Information Society and telecommunications policies to the Presidency of the Portuguese Republic and in 2008 he was chosen by the World Economic Forum as a Young Global Leader. He is co-editor, with Manuel Castells, of the book *Network Society: from Knowledge to Policy* (Centre for Transatlantic Relations, 2005) and associate editor at the peer-reviewed journals IJOC at USC Annenberg and IC&S at Routledge and editor of the international peer-reviewed Observatorio (OBS*) Journal. He is a member of the evaluation panels of the European Research Council (ERC) and of the ESF (European Science Foundation). During the last 5 years he has been the Director of OberCom, the media observatory in Lisbon, and a member of the board of LUSA, the Portuguese News Agency.

Dana E. Chisnell is an independent researcher currently working on usable security and research methods for social media usability. Dana has helped thousands of people learn how to make better design decisions by giving them skills to gain knowledge about the people using the designs. She has observed hundreds of study participants to learn about design issues in software, hardware, web sites, online services, games, and ballots, and helped organisations perform usability tests and user research to inform design decisions for products and services. She's the co-author, with Jeff Rubin, of *Handbook of Usability Testing* Second Edition (Wiley 2008).

Alexander van Deursen is an Assistant Professor at the University of Twente in the Netherlands. His dissertation, called *Internet Skills, Vital Assets in an Information Society* (University of Twente) was released in December 2010. His research covers the digital divide, internet skills, and social inequality. He has published the results of his studies in several journals. His first book, co-authored with Jan van Dijk, is soon to be published.

Rita Espanha is a Professor at ISLA-Campus Lisboa (Laureate International Universities) and at ISCTE-IUL (Lisbon University Institute). She is a researcher at CIES-IUL, developing research in the areas as young people and ICTs, e-health and e-democracy. She is member of the Executive Commission and a researcher at OberCom (Media Observatory) and participates in international research networks (WIP – the World Internet Project at USC Annenberg, and COST Action IS0903 (Enhancing the role of medicine in the management of European health systems – implications for control, innovation and user voice). Her main areas of research focus on developing knowledge of ICTs use and social appropriation in the fields of health and media. She is editor of the international peer-reviewed Observatorio (OBS*) Journal.

Jan-Erik Hagberg is an Associate Professor in technology and social change. He is a fellow of The National Institute for the Study of Ageing and Later Life at Linköping University in Sweden. For over two decades he has been doing research on the history of everyday technology, technology education, and old people's use of technology during their life course. He has been the director for the research program on "Ageing in Time and Space: Home, Housing and Technological Landscapes". At present he is leading a research program on ageing in rural areas with a special focus on housing, communications and the importance of place.

David Kurt Herold is a lecturer in Sociology at the Hong Kong Polytechnic University, where he leads a multi-faculty project to establish a virtual campus for the university in the 3D online world Second Life. For the past 15 years, he has worked on the culture and society of the People's Republic of China, with a specialisation in online China. His work has focused on online vigilantism, citizen activism online, virtual encounters between Chinese and non-Chinese, and online community building. As part of his teaching, he has also conducted research into online education, and into the ICT skills of university students, which has led to an interest in wider questions about Human-Computer interactions and the place of ICTs in human societies. He has presented at numerous conferences and published a number of journal articles and book chapters, and has co-edited several special issues in journals and a book on online China.

Tiago Lapa holds an MPhil in Modern Society and Global Transformations from the University of Cambridge and is currently a PhD student of sociology at the Lisbon University Institute (ISCTE-IUL). He was an Assistant Professor at the School of Education and Social Sciences of the Polytechnic Institute of Leiria and is a Research Assistant at the Center for Research and Studies in Sociology (CIES-ISCTE) and at the Portuguese Observatory of Communication. His research interests concern the intersection between the sociology of communication and the sociology of family. For the past 5 years, he has worked on the relationship between media and children and its impact on family life.

Giuseppe Lugano is the ICT Science Officer at the COST Office in Brussels. He manages 24 scientific projects on technology and society, which involve thousands of senior and young researchers from all European countries and beyond. Giuseppe received a Master's degree in computer science from the University of Bologna (Italy) and a PhD in cognitive science from the University of Jyväskylä (Finland). He is author of the book *Comunicazione Mobile* (Ed. Cierre, 2007). His research focuses on the conceptual design of technologies and services empowering digital communities to promote more sustainable futures. He has worked for ICT companies like TeliaSonera and Nokia, collaborated on educational technology projects with several NGOs and published viewpoints on ICT and Society as a freelance journalist for the Helsinki Times. More at http://mobspace.cosix.it

Eva Mayr is a research associate at the Research Center KnowComm at Danube University Krems in Austria. Her research interests focus on the question how to design information and media to support informal learning. Eva Mayr has a PhD in applied cognitive and media psychology from the University of Tübingen in Germany.

Peter Peltonen is a doctoral student in social psychology at the University of Helsinki who works as a researcher in a project studying collaboration in online environments funded by the Network for Higher Education and Innovation Research (HEINE). He has previously worked in the Helsinki Institute for Information Technology (HIIT) studying interaction with ubiquitous technology, such as multi-touch displays, mobile augmented reality and social media, in real-life settings. He has co-authored an article in *Computer and Graphics* in 2011, a book chapter in Willis et al. (eds), *Shared Encounters*, published by Springer in 2010 and in 2007-2009 he has published several full papers in conference proceedings.

Janice (Ginny) Redish is president of Redish & Associates, Inc., a small consultancy based in Bethesda, Maryland, USA. For more than 30 years, Redish has helped clients and colleagues focus on the people for whom they are writing or developing products. She has trained thousands of designers, developers, managers, writers, lawyers, and other subject matter specialists in clear writing and usability. Known as a highly-interactive workshop leader and speaker, she has keynoted conferences in 8 countries. She is co-author of two of the classic texts in usability, as well as many journal articles and book chapters. Her latest book, *Letting Go of the Words – Writing Web Content that Works*, brings together her background as a linguist with her research and practice in plain language and user-centred design. Among her many research projects, she conducted ground-breaking studies of older adults using the web and the value of plain language in ballots, both with her chapter co-author, Dana Chisnell. More at http://www.redish.net

Günther Schreder received his diploma in psychology from the University of Vienna and has been working as a freelance scientist since 2004. His major projects involved research on eye-movement analysis for the Austrian Road Safety Board. He is an associate member of the Research Center KnowComm at Danube University Krems in Austria and is currently working in the fields of information design and human-computer interaction.

Karin Siebenhandl is head of the Research Center KnowComm at Danube University Krems in Austria. Her research interests focus on perspectives on information design (related to traffic applications), gender aspects in IT and usability. She has a PhD in landscape planning and architecture from the University of Natural Resources and Applied Life Sciences, Vienna, Austria.

Michael Smuc studied Psychology at the University of Vienna with an emphasis on methodology, empirical research, and cognitive science. He worked for several years as a traffic psychologist at the Austrian Road Safety Board, managing interdisciplinary projects that addressed driver's interaction with new technologies and telematics. Since 2007, he has been working at the Danube University Krems in Austria as research associate focusing on usability, Human Computer Interaction, and participatory information design.

Introduction

Eugène Loos, Leslie Haddon and Enid Mante-Meijer

Younger and Older Generations Living in a Multimedia Landscape

As inhabitants of a multimedia landscape[1] we are increasingly being confronted with new digital roadways intended to lead us to a range of new possibilities. The well-trodden paths, the traditional routes via the old media, cannot so easily lead us to these new destinations. The question is whether all generations are able to appreciate and find these new routes, use them and use them safely – if they wish to. All citizens, including young and old, should at least be entitled to have access to this new realm of online and multimedia possibilities so that they will be able to participate more fully in societies in which these technologies and facilities are increasingly prevalent and increasingly confronting us in our everyday lives. However, 'entitlement' and 'access' do not in themselves guarantee that users can or choose to engage with them.

In fact, both younger and older generations are only too often regarded as being homogenous entities. It is essential that we recognise the differences and the similarities between younger and older people using new media such as websites, but we also have to pay attention to the various sub-populations, especially within the broader group of senior citizens. Individual differences increase as people age. This is termed 'aged heterogeneity' by Dannefer (1988: 360); see also Chapter 5 by Hagberg, Chapter 6 by Chisnell and Redish, Chapter 7 by Schreder et al. and Chapter 10 by Loos and Mante-Meijer in this volume).

What we require is insight into and research on the role of new media in the lives of both diverse younger people and for various groups of older people (such as males/females, those with higher and lower levels of education and a different degree of internet experience). The volume *Generational Use of New Media* offers insights in this respect by presenting the results of research on the way in which both younger and older generations use new media, for example, when searching for information about products and services that may be beneficial to them – or, indeed, which they sometimes need in order to survive in our information society.

1 Hagberg (2004: 163) argues we all live, literally and metaphorically, in a technological landscape. See also Loos (2010), Chapter 5 by Hagberg and Chapter 10 by Loos and Mante-Meijer in this volume.

Generations: A Multifaceted Notion

Before we elaborate the topic of this volume it is important to explain what we understand by 'generation'.[2] This notion is often used in two different ways, underlying distinct concepts:

1. Generation as *a period in the life course*, for example being an adolescent or being retired.
2. Generation as *a grouping of cohorts*, to indicate all individuals born between specific years, for example the baby boomers, born in time interval after World War II, and the digital generation, who grew up during the years when digital media were introduced.

Sometimes 'generation' refers to both concepts, for example if we discuss the question if the current older generation (for example retired people, born before the end of World War II) can be considered as 'digital immigrants' and the younger generation (adolescents, born these last decades) as 'digital natives'.[3] But if we discuss whether the problem of the older generation not using new media will go away by itself as time passes, the distinction between generation as a *period in the life course* and *a grouping of cohorts* makes sense. In that case generation should not be considered as a grouping of cohorts who will 'die away' in a near future but as a period in the life course (Loos, 2010: 16; Sourbati, 2010: 115). In the course of history there will be always a new old generation that has difficulties of coping with an emerging new technology. De Haan and Adrichem (2010: 105–106) illustrate this general point more specifically by providing a concrete example from the possibilities being made available via mobile technologies:

> This [kind of] information is increasingly coupled to locations, and with the help of the *global positioning system* (GPS) and digital maps we can now determine exactly where we are and to see what our surroundings have to offer. For example, it is possible to see where your husband is, where the nearest cafe is and to find visitors' reviews of that cafe, or where the theatres are, find out what is playing and check the reviews.[4] We are increasingly surrounded by

2 See also Becker (1992a/b, 1993: 837–838), Edmunds and Turner (2002), Buckingham and Willett (2006: 2–4, 11–12) for a historical and sociological discussion of this notion, and Buckingham and Willett (2006: 4–12) and Aroldi (2011) for a discussion on the role of media related to generations.

3 It was Prensky (2001) who coined the terms 'digital natives' (the younger generation who grew up in a digital world and capable of using new media without any problem) and 'digital immigrants' (the older generation who, with much effort can learn to use digital media up to a certain point). See Schulmeister (2008) and Bennett et al. (2010) for a critical review of Prensky's rigid division and his lack of empirical evidence to support this.

4 See also Von Bredow et al. (2010) for more examples.

> information and no longer surf the net but *live in* the web (Van 't Hof, Daemen and Van Est, 2010). (…) It may confidently be expected that, again, the same groups will take the lead and that again, senior citizens, those with a low level of education and the inactive part of the population will move far more slowly towards a life in the web. [translation]

Let us finally have a look at the various labels that have been invented to describe younger and older generations' (non) use of new media in order to appreciate how society perceives online activities by younger and older generations. Table I.1 shows us clearly that there are no specific labels for younger generations not being able to and/or willing to use new media. At first sight this may sound logically, but in Chapter 4 Herold shows us that 'existence of technology does not automatically lead to a proficiency of its users – even if the users grew up with it' (see also part III of this volume). While there are many labels characterising younger generations using new media, we found only one label for older generations' activities on the web (silver surfers[5]) and two labels for the older generational non-users (digital immigrants and non-liners[6]).

Digital Divide or Digital Spectrum?

The research for this volume has been conducted in different countries (EU, Hong Kong and USA) by international experts. Some of them were part of the COST 298 Action.[7] Others are national experts on the use of new media by younger and/or older people. The idea of assembling this volume emerged from discussions and research papers in the strand "The future in young and old hands: Towards an inclusive broadband society" at a COST 298 conference in Copenhagen, 13–15 May 2009.

One key question to be addressed is how we can ensure that digital information about services and products is presented through new media in such a way that this remains accessible to and usable by various age groups. There are various assumptions about the degrees to which younger and older people are more or less willing to use, or are capable of using, new media in order to gain access to the information that can help them to participate in a broadband society. Some researchers argue that there is a widening 'digital divide' between younger users of new media and older non-users (e.g. Prensky, 2001; see also Chapter 8 by

5 See Sourbati (2010: 108–111) for a discourse analysis of this label.

6 See Duimel (2007: 24–57, 104–105) for more information on 'non-liners'.

7 From 2006 to 2010 COST 298 "Participating in the Broadband Society" (http://www.cost298.org/) was a network of European researchers from telecommunication departments, universities and operators together with independent consultants that collaborated in cross-disciplinary groups to analyse social dimensions of people's relationships to information and communication technologies. The editors of this volume were members of this network.

Table I.1 Denominations for younger and older people (not) using new media

Denomination for younger generations using new media	Denomination for younger generations not being able and/ or willing to using new media	Denomination for older generations using new media	Denomination for older generations (not) being able to and/or willing to use new media
Digital natives (Prensky, 2001)		Silver surfers (Ofcom[8])	Digital immigrants (Prensky, 2001)
Cyberkids (Valentine and Holloway, 2002; Holloway and Valentine, 2003)			Non-liners (Duimel, 2007: 24–57, 104–105)
Cyberteens (Bauwens et al., 2009)			
Cyborg babies (Davis-Floyd and Dumit, 1998)			
Digital generation (Papert, 1996)			
e-generation			
Google generation[9]			
Generation Next (Tapscott, 2009)			
Internet generation			
Millennials (Howe and Strauss, 1991, 2000)			
Net generation (Tapscott, 1998)			
Nintendo generation (Green and Bigum, 1993)			
Playstation generation (Blair, 2004)			
Screenagers (Rushkoff, 2006)			
Screen generation (Rivoltella, 2006)			
Thumb generation[10] (Brooke, 2002)			
Web generation (Hartmann, 2003)			

8 'Over the past couple of years Silver Surfer news have featured regularly in Ofcom's [ ] Media Literacy Bulletins published on line at: www.ofcom.org.uk/advice/media_literacy/medlitpub/bulletins (see, for example, issues 7, 9 and 10).' Sourbati (2010: 110)

9 'The University College London (UCL) CIBER group will be conducting a study for the JISC and the British Library to investigate how the Google generation searches for information and the implications for the country's major research collections.' http://www.jisc.ac.uk/whatwedo/programmes/resourcediscovery/googlegen.aspx

10 'Young people who have apparently developed a new dexterity in their thumbs as their use of game consoles and mobile phones.' Buckingham and Willett (2006: 1)

Lugano and Pettonen). Others think that the situation is better characterised by the notion of a 'digital spectrum', with people using new media to varying degrees depending on factors such as age, life events, gender and education (e.g. Lenhart and Horrigan, 2003; see also Chapter 10 by Loos and Mante-Meijer).

How can we guarantee that the digital information presented through new media such as websites is accessible to, usable by and useful for different age groups so they all can continue to have access to the digital information about the services and products that can benefit them in our information society? On the one hand we need insight into which factors are facilitating access to and use of websites. Chapter 6 by Chisnell and Redish, and Chapter 10 by Loos and Mante-Meijer address this point. On the other hand we need to know if older people use new media differently than younger people. This is discussed in Part III of this volume. And, drawing on debates relating to 'digital divide'[11], what is the nature of their various skills in using new media, from more operational ones to formal, information, and strategic searching skills? This question is answered in Chapter 9 by Van Deursen.

Outline of the Three-Part Volume

This volume focuses on how do new media fit into the lives of younger and older generations, or not, and indeed what makes various new media interesting for or attractive to the younger and older generations. The first part of this volume deals with young people using new media. Leslie Haddon, Joke Bauwens and Gustavo Cardoso, Rita Espanha and Tiago Lapa report the results of studies focused on the way children in families use new media. These studies range from parent relations with young children (Haddon), through the influence of peer culture on morality (Bauwens) to parental control and autonomy of children (Cardoso, Espanha and Lapa). David Herold examines the information literacy of students. In the second part Erik-Jan Hagberg, Dana Chisnell and Janice (Ginny) Redish, Günther Schreder, Karin Siebenhandl, Eva Mayr and Michael Smuc provide us with insights into older people's experiences with such media, focussing on barrier free information. In the third part Giuseppe Lugano and Peter Peltonen, Alexander van Deursen, and Eugène Loos and Enid Mante-Meijer contrast the way younger people use new media with the way older people proceed.

In order to get a better understanding of what is really going on *Generational Use of New Media* presents results of literature reviews and empirical studies in this field conducted in the EU, Hong Kong and the USA, that contain theoretical reflections on these societal practices and practical implications for the use of new media by children in family life and the enhancement of an *inclusive society* where older people also can make use of new media. All the literature reviews and empirical

11 See Van Ingen et al. (2007: 14) on the 'digital divide', according to them a term coined in 1995 by two journalists, Jonathan Webber and Amy Harmin of the *LA Times*, after which Al Gore further popularized the term in May 1996.

Table I.2 Chapter overview

Chapter	Author(s)
Introduction	Eugène Loos, Leslie Haddon and Enid Mante-Meijer
Part I Young people using new media	
1. Parental Mediation of Internet Use: Evaluating Family Relationships	Leslie Haddon
2. Teenagers, the Internet and Morality	Joke Bauwens
3. Family Dynamics and Mediation: Children, Autonomy and Control	Gustavo Cardoso, Rita Espanha and Tiago Lapa
4. Digital Natives: Discourses of Exclusion in an Inclusive Society	David Herold
Part II Barrier free information for older people	
5. Being the Oldest Old in a Shifting Technology Landscape	Jan-Erik Hagberg
6. Modelling Older Adults for Website Design	Dana Chisnell and Janice (Ginny) Redish
7. The Ticket Machine Challenge: Social Inclusion by Barrier-free Ticket Vending Machines	Günther Schreder, Karin Siebenhandl, Eva Mayr and Michael Smuc
Part III Younger and older people using new media: a contrastive analysis	
8. Building Intergenerational Bridges between Digital Natives and Digital Immigrants: Attitudes, Motivations and Appreciation for Old and New Media in Finland	Giuseppe Lugano and Peter Peltonen
9. Age and Internet Skills: Rethinking the Obvious	Alexander van Deursen
10. Getting Access to Website Health Information: Does Age Really Matter?	Eugène Loos and Enid Mante-Meijer
Conclusion	Eugène Loos, Leslie Haddon and Enid Mante-Meijer

studies are carried out from a *user perspective*[12], focusing on the *everyday life*[13] of the younger and older generations inhabiting the multimedia landscape.

Finally, Table I.3 presents an overview of the way the literature reviews and empirical studies have been set up.

Table I.3 Overview set up literature reviews and empirical studies

Chapter	Younger/ Older users	Users' geographical background	Medium	Everyday online practices ...
1.	Children	EU	Internet	By children and the role of their parents
2.	Children	Belgium	Internet	By children and the role of their parents
3.	Children	Portugal	Internet, Mobile Phone, Television	By children and the role of their parents
4.	Students	Hong Kong	Twitter, YouTube, Blogs, Social Networking Sites	By students for educational use
5.	Older users	Sweden	New technology	And their significance for the oldest old
6.	Older users	USA	Websites	To find information
7.	Older users	Austria	Ticket machines	To get a transportation ticket
8.	Younger vs older users	Finland	Letters, Postcards, Phone calls, SMS, Email, Instant Messaging, Blogs, Social Networking Sites	Compared with traditional media to send a message
9.	Younger vs older users	The Netherlands	Websites	to find information
10.	Younger vs older users	The Netherlands	Websites	to find information

12 See also COST 298 (http://www.cost298.org/) and Haddon et al. (2005).

13 For a theoretical discussion on the notion of 'everyday life' we refer to Schutz and Luckman (1983), De Certeau et al. (1984), Highmore (2002) and Sheringham (2006). For a discussion of the relevance of this notion for media and technology use we refer to Bakardjieva (2005), Haddon et al. (2005) and Hartman (2008).

References

Aroldi, P. (2011), 'Generational belonging between media audiences and ICT users', in Colombo, F. and Fortunati, L. (eds), Broadband Society and Generational Changes (Frankfurt am Main etc.: Peter Lang).

Bakardjieva (2005), Internet Society: The Internet in Everyday Life (London etc.: Sage).

Bauwens, J., Pauwels, C., Lobet-Maris, C., Poullet, Y. and Walrave, M. (2009), Cyberteens, Cyberrisks, Cybertools: Tieners en ICT, Risico's en Opportuniteiten [Cyberteens, Cyberrisks, Cybertools: Teenagers and ICT, Risks and Opportunities] (Gent: Academia Press).

Becker, H.A. (ed.) (1992a), Dynamics of cohort and generation research: Proceedings of a symposium held on 12, 13 and 14 December 1991 at the University of Utrecht, the Netherlands (Amsterdam: Thesis publishers).

Becker, H.A. (1992b), Generaties en hun kansen (Amsterdam: Meulenhoff).

Bennett, S., Maton, K., and Kervin, L. (2008), 'The 'digital natives' debate: A critical review of the evidence', British Journal of Educational Technology, 39 (5), 775–786.

Blair, A. (2004), 'Playstation generation could be alone for life'. Available at: <http://www.timesplus.co.uk/welcome/index.htm>

Brooke, J. (2002), 'Youth let their thumbs do the talking in Japan', New York Times, April, 30, 2002. Available at: <http://www.nytimes.com/2002/04/30/technology/30THUM.html>.

Buckingham, D. and Willett, R. (2006), Digital Generations. Children, Young People, and New Media (Mahwah, NJ: Lawrence Erlbaum).

Dannefer, D. (1988), 'What's in a name? An account of the neglect of variability in the study of aging', in Birren, J.E. and Bengtson, V.L. (eds), Emergent Theories of Aging (New York: Springer).

Davis-Floyd, R. and Dumit, J. (eds) (1998), Cyborg Babies: From Techno-Sex to Techno-Tots (London, New York: Routledge).

De Certeau, M., Giard, L. and Mayol, P. (1984), The Practice of Everyday Life, Vol. 2 (Minneapolis, MN: University of Minnesota Press).

De Haan, J. and Arichem, L. (2010), 'Meedoen of buitenspel staan in de digitale leefwereld', in Frissen, V. and J. Steenhoven, J. van den (eds), De duurzame informatiesamenleving (Gorredijk: Media Update).

Duimel, M. (ed.) (2007), Verbinding maken: Senioren en internet (The Hague: Sociaal en Cultureel Planbureau).

Edmunds, J. and Turner, B. (2002), Generations, Culture and Society (Buckingham: Open University Press).

Green, B. and Bigum, C. (1993), 'Aliens in the classroom', Australian Journal of Education 37 (2), 119–141.

Haddon, L., Mante, E., Sapio, B. Kommonen, Fortunati, L. and Kant, A. (2005), Everyday Innovators: Researching the Role of Users in Shaping ICTs (Dordrecht: Springer).

Hagberg, J.-E. (2004), 'Old people, new and old artefacts: Technology for later life', in Öberg, B.-M., Närvänen, A.-L., Näsman, E. and Olson, E. (eds), Changing Worlds and the Ageing Subject: Dimensions in the Study of Ageing and Later Life (Aldershot: Ashgate).

Hartman, M. (2003), The Web Generation? The (De)Construction of Users, Morals and Consumption (Brussels: SMIT-VUB, Free University of Brussels).

Hartman, M. (2008), 'Everyday life: Domesticating the invisible', in Pierson, J., Mante-Meijer, E., Loos, E. and Sapio, B. Innovating for and by Users. (Luxembourg: Office for Official Publications of the European Communities).

Highmore, B. (2002), Everyday Life and Cultural Theory: An Introduction (London, New York: Routledge).

Holloway, S. and Valentine, G. (2003), Cyberkids: Children in the Information Age (London: Routledge Falmer).

Howe, N. and Strauss, W. (2000), Millennials Rising: The Next Great Generation (New York: Vintage books).

Ingen, E. van, Haan, J. de and Duimel, M. (2007), Achterstand en afstand: Digitale vaardigheden van lager opgeleiden, ouderen, allochtonen en inactieven (The Hague: Sociaal en Cultureel Planbureau).

Lenhart, A. and Horrigan, J.B. (2003), 'Re-visualizing the digital divide as a digital spectrum', IT & Society, 5, 23–39.

Loos, E.F. (2010), De oudere: een digitale immigrant in eigen land? Een terreinverkenning naar toegankelijke informatievoorziening [Senior citizens: Digital immigrants in their own country? An exploration of accessible information delivery]. [Inaugural lecture] (The Hague: Boom/Lemma).

Papert, S. (1996), The Connected Family: Bridging the Digital Generation Gap (Atlanta, GA: Longstreet).

Prensky, M. (2001), 'Digital natives, digital immigrants', On the Horizon, 9 (5), 1–6.

Rivoltella, P.C. (2006), Screen Generation: Gli adolescenti e le prospettive dell'educazione nell'età dei media digitali (Milan: V&P Università).

Rushkoff, D. (2006), Screenagers: Lessons in Chaos form Digital Kids (Cresskill: Hampton Press).

Schulmeister, R. (2008), Gibt es eine »Net Generation«? Work in Progress. Hamburg, (Universität Hamburg: Zentrum für Hochschul- und Weiterbildung). Available at: <http://www.zhw.uni-hamburg.de/uploads/schulmeister-net-generation_v2.pdf> (accessed 20.07.2011).

Schutz, A. and Luckman, T. (1973), The Structures of the Life-World (Evanston, IL: North-Western University Press).

Sheringham, M. (2006), Everyday Life: Theories and Practices from Surrealism to the Present (New York, Oxford: Oxford University Press).

Sourbati, M. (2010), 'Non-users in the information society: Learning from the older generation', in Gebhardt, J., Greif, H., Raycheva, L., Lobet-Maris, C. and Lasen, A. (eds), Broadband Society and Generational Changes (Frankfurt am Main etc.: Peter Lang).

Tapscott, D. (1998), Growing up Digital: The Rise of the Net Generation (New York: McGraw-Hill).
Tapscott, D. (2009), Grown up Digital: How the Net Generation is changing your World (New York: McGraw-Hill).
Van 't Hof, C. , Daemen, F. and Est, R. van (2010), Check in / check uit. Digitalisering van de openbare ruimte (Rotterdam: NAi Uitgevers).
Valentine, G. and Holloway, S.L. (2002), 'Cyberkids? Exploring children's identities and social networks in on-line and off-line worlds', Annals of the Association of American Geographers, 92 (2), 302-319.
Von Bredow, R., Dworschak, M., Müller, M.U. and Rosenbach, M. et al. (2010), 'Ende der Privatheit', Der Spiegel, 2, 11.01.2010, 58–69.

PART I
YOUNG PEOPLE USING NEW MEDIA

Chapter 1
Parental Mediation of Internet Use: Evaluating Family Relationships

Leslie Haddon

Introduction

One of the major claims regarding changes in contemporary parent-child relationships is that there has been a detraditionalisation of various institutions, including the family (Giddens, 1991; Beck et al., 1996). A review of the related literature on 'new' parent-children relations, points to European discussions of 'negotiated childhood', the shift from authoritarian households, changes in power relations within families, and greater intimacy and openness between parents and children (Williams and Williams, 2005). It is argued that such developments have led to more autonomy being experienced by children, and more democratic interactions within the home (Livingstone, 1997). Some writers have contested these developments, emphasising the social control exercised by parents, and hence the power differences that continue to exist in parent-child relations (Jamieson, 1998). Meanwhile, Vestby (1994) paints a more negative picture on the basis of her empirical studies, arguing that in some ways there has actually been a move away from children having autonomy and responsibility to being more protected, making less decisions and experiencing more restrictions in their daily activities. In this volume Chapter 2 by Bauwens and Chapter 3 by Cardoso et al. present more insights into this field by presenting the results of empirical studies conducted, respectively, in Belgium and Portugal.

Of interest in this chapter, this view of increasingly democratic, sometime intimate, families has been explored and used as a framework in western empirical studies of how parents mediate their children's experience specifically of information and communication technologies (ICTs). For example, this thesis is drawn upon in studies of parents' mediation of children's mobile phone use (Williams and Williams, 2005). Moreover, to illustrate the fact that these developments may not be simply a Western experience, the challenge to the hierarchical family and greater influence of children in domestic negotiations has also been mentioned in some ICT studies in Asia (e.g. Lim, 2005, on China).

Coming from a different mode of analysis, the sociological literature examining the social construction of childhood would suggest that if some degree of detraditionalisation of family life is occurring this in part reflects societal expectations of children, of their independence, of their roles, of what they should know or not know, and these expectations can be different in different countries and at different points in time (e.g. see James and Prout, 1997). Beyond the family, such expectations are embodied in wider public discourses about children and parent-children relationships, as reflected in media representations, expert advice, the practices of institutions and legal frameworks. Indeed, we can see certain broader developments that fit in with less hierarchical families, such as demands for children's rights and the academic call to give children more of a voice in research and to hear children's perspectives (Lobe et al., 2007).[1] At the same time the writings on the complementary social construction of parenthood would draw attention to the changing expectations we have of parents, where one key element of relevance here would be that parents may be influenced by the more general pressures for adults to increase the regulation and risk management of children (Livingstone, 1997).

In addition, and sitting alongside these more general claims about the changing experiences of children and of parent-child relations, there is the literature referring to a longer history of anxieties about children's specific relation to ICTs (Drotner, 1999; Critcher, 2008). For example, concerns about the effects of TV on children (e.g. whether it made them aggressive, how much time it took up in their lives) emerged almost as soon as TV appeared (Spigel, 1992), and there were subsequent concerns about children's experience of videos (specifically, 'video nasties' – Barker, 1984), the addictiveness of video games (Haddon, 1988) and how too much time spent using home computers might adversely effect children's social skills (Turkle, 1984). The point is that whatever generalised changes in parenting may (or may not) be occurring, these specific discourses and related advice to parents may have a bearing upon how parents engage with the children's use of these technologies.

Currently these and other concerns have been translated into even more specific discussions of the risks children face when using the internet, including ones where children themselves are the perpetrators, as in cyberbullying. To codify some of the major concerns into a taxonomy, the first *EU Kids Online* project produced to Table 1.1, indicating the content, contact and conduct risks[2], where children's roles varied for these three different categories.

For the purposes of this chapter the outline of concerns in Table 1.1 provides a sense of what potential 'dangers' parents (and other adults dealing with children) are currently supposed to be sensitive to, and these are in many (certainly European) countries the subject of public awareness campaigns, including advice to parents (e.g. to pay attention to what they children do online). Again, we may

1 In fact, this call to hear children's voices informed the *EU Kids Online II* survey reported later in this chapter.

2 One other key concern that parents have is about the time their children spend online. This is not reflected in the classification in Table 1.1 and although data was collected on 'excessive internet use' in the *EU Kids Online* survey, that material was not used in this chapter.

anticipate some cultural variation in the extent to which different risks have more prominence in different national contexts. For example, an *EU Kids Online* study of press coverage showed the media prominence of the different risks varied across the European countries examined (Haddon and Stald, 2009).

Table 1.1 Concerns about children's online experiences [Adapted from Livingstone and Haddon (2009: 8)]

	Content: child as recipient	**Contact: child as participant**	**Conduct: child as actor**
Commercial	Advertising, spam, sponsorship	Tracking/ harvesting personal info	Gambling, illegal downloads, hacking
Aggressive	Violent/ gruesome/ hateful content	Being bullied, harassed or stalked	Bullying or harassing another
Sexual	Pornographic/ harmful sexual content	Meeting strangers, being groomed	Creating/ uploading porn material
Values	Racist, biased info/ advice (e.g. drugs)	Self-harm, unwelcome persuasion	Providing advice e.g. suicide/ pro-anorexia

To add one final layer of complexity, as also noted by other authors in this volume, there are yet other ongoing developments that can influence parents' very ability to implement certain mediation practices. One, occurring in some countries more than others (Haddon, 2004), is the rise of what has been called 'bedroom culture', where children spend more time in the increasingly media rich private space of their bedroom (Bovill and Livingstone, 2001). For example, in 2010 49% of children in the *EU Kids Online II* European survey presented later in this chapter accessed the internet from their own room (Livingstone et al., 2011). This can have some bearing on parents' ability to supervise what their children do online. Another development is children's evolving use of technologies, for example, when parents are either less familiar with the internet in general or with the specific applications that the children use. Meanwhile, the use of mobile devices to access the internet, like smartphones, can once again make surveillance of children's internet use problematic. In fact, in the *EU Kids Online II* survey 33% of the children accessed the internet from a mobile phone or other handheld device (Livingstone et al., 2011).

The EU Kids Online II Study

EU Kids Online II built on the work of a prior project, *EU Kids Online*, which had mapped and summarised existing European research on children and the internet. The *EU Kids Online II* goal was to conduct a survey in 25 European countries examined the risks faced by children when using the internet.[3] The study was funded by the European Commissions' Safer Internet Programme in order to strengthen the evidence base for policies regarding online safety – policies which include advising children, parents and others, noted above, as well setting up supporting helplines and dealing with the internet industry.

The survey, where questionnaires were administered in people's homes, involved a random stratified sample of 25,142 children aged 9–16 who use the internet, plus one of their parents. These were interviewed during Spring/Summer 2010. The focus was on pornography, cyberbullying, sexting (sending and receiving sexual messages or images) and meeting strangers offline who had first been meet on the internet (what has been popularly called 'stranger danger'). Hence there were questions about how offline experiences compared to online ones (e.g. bullying versus cyberbullying); whether the experiences were negative (or not) and if negative and to what degree; and how children tried to cope or deal with the experience. Examples of contextual data to help understand responses to risk included socio-demographics, psychological profiles of the children, the range of technologies accessed and how they were used, and parental strategies to mediate their children's online experiences.

This chapter mainly makes use of some of the parental mediation data, combined with some of material on risks when this casts further light on parent-child relationships. It is never going to be straightforward to 'test' some of the claims about changes in family life noted above. There is no before and after measurement of change. The literature reviewed itself indicates that multiple processes may be at work, some specific to ICTs, which could influence the way in which parents engage with their children in this field. Yet, the data captured in the above survey can at least be suggestive concerning relationships between parents and children. First, however, it is important to clarify how the different forms of mediation measured in the survey relate to the earlier discussions of what may be happening in families.

Parental Mediation of the Internet

Over the years there have been a number of ways of differentiating and characterising the approaches that parent's use to mediate their children's experiences of ICTs (reviewed in Kirwil et al., 2009, which also shows the balance of evidence about patterns from previous studies). Building upon and developing the work from this review, the *EU Kids Online II* survey used the following distinctions:

- *Active mediation of the child's internet use* – the parent is present, staying nearby, encouraging or sharing or discussing the child's online activities.
- *Active mediation of the child's internet safety* – whether before, during or

3 More information at www.eukidsonline.net

after the child's online activities, the parent guides the child in using the internet safely, also possibly helping or discussing what to do in case of difficulty.

- *Restrictive mediation* – the parent sets rules that restrict the child's use (of particular applications, activities, or of giving out personal information).
- *Monitoring* – the parent checks available electronic records of the child's internet use afterwards.
- *Technical mediation of the child's internet use* – the parent uses software or parental controls to filter or restrict the child's use.

The first task is to reflect on how the different forms of mediation fit in with or are in conflict with the claims about the way families are becoming less authoritarian. The first two forms of mediation in the above list would count as variations on a social approach to mediation, the second focusing specifically on safety issues. Arguably both forms of active mediation would in many ways fit in with the claims about detraditionalised parent-child relationships. They contain a mix of elements, as will be clearer in Table 1.2, but perhaps various forms of talking with the child, showing an interest, engaging with the child, including giving advice, would be the aspects most if keeping with the changes in family life noted earlier, while the being nearby and observing elements are more akin to a social form of monitoring.

Evaluating restrictive mediation can be quite complex, since this can range from simply laying down rules (in what might be seen as a more authoritarian style) to explaining why certain activities need to be avoided because they are potentially problematic (which, in another light, might be considered to be a softer exercise of power). Indeed, the cognitive testing of the survey questionnaire showed that rules can be quite complicated, involving a mix of outright prohibition and allowing permission to do things only under certain circumstances (Haddon and Ponte, 2010).

Monitoring children's internet use, this time via the automatic electronic records kept of that use, might again be difficult to evaluate in relation to claims about the changing family. Such technical monitoring can in principle threaten trust between parents and children, where the importance of trust has been identified as one key principles of intimate relationships such as those in the family (Giddens, 1990; see also Chapter 3 by Cardosa et al. in this volume). Such monitoring can be seen by children to be an invasion of their privacy (and privacy from parents can be very important to children – Pasquier, 2008). But there might be situations where children accept this checking as a sign of parental interest, or else see it as a trade-off to obtain other rights (an example in the case of mobile phones being the right to stay out longer with friends if teenagers check in from time to time to let parents know their location and plans – Williams and Williams, 2005).

Arguably technical interventions in the form of filters and blocking certain activities are the least in keeping with a non-authoritarian approach and can be taken to indicate a lack of trust – it is the equivalent of the imposition of a rule. Yet part of the safety advice given to parents is to be aware of and consider such options and there is a good deal of effort at the policy and company level to develop and make visible these parental controls.

Having set the scene, the review of findings in the next section, examines the actual patterns of mediation by parents, in terms of comparing the five different types of mediation, reflecting on individual strategies within these five where this seems particular relevant to claims about contemporary family life, and commenting on what picture the specific percentages help to paint, in terms of whether some figures should be seen as being high or low.

Of course, any broad claims about parent-children relationships would require some caveats. For example, there might be somewhat different interactions between parents of younger as compared to older children, reflecting the capabilities of the children, their understanding of the social world and their social skills. Hence the review of findings below specifically compares the experience of younger and older children to see how much difference this makes.

In addition, we might also anticipate some variation within and between countries – for example, previous research on parental mediation has shown variation between households of different socio-economic status and national differences even within Europe (Pasquier et al., 1998; Hasebrink et al., 2008). Therefore some attention is paid to national variation in the figures that might be hidden by looking at averages, but also to the degree to which some patterns seem fairly common across these countries.

Parent's Mediation Strategies

The above indicates that were might anticipate a somewhat complex set of parental mediation strategies to emerge as parents grapple with these various considerations.

Table 1.2 Percentages of active mediation of the child's internet use (reported by the child)

The above indicates that were might anticipate a somewhat complex set of parental mediation **Parents sometimes…**	**% of all children**	**% of 9–12 year olds**	**% of 13–16 year olds**
talk to you about what you do on the internet	70	73	66
stay nearby when you use the internet	58	68	48
Encourage you to explore and learn things on the internet on your own	47	51	54
sit with you while you use the internet	44	53	50
do shared activities together with you on the internet	42	50	35

One of the most striking results in Table 1.2[4] is that seven in ten parents (70%) talk to their children, and nearly half encourage them, which is in keeping with both a more negotiated mediation and advice to parents to show an interest in what their children are doing online. Obviously there is also a fair degree of informal observation of what children are doing, a form of social monitoring, given the 58% who stand nearby and 44% who sit with children when they are online.

The breakdown by age immediately underlines the fact that, as anticipated, the age of the child can really make a difference to how parents mediate that child's online experience. Parents actively mediate younger children's use of the internet much more in all the ways outlined above. The gap is smallest for talking and encouraging, suggesting that many parents continue to take an interest in what older children do, but nevertheless check on them far less and work with them far less.

Table 1.3 Percentages of active mediation of the child's internet safety (reported by the child)

Parents sometimes …	% of all children	% of 9–12 year olds	% of 13–16 year olds
Explained why some websites are good or bad	68	72	63
Helped you when something is difficult to do or find on the internet	66	75	58
Suggested ways to use the internet safely	63	68	51
Suggested ways to behave towards other people online	56	58	54
talked to you about what to do if something on the internet bothered you	52	55	50
helped you in the past when something has bothered you on the internet	36	37	34

Table 1.3 shows more detail of what that talking process can involve, here in terms of talking about safety and it includes advice to children about how to evaluate and respond to what they encounter. The fact that roughly two-thirds explain how to evaluate websites (68%), help when children are in difficulties doing or finding something (66%) and give safety advice (63%) is once again in keeping with the

4 As the sample is very large traditional significance testing does not really add any useful information about the accuracy of the findings, and this is true for all subsequent tables. The margin of error for the percentages is in most cases around 1 percentage point or even less.

vision of more supportive parents, and ones who themselves have listened to the safety advice given to parents. That degree of active engagement is also clear when half (56%) had also talked to their children about appropriate behaviour online and talked about how to deal with something if it bothered them (52%). The lower figure for whether parents actually helped them when they were bothered (36%) reflects the fact that in practice many children have not been bothered by what they encountered online – so in many families the situation never arose.

Once again, when we look at age younger children receive more guidance in mediation to help them develop their critical faculties – in evaluating websites, and in managing internet use effectively – as well as being helped when in difficulty. But to put that in perspective, half or more of the older children also receive these various forms of support and guidance, so it is not as if they have been simply left on their own by their parents. This should be kept in mind in the discussion below of how much parents know about the internet compared to (especially older) children and by implication, how much they are actually in a position to help them.

In Table 1.4 showing the case of restrictive mediation (and here the figures cover any form of rules, even conditional ones), the list of options is dominated by rules about children disclosing personal information – in fact, if parents make any rules at all, it includes rules about this issue. The second most common rules, about uploading material (63%) may be high because they can include photos or videos of the children themselves – again, a form of self-disclosure. The fact that downloading is also fairly strongly regulated or restricted (57%), arguably reflects wider discussions about copyright issues and illegal downloads.

Table 1.4 Percentages of parents using restrictive mediation of the child's internet use (reported by the child)

Rules apply about....	% of all children	% of 9–12 year olds	% of 13–16 year olds
giving out personal information to others on the internet	85	93	78
Uploading photos, videos or music to share with others	63	71	46
downloading music or films on the internet	57	77	40
having your own social networking profile	47	70	28
watching video clips on the internet	39	58	22
using instant messaging	38	59	21

When we look in more detail at age, yet again 9–12 year olds experience far more restrictions for each activity in general compared to 13–16 year olds, the one exception being the issue of giving out personal information, where the figure of 78% is still high, even for the older children. But for uploading, downloading, watching video clips, instant messaging and especially having an SNS profile, the overall figures for children are as high as they are mainly because of the restrictions on young children. Some of the figures for the older children are quite low.

Table 1.5 Percentages of parents monitoring the child's internet use (reported by the child)

Parents sometimes check …	% of all children	% of 9–12 year olds	% of 13–16 year olds
Which websites you visited	46	59	36
Your profile on a social network or online community	40	57	33
Which friends or contacts you add to social networking profile	36	52	28
The messages in your email or instant messaging account	25	41	18

It seems that the various electronic monitoring strategies that involve checking children's internet use are less favoured in comparison to positive support, safety guidance or making rules about internet use. Nevertheless, in Table 1.5 just under half (46%) still check which websites children visit and around four in ten check their children's social networking profiles (40%) or the friends who are added to those profiles (36%). A quarter (25%) even check actual messages, which from the child's perspective can be very personal and might well be seen as a greater invasion of their privacy than some of the other interventions. Once again, the overall figure for children hides the fact that there are notable age differences where parents may be trying to respect teenager's privacy especially.

Table 1.6 Percentages of parents using technical mediation of the child's internet use (reported by the child)

Parents make use of …	% of all children	% of 9–12 year olds	% of 13–16 year olds
software to prevent spam/junk mail or viruses	73	74	73
parental controls or other means of blocking or filtering some types of website	28	37	25
parental controls or other means of keeping track of the websites you visit	24	33	20
A service or contract that limits the time you spend on the internet	13	17	11

In Table 1.6, the major form of technical intervention observed in this survey – the three-quarters of parents using spam protection software (73%) – does not relate so much to taxonomy of risks and is unlikely to be an issue of contention with the child. Beyond this, use of technical tools is relatively low, especially in comparison to other parental mediation strategies, and this would count as evidence for the spread of less authoritative parenting. That said, roughly a quarter of parents block or filter websites (28%) and/or track the websites visited by the children (24%), a sign that a significant minority have been influenced by concerns and the promotion of these control tools. In line with the results for the other forms of mediation, there are major age differences (apart from the case of spam and virus software) with parents being more willing to consider technical controls for the younger children.

To finish this section it is important to reflect on potential national differences since it noted earlier that the previous figures are all averages from the whole European sample, and so one question is whether this hides substantial European variation. Given the social construction of parenthood writings point to potential country variation, can we find any clues of this within a European sample, or is Europe relatively homogenous in its parent-children relationships – at least specifically in relation to internet use?

Table 1.7 Country variation in mediation practices (reported by the child)

General forms of parental mediation	% adopting one of more examples of mediation according to the child	Country range according to child (%)
Active mediation of the child's internet use	87	73–97
Active mediation of the child's internet safety	86	70–97
Restrictive mediation	85	54–92
Monitoring	50	26–61
Technical mediation of the child's internet use: Parental controls	28	5–46

In Table 1.7 we see a version of the data that, for most types of approaches to mediation, combine the different individual strategies – e.g. as regards active mediation, did the parents ever talk to the child, stay by them, encourage them, sit with them or engage in shared activities. When comparing our five approaches, active mediation of use and of safety information have the lower ranges, and they would be lower still if not for Turkey being an outlying in both cases (low on both: 73 and 70 respectively). In other words, most countries scores were similar, with only a relatively few percentage points difference. In the case of restrictive mediation, there are three countries with low scores (Lithuania at 54%, Estonia at 73% and Poland at 65%). If not for these countries, the overall range would be narrower, although slightly less so than in the case of the two forms of active mediation. But the range is wider for monitoring and technical mediation, (in the latter case only the one activity of using parental controls is considered). Here the countries are just a little more diverse with more spread about from the average. In other words, one can argue that the averages discussed in previous tables provide a reasonable guide to what is happening across Europe for the two forms of active mediation and to some extent restrictive mediation. But perhaps in part reflecting the complex picture of different national discourses about parental-child relations and about internet safety in particular, we seem to have more variation in the case of monitoring and using parental controls. The fact that we had some countries with low scores noted above also shows where the national variation may lie.

Responses to and Evaluations of Mediation Strategies

The results so far have shown the patterns of parental mediation, and these have been evaluated in large part in terms of what they suggest about the broader nature of parent-child relations. But the survey also collected data not captured in previous research on children's evaluation of and response to mediation. This can provide further clues about how the children see those relations with parents, at least as it pertains to their internet usage.

But first, to provide a wider context, one observation made by several researchers is that parents often know less about the internet than their children, a theme highlighted in characterising parents as 'digital immigrants' compared to children who had grown up with the internet as being 'digital natives' (Prensky, 2001), discussed at length in the introduction, the conclusion, Chapter 4 by Herold, Chapter 8 by Lugano and Peltonen and Chapter 10 by Loos and Mante-Meijer in this volume. In fact one change noted in an earlier review of evidence conducted by *EU Kids Online I* is that this was becoming less the case as more parents were using the internet (Hasebrink et al., 2008). Moreover, the *EU Kids Online II* survey indicates that parents often know more than specifically younger children – or at least 63% of 9–10 year olds claim this. But over and above this, even for parents less skilled in internet use it is still the case that they can, for example, ask about their children's use. This awareness is not only potentially important for their ability to support their children (when faced with things that make them uncomfortable) but the extent of that knowledge can also be indicative of the general relationship they have with their children.

When we check the actual survey findings, Table 1.8 shows that two-thirds of children (68%) think their parents know a lot or quite a bit about the children's internet use, only 7% claiming that their parent knows nothing. This suggests that some of the prevalent forms of mediation we observed earlier, such as talking, but also observing, have led to an understanding of this part of their child's life, more in

Table 1.8 How much parents know about their child's internet use (reported by the child)

Parents know about their child's internet use (reported by the child):	% of all children	% of 9–12 year olds	% of 13–16 year olds
a lot	32	44	22
quite a bit	36	33	39
just a little	24	16	6
nothing	7	6	9

keeping with the view of the more engaged parents.[5] In particular younger children are more likely to think their parents know a lot, which is in line with the finding that parents mediate their experiences more than they do those of older children.

When charting children's multifaceted evaluation of and response to parental mediation of their experience of the internet, one first question asked of the children was whether they thought that overall that mediation had a positive outcome. In fact, in Table 1.9 over two-thirds of children (70%) say it helps a lot or a little. Younger children aged 9–12 years old were even more positive, perhaps reflecting their relative lack of skills; for them, parental mediation may indeed be more helpful. That said, nearly two-thirds (63%) of older children also said that parental mediation helps. Clearly this is moving away from an image of parents as digital immigrants who are in no position to support their child online.

A second dimension of children's evaluation was how constraining the children felt parental mediation is felt to be, since if it is seen to be a major limitation then children might have a more negative evaluation of that intervention. In practice Table 1.9 shows that a majority (56%) do not find mediation burdensome in this respect, and of the remainder, only 11% say it limits their activities a lot. The younger children are somewhat more likely to say it limits them, and that it limits them a lot – which reflects the reality that parents mediate their use more.

Finally, when we look at how the children respond to that parental mediation, only a small proportion of children (7%) in Table 1.9 say they simply ignore it – this is more likely amongst teenagers. While over a quarter (29%) may not always follow their parents advice (or instructions), saying they ignore them a little, perhaps the most striking figure is that nearly two-thirds (64%) say they do not simply ignore that mediation – and that includes 59% of older children. In other words, and in keeping with the fact that they do not find it overly limiting, the

5 In may be partly because of this level of engagement that the majority of parents (85%) are confident about their role, feeling that they can help their child a lot or a fair amount if their child encounters something that bothers them online.

Table 1.9 Evaluation of and response to parental mediation (reported by the child)

Whether parental mediation helps (reported by the child)	% of all children	% of 9–12 year olds	% of 13–16 year olds
Yes, a lot	27	35	20
Yes, a little	43	43	43
No	30	21	38
Whether parental mediation limits the child's activities	% of all children	9–12 year olds	13–16 year olds
Yes, a lot	11	15	8
Yes, a little	33	37	33
No	56	30	62
Whether the child ignores what parents say when they use the internet	% of all children	9–12 year olds	13–16 year olds
Yes, a lot	7	6	8
Yes, a little	29	25	30
No	64	69	62

clear majority pay attention to their parents' interventions, rather than exhibiting outright resistance.

Pulling these different strands together what emerges is a fairly positive evaluation that does not in itself prove that less authoritarian parenting is taking place but does suggest reasonably good relations between parents and children, where mediation is by and large acceptable. Parental mediation can at worst limit the activities of some children, but for most is not too onerous. Many children appear to value that parental engagement, saying it helps, and by and large they are willing to listen to it (at least some of the time). Although there are age differences as has been consistently true across all these results, this applies to many of the older children as well.

Given this overview, the test of the acceptability of this mediation was a final question asking whether the children thought parents should take more or less interest in what they do online. In Table 1.10 most children (72%), and even more so for teenagers, judge that parents have got it about right, since these children think the level of parental interest in their online activities should stay the same. In fact, while 13% would like their parents to do rather less, 15% would even

Table 1.10 Whether the child would like his/her parent(s) to take more or less interest in what they do online (reported by the child)

Whether a child would like his/her parent(s) to take more or less interest in what he/she does online	% of all children	% of 9–12 year olds	% of 13–16 year olds
A lot less	3	3	4
A little less	9	9	9
Stay the same	72	69	75
A little more	10	12	8
A lot more	5	7	4

like their parents to do a little or a lot more, welcoming greater engagement. For once there were limited differences between older and younger children, so to finish of the picture of parent-child relationships in this field, both age groups were overwhelmingly positive about the level of parental engagement.

Risk Areas

While the above outline provides a picture of children's general responses to and evaluations of parental mediation, it is possible to seek an even more nuanced picture by looking more in detail at specific risks investigated, given that these might be potentially 'sensitive' experiences where the child might not want to alert the parent.

As noted earlier, the areas covered in some detail were encounters with pornography, cyberbullying, sexting and contact with strangers. The experience of risk itself is not the main interest of this chapter, but it is worth pointing out that the incidence of these experiences is not so high anyway[6] (Livingstone et al., 2011). Moreover, when asked whether (and if so how much and for how long) they were bothered by these experiences, only small proportions of children had very negative or long lasting experiences.

What Table 1.11 shows is, in cases where the child has had one of the four experiences listed above, whether the parent (a) thinks their child has had the experience, (b) thinks they have not, or (c) does not know. Only in the case of meeting an online contact offline did the majority of parents know about this. The overall message from this set of questions is that although parents may talk a good deal with their children, and many in general know what their children are doing,

6 The lower numbers of children mean that it is not possibly to even consider more detailed cross-national comparison.

Table 1.11 Parents' knowledge of those children who have had various risk experiences (reported by the parents)

Parents knowledge of those children who had various risk experiences (reported by parents)	% of parents saying child has no experience	% of parents saying child has experience	% of parents saying they do not know
Seen online pornography	40	35	26
Been bullied online	56	29	15
Received sext messages	52	21	27
Met an online contact offline	28	61	12

there are some experiences online parents do not know about, more so for some risk areas than others – e.g. only a fifth (20%) knew their child sext messages and three in ten (29%) knew their child had been bullied. In fact, the bottom row indicates that some parents are aware that they simply do not know about whether their child has had these experiences.

Table 1.12 Whether children talk to parents or others about negative experiences (reported by the parents)

Children talking about negative experiences (reported by the parents)	% who talked to someone about it	% who talked to a friend	% who talked to mother or father
Seen online pornography and was bothered	53	33	25
Been bullied online	77	50	40
Received sext messages and was bothered	60	37	29
Met an online contact offline and was bothered	62	35	28

The fact that this lack of parental awareness may be because the children do not want to talk to them about certain aspects of their lives appears to be supported by the evidence in Table 1.12 showing whom the children talked to if they had a negative experience.[7] Arguably it is a good thing that for each experience a majority talked to someone about something that was problematic, more so for bullying (77%) and least so for pornography (53%). But for each of the four

7 It was assumed that being bullied is by its nature always negative.

experiences more children preferred to talk to peers about it and only between a quarter (25% for pornography) and four in ten (40% for bullying) wanted to talk to a parent. This reminds us that whatever the general rapport and understanding between parent and child, and there has been plenty of evidence of that, some things remain relatively private from parents.

Conclusions

Using survey material to reflect upon major claims about developments in family relations is problematic because we have at best a snapshot of what is supposed to have been a process of change over time. Moreover, this is compounded by the fact while the claims about greater negotiation in families are very general, the particular area researched in the survey has associated with it a history of anxieties about children and ICTs, and indeed an ongoing set of social discourses and actions, manifest in advice to parents about what they should be doing. Therefore, one would expect complex results from multiple considerations.

The questions in this survey may not have been developed specifically to measure parent-child relations per se, but when combining different data, measuring a variety of dimensions, it is possible to build up some picture of those family relationships, at least a regards parental mediation of ICTs. Generally relationships appear to be positive, the interventions are regarded as helpful, they are often heeded (at least far more than would be anticipated in some accounts of rebellious teenagers) and appreciated. One could argue that this could all hold true if more authoritarian relationships in families existed, but in keeping with the similar conclusion reached in Chapter 3 by Cardoso et al. in this volume, it seems much more plausible that these sentiments would be expressed in less hierarchical families, experiencing more negotiation. However, the last section reminds us that these good relations do not always translate into transparency in sensitive areas where children would still like to keep some privacy from parents, and prefer support from peers.

References

Barker, M. (1984), The Video Nasties: Freedom and Censorship in the Media (London: Pluto Press).

Beck, U., Giddens, A. and Lash, S. (1996), Reflexive Modernisation: Politics, Tradition and Aesthetics in the Modern Social Order (Cambridge: Polity Press).

Bovill, M. and Livingstone, S. (2001), 'Bedroom culture and the privatization of media use', in Livingstone, S. and Bovill, M. (eds), Children and their Changing Media Environment: A European Comparative Study (Mahwah, NJ: Lawrence Erlbaum).

Critcher, C. (2008), 'Making waves: Historical aspects of public debates about children and the media', in Drotner, K. and Livingstone, S. (eds), The International Handbook of Children, Media and Culture (London etc.: Sage).

Drotner, K. (1999), '"Dangerous media?" Panics discourses and dilemma of modernity', Paedogogica Historica, 23 (4) 593–619.

Giddens, A. (1990), The Consequences of Modernity (Cambridge: Polity Press).

Giddens, A. (1991), Modernity and Self-Identity (Cambridge: Polity Press).

Haddon, L. (2004), Information and Communication Technologies in Everyday Life: A Concise Introduction and Research Guide (Oxford: Berg).

Haddon, L. (1988), 'Electronic and computer games', Screen, 29 (2), 52–73.

Haddon, L. and Ponte, C. (2010), 'A pan-European study on children's online experiences: Contributions from the cognitive testing', presentation at IAMCR Conference, Braga, Portugal, 18–22 July 2010.

Haddon, L. and Stald, G. (2009), 'A comparative analysis of European press coverage of children and the internet', Journal of Children and the Media, 3 (4): 379–93.

Hasebrink, U., Livingstone, S. and Haddon, L. (eds) (2008), Comparing Children's Online Opportunities and Risks across Europe: Cross-national Comparisons for EU Kids Online, a report for the EC Safer Internet Plus Programme.

James, A. and Prout, A. (eds) (1997), Constructing and Reconstructing Childhood: Contemporary Issues in the Sociological Study of Children (London: Falmer Press).

Jamieson, L. (1998), Intimacy, Personal Relationships in Modern Societies (Cambridge: Polity Press).

Kirwil, L., Garmendia, M., Garitaonandia, C. and Martínez, G. (2009), 'Parental mediation', in Livingstone, S., and Haddon, L. (eds), Kids Online: Opportunities and Risks for Children (Bristol: Policy Press).

Lim, S.S. (2005), 'From cultural to information revolution: ICT domestication by middle-class Chinese families', in Berker, T., Hartmann, M., Punie, Y. and Ward, K. (eds), Domestication of Media and Technologies (Maidenhead: Open University Press).

Livingstone, S. (1997), 'Mediated childhoods: A Comparative approach to young people's changing media environment in Europe', European Journal of Communication, 13 (4), 435–56.

Livingstone, S., and Haddon, L. (eds) (2009), Kids Online: Opportunities and Risks for Children (Bristol: Policy Press).

Livingstone S., Haddon, L., Görzig, A. and Ólassson, K. (2011), Risk and Safety on the Internet: The Perspective of Children: Full Findings and Policy Implications from the EU Kids Online Survey of 9–16 Year Olds and their Parents on 25 Countries (London: LSE).

Lobe, B., Livingstone, S. and Haddon, L. (2007), Researching Children's Experiences Online across Countries: Issues and Problems in Methodology (London: LSE).

Pasquier, D. (2008), 'From Parental Control to Peer Pressure: Cultural Transmission and Vonformism', in Drotner, K. and Livingstone, S. (eds), The International Handbook of Children, Media and Culture (London etc.: Sage).
Pasquier, D., Buzzi., C., d'Haeevens, L. and Sjöberg (1998), 'Family lifestyles and media use patterns: An analysis of domestic media among Flemish, French, Italian and Swedish children and teenagers', European Journal of Communication, 13 (4), 503–519.
Prensky, M. (2001), 'Digital natives, digital immigrants', On the Horizon, 9 (5).
Spigel, L. (1992), Make Room for TV: Television and the Family Ideal in Postwar America (Chicago: University of Chicago Press).
Turkle, S. (1984), The Second Self: Computers and the Human Spirit (London: Granada).
Vestby, G. (1994), 'Constructing childhood: Children interacting with technology', in Berg, A. and Aune. M. (eds), Proceedings from COSTA4 workshop Domestic Technology and Everyday Life: Mutual Shaping Processes, 28–30 November 1994, Centre for Technology and Society, Trondheim, Norway: University of Trondheim, 97–118.
Williams, S and Williams, L. (2005), 'Space invaders: The negotiation of teenage Boundaries through the mobile phone', The Sociological Review, 53, 314–331.

Chapter 2
Teenagers, the Internet and Morality

Joke Bauwens

Introduction

The prominent meaning of the internet in teenagers' everyday life has prompted many to conclude that the culture of today's adolescents is increasingly shaped by their online activities and interactions. Because of their intense communicative practices on the internet (e.g. instant messaging, social networking sites, personal web pages) and their receptivity to new online trends, the internet is considered to be a space where young people are increasingly socialised and 'culturalised' by peers (Valentine and Holloway, 2002; Livingstone and Bober, 2005). Although today's parents, especially in high SES families, and teachers are managing reasonably well to keep pace with internet developments (see for example Livingstone et al., 2010: 35), it is often assumed that the role of the traditional pedagogic institutions is challenged and reconfigured by the internet, which transcends the role of adults in mediating young people's access to the lessons of life (Palfrey and Gasser, 2008 – but by contrast see also Chapter 1 by Haddon and Chapter 3 by Cardoso et al.). Vertical processes of adolescent socialisation by adults, i.e. parents and teachers, are, it is claimed, increasingly juxtaposed to and undermined by horizontal or peer-to-peer processes of adolescent socialisation.

This field of tension is not new and has already been discussed and investigated with respect to adolescents' uses of other media (e.g., Arnett, 1995; Thomson and Holland, 2002). However, because of young people's intense and significant use of the internet as a communicative space and sounding board for identity construction, scholars point out a qualitative change in the way young people inherit the norms, skills, habits, customs, values, social roles, symbols and languages that they need for participating in society (James et al., 2009). Hence, it is assumed that we are witnessing a generation which, unlike previous generations of young people, draws upon an internet-mediated culture where they pre-eminently meet and interact with peers, but also with the symbolic resources provided by the cultural industries (Drotner, 2000; Pasquier, 2005: 160; Batat, 2008). Parents and teachers, the traditional agents of primary and secondary adolescent socialisation, are still present but they stay in the background (Pasquier, 2005; De Haan et al., 2006: 16). Others, Drotner (2000: 159) for example, argue that the communicative practices of the multimedia generation resemble the patterns of socialisation that were 'prevalent with most children and young people until the late 19th century, when older siblings, cousins or adults of authority operated as foci of everyday interaction'. Whether these dynamics indicate a new generation conflict, a generation gap, 'cohabitation indifférente' (Pasquier, 2005), 'generational silence' (De Haan et al., 2006: 16) or the coming of 'the adultlike child and the childlike adult' (Meyrowitz, 1984) is not clear. Yet they show that whenever media technologies are used and made sense of in everyday life, they both impinge upon and are the expression of the prevailing social relations and cultures, in this case the way young people relate to adults and vice versa (see a.o. Moores, 1993).

One particular field where the social relations and balance of power between adolescents and adults is negotiated in a lively manner is that of morality. Bringing to mind Friedrich Nietzsche's words that '[W]hatever passes as 'good' or 'bad' has [...] something to do with hierarchy, superiority and inferiority, domination and rule', Bauman's (1994: 26) ideas about the social specificity and contextuality of morality, guides the theoretical approach taken in this chapter. It discusses peer culture as a sphere where teenagers explore and construct a morality of their own, sometimes imagining themselves beyond parents' and teachers' scope, but more often negotiating with the values they get from adults, i.e. parents, but also media discourses. The chapter draws on the Belgian research project TIRO (Teens, ICT, Risks and Opportunities), undertaken between 2006 and 2008, which involved a range of data sources including questionnaires among students at secondary schools and their parents, focus group discussions with teenagers, parents and teachers, individual interviews with adolescents and their parents and observations of young people's online practices. Although ethics and morality were not the main focus, throughout the research it quickly became clear that internet usage is deeply entrenched in social, and hence moral, life. This chapter discusses teenagers' response to adults' moral guidance in dealing with the internet.

Other Times, Other Manners

Building on Bauman's (1994) appraisal of morality without ethics, the approach taken in this chapter is not ethical, but sociological and ethnographical. It is a description of what young people do to each other and to themselves, and how they evaluate their acts. Hence we are involved in what is called 'ethnoethics', which 'tells us what certain people ('ethnos') believe to be right or wrong, without telling us whether these beliefs themselves are right or wrong' (Bauman, 1994: 1). Bauman (1994: 2) stresses that '[M]ost of the people, most of the time (…) can do very well without a code and without official stamps certifying its propriety.' The reason for that is sociological. 'Most of the people – most of us – follow, most of the time, the habitual and the routine; we behave today the way we behaved yesterday and people around us go on behaving the same, too.' (Bauman, 1994: 3)

Morality is inherently social, and hence contingent (Bauman, 1994: 7). 'It builds itself up, as it may dismantle itself and rebuild in a different fashion, in the course of *sociality* – people coming together and taking their leave, joining forces and falling apart, coming to agreement and falling out, patching up and tearing down the bonds and the loyalties and the solidarities that unite them.' (Bauman, 1994: 8)

Bauman's social approach to morality also foretells the ideas expressed in many works on the participatory, grassroots and bottom-up functioning of the internet, as he envisions the coming of an age in which people increasingly fall back on each other to make sense of 'the' truth, of the meaning of life, of what they know and what they want. However, the downside of this upsurge of agency is ambiguity and disorientation. After the age of modernity, in which 'ethical clouds [...] tightly wrapped and obscured the reality of the moral self' (Bauman, 1994: 31) – people are thrown upon themselves 'to face the moral issues point blank, in all their naked truth, as they merge from the life experience of men and women, and confront moral selves in all their irreparable and irredeemable ambivalence' (Bauman, 1994: 31).

Exactly this ambiguity slumbers in the discussions about young people's moral deeds in online surroundings. This not only shows itself in the double-sided perspective often taken in studies of young people's use of the internet (the title of the research project presented in this chapter is but one example), but also in the way – mostly adult – researchers deal with and evaluate adolescent behaviour on the internet. If we are indeed facing a new generation, socialised through and in digital media, and therefore, as James (2009 et al.: xiv) argues, dealing in a qualitatively different way with moral issues related to identity, privacy, ownership and authorship, credibility and participation, what role then should or could parents and other adults, 'coloured' by other forms of media reception (Drotner, 2000: 149), play in this process of change? Should we hold on to 'old' ideas about these issues, and re-educate the young ones? Should we trust in the competences of our children and students, and wait for a new morality, rebuilding itself in peer-to-peer culture?

Adolescents, Morality and the Internet

One of the first authors who drew a connection between, on the one hand, the specificities of the internet and, on the other hand, adolescents' day-to-day efforts to explore and construct their identity and self, was Turkle (1995, 2005). In *Life on the Screen*, building on Erikson's theories about adolescent identity development, she describes the internet in terms of 'a significant social laboratory' (Turkle, 1995: 180) and 'a psychosocial moratorium' (Turkle, 1995: 203). Both notions refer to the openness of the internet to experiments and time outs. Acknowledging the virtual character of the internet, she notes that this communication technology provides a space that is real since it entails experiences and consequences with a real impact on people's feelings, thoughts and life, but it is one that at the same time challenges the meaning of actual existence (Lévy, 1998). Turkle notices an interesting parallel between what Erikson has called an adolescent moratorium and young people's intense engagement within virtual realms. Rather than considering these processes as a withdrawal from or in opposition to 'real' social life, Turkle states that the internet has tacitly become understood as the space where adolescents can try new things and are given permission to have experiences that 'feel removed from the structured surroundings of one's normal life' (Turkle, 1995: 203). Hence, the moratorium, i.e. the necessary stage of adolescent's identity development, now increasingly takes place in online surroundings or virtual communities, which makes them so attractive for most young people (Turkle, 1995: 204).

Moral reasoning is a substantial part of adolescents' identity exploration. The process of questioning values, laws, beliefs, norms, and standards, and engaging in experimentation with possible roles, begins in adolescence (Erikson, 1968). In today's youth culture this process coincides with an intensified use of the internet. Many scholars and policymakers look at this with apprehension. Transgression, risk behaviour and amoral conduct in online settings take the lead in a significant portion of research on young people's usage of the internet. The focus on teenagers' dangerous forms of play seems to be part of a more general concern about young people's moral decline (Fabes et al., 1999; Thomson and Holland, 2002; Padilla-Walker et al., 2008). However, other studies, although smaller in number, furnish evidence that young people also exhibit so-called positive orientations, in terms of pro-social behavioural tendencies and internalisation of pro-social values (Padilla-Walker et al., 2008).

Both psychological and sociological explanations help us understand how young people become competent moral agents (Fabes et al., 1999: 8–9; Thomson and Holland, 2002; Padilla-Walker et al., 2008: 453). First, advances in social cognition enable more sophisticated moral reasoning (e.g., empathy, perspective-taking skills). Pubertal changes foster the growing importance of interpersonal relationships (i.e., increased interest in intimate relationships, romantic and sexual relationships). Second, the changes in the social context (e.g., participation in small scale local cultures, family life, school culture, friendships and consumption practices) encourage the substantial development of a variety of types of pro-social behaviour from adolescence onward. Likewise, studies on young people, morality and media, suggest that the proliferation of media and mediated discourses result in an increasing ethical and/or moral complexity[1] within media and popular culture, which may be accompanied with or contribute to more sophisticated skills in moving and negotiating between competing discourses and identities in the construction of a moral self (Thomson and Holland, 2002: 113; Jenkins, 2008: 26). According to these authors, the media, often blamed for eroding young people's moral values, add to the process of 'negotiating the various boundaries of their

---

1 Although some authors advocate a strict distinction between morality and ethics and hesitate to use the terms as synonyms (see Stevenson, 2002), Bauman (1994: 9) argues that '[E]thics and morality (if we insist on separating them still) grow of the same soil: moral selves of not 'discover' their ethical foundations, but (much like the contemporary work of art which must supply its won interpretative frame and standards by which it is to be judged) build them up while they build up themselves.'

moral landscape (for example between home, school, and peer group) as well as actively engaging with the constitution of moral authority by ceding and denying legitimacy' (Thomson and Holland, 2002: 113).

Where Have all the Adults Gone?

In popular debates about children, teenagers and the internet, it is often assumed that young people's moral agency and reasoning are isolated from or even opposed to adults' views on what is right and wrong. Yet, taking the substantial field of research on adolescents' moral socialisation into consideration, there is ample evidence that the internalisation of values is a process in which both parents and peers play a role. As Brody and Schaffer (1982: 38) argue, parents use disciplinary techniques in an attempt to move from externally controlling their children's moral agency (through discouraging morally unacceptable thoughts, feelings and actions) to the internalisation of a set of moral standards and values that provide a basis for self-controlled behaviour. However, children themselves also determine what disciplinary practices their parents – often inconsistently – will use. Not only children's characters, but also their gender and their accompanying socio-cultural beliefs often play a decisive role in interactions with parents. With regard to parental mediation of their children's internet use, children's age is equally an influential characteristic, as parents interfere less as their children get older (Livingstone and Helsper, 2008).

Furthermore, as Grossbart et al. (2002: 66–67) argue, the parent-child relationship leaves room for 'reverse socialisation' (see also Buckingham, 2006: 3), a term borrowed from Margaret Mead, in which parents learn from their children. In particular in areas in which adolescents are seen as having expertise, for example, in relation to digital media, young people are expected to be resources for parents to learn about unfamiliar and changed circumstances. Notably in families where young people (are perceived to) have more expertise about the internet than parents, it is assumed that children teach their parents more about this communication technology, than the other way round (see also Chapter 3 by Cardoso et al.). Recent evidence suggests that the generation gap and the reversal socialisation that might accompany it, is related to social stratification, since the lower the educational level of the parent, the more children say they know more about the internet than their parents (Paus-Hasebrink et al., forthcoming). However, it remains unclear, and under-researched, whether and how young people's pole position in terms of technical and instrumental competencies is also creating 'a significant reversal in parent-child knowledge hierarchy' (Grossbart et al., 2002: 67) in the field of moral values.

All this suggests that rather than considering socialisation in terms of a linear transmission of values from one side to another, it should be seen as a process in which negotiation and reversal shape the lived experience of moral values. Hence, young people's moral landscape is in considerable measure shaped through parental socialisation, but as children grow up, they come in contact with other people, both peers and adults, who moderate or challenge parental influence in this domain. The likelihood of this so-called additive-influence model (Brody and Schaffer, 1982: 59), is a more useful point of departure and comes much closer to the complexity of young people's moral agency, characterised by cross-pressures (i.e. conflicts between parents and peers' morality), but also by synergies between peer group norms and parents' norms. In the latter case the peer group sometimes acts as a gatekeeper for the norms and practices of 'average' parents, i.e. the average level of support for particular acts, thoughts and feelings among the parents of all peer group members. In that way, adolescents themselves often reproduce parental standards (Brody and Schaffer, 1982: 66–69).

Research Method and Material

In order to reflect on ICTs and young people's moral practices, we draw upon the Belgian research project 'Teens and ICT: Risks and Opportunities' (acronym: TIRO). In this study, together with other colleagues, we examined how Belgian teenagers (aged 12 to 18) made use of the internet and mobile phones, how their usage was related to their social background, and how they experienced these communication technologies in different contexts and in the practices of their everyday life. In this chapter we will only report and discuss findings related to the usage of the internet. The research consisted of datasets that were gathered in collaboration with colleagues from other universities.[2]

First, we report on the data from a representative survey conducted among 1318 teenagers at secondary schools in the Flemish and French-speaking community, and the bilingual metropolitan district of Brussels. In addition, 571 parents (response rate 43%) participated in the study by filling in a questionnaire passed on by their children. Second, we examine the findings fro, an in-depth panel study

2 The TIRO research project ran from February 2006 until December 2008 and was funded by the Belgian Federal Science Policy Office. Four research groups were involved in the project. Joke Bauwens and Caroline Pauwels (IBBT-SMIT, Vrije Universiteit Brussel - Free University of Brussels) coordinated the whole research and conceptualised the qualitative methodology of the study. They equally carried out the qualitative panel research in the Dutch speaking part of Belgium. Claire Lobet-Maris (CITA, Facultés Universitaires Notre-Dame de la Paix de Namur – University of Namur) coordinated the qualitative panel study in the French speaking community of Belgium. Michel Walrave (MIOS, Universiteit Antwerpen – University of Antwerp) developed and directed the quantitative survey among students and parents, as well as the focus groups on risk scenarios and coping strategies. Yves Poullet (CRID, Facultés Universitaires Notre-Dame de la Paix de Namur – University of Namur) supervised the analysis of legislation and made the policy recommendations. All quantitative data as well as the focus group findings presented in this book chapter are drawn from Bauwens et al. (2009). The qualitative findings originate from the author's personal re-reading of the material gathered in the Dutch-speaking panel study.

involving 34 Belgian teenagers (15 boys; 19 girls) who were selected through theoretical sampling. In accordance with ethnographical methods (see a.o. Walsh, 2004), we originally started up a panel study using a variety of techniques. During ten months we had regular contact with the participants, by means of face-to-face in-depth interviews, instant messaging and e-mail, and participant observations in their home environment. Furthermore, we let them report their use of ICTs in a diary and looked at the content that they published online (e.g. on personal webpages). We also took into account the technologically mediated content that was not published online, but nevertheless shared with us (e.g. photos). While the in-depth interviews and the diaries were clearly elicited by the researchers, the conversations through instant messaging and e-mail were more spontaneous and informal. Third, a series of focus groups with students, parents, teachers and heads of school are examined. The discussions aimed at confronting both young people and adults with possible online risks (e.g. privacy risks, identity theft, unwanted exposure to harmful content, spam, corruption of language) and learning from them how they thought about these risks, and how they should cope with them.

All quantitative data as well as the focus group findings presented here are drawn from Bauwens et al. (2009). The panel study among French and Dutch speaking teenagers is also an important source of data in this chapter. We add to all this qualitative findings originating from the author's personal re-reading of the material gathered in the Dutch-speaking panel study. We decided to use the past tense to present our data, since the young people moved to another life stage and most probably developed different patterns of internet usage and moral agency.[3]

Culture of Surveillance in Everyday Life

From young people's answers to the survey questions we learned that the number of adolescents that completely feels footloose and fancy-free in their usage of the internet was significantly smaller than the group that had to deal with either parental control of their online activities, or at least the presence of their mother, father or carer when they were going online. This emerged very clearly when we triangulated the different data sources. For example, only 18.4% of the teenagers had their own personal computer, whereas the rest (81.6%) had to share the computer with other family members. But at the same time, 56% of adolescents reported they used the computer in a separate room, mostly their bedroom of the study.

An overwhelming majority of the young people (93.4%) stated that they were allowed to use the internet when they were alone at home. The majority of parents (80.3%), albeit smaller in number than the young people, answered that they did

3 This is something we learned from a return to the participants of the panel study two years after finishing the study. There it showed that young people looking back on their previous internet habits self-reflexively commented upon them as something in motion (see Bauwens and Vleugels, forthcoming).

not forbid their children to go online when they were alone. However, when asked who was usually at home when they went online (multiple responses question), 44.4% of young people responded that generally an adult (parent or another carer) was present when they went online; 35.3% of the teenagers replied that they were mostly alone. 38.4% reported the presence of a younger sibling, 28.4% the presence of an older one. Hence, although the percentages where in the same region, the most frequent answer indicated the presence of an adult. And in case their parents were at home when they went online, 69.8% told us that they were asked questions by their parents about their activities on the internet. Moreover, 49.6% of the teenagers stated that at least sometimes they surfed on the internet together with their parents. Although this equally means that 50.4% of the children were never accompanied by their parents when they went online, the percentage of active co-use, which is a form of evaluative mediation (Eastin et al., 2006), was rather high, especially considering the specificities of computer and internet use (i.e. individualised use, interactivity – Lister et al., 2003). So, whereas, on the one hand, the quantitative data portrayed a group of young people that made use of the internet in the absence of their parents, teenagers also indicated that their parents were not on the sidelines, but shaping the environment in which they went online and became familiar with the internet.

From the qualitative panel study we learned that parents were susceptible to what Furedi (2001) has termed the culture of 'paranoid parenting', based on a structural feeling of fear, anxiety and insecurity. In our study, the fear of a stranger intruding into their children's personal space often emerged in the interviews. In particular chat rooms were seen as at-risk areas and parents made it clear that they taught their daughters to approach unknown others with due suspicion, rather than with an open mind.[4] Although it transpired from the parents' stories that media coverage stimulated the worrisome imagination about what might go wrong, it equally triggered conversations between parents and their daughters about their own unpleasant internet experiences, and how they thought they had to deal with them. These conversations varied significantly depending on the adolescent's age and parenting culture. In the case of younger girls and of parenting cultures that were more based on power assertion (Brody and Schaffer, 1982), the moral socialisation about virtual communication and contact with unknown others was articulated through top-down, albeit emotional, instructions; among older girls and families that were organised according to a deliberative parenting model, we found evidence of the use of more inductive moral socialisation (Brody and Schaffer, 1982), built on rationality (i.e. reasoning and understanding). All the young people we talked to understood and appreciated their parents' concerns about this widely

4 Our study was conducted before the breakthrough of Facebook. During our research the market of social networking websites and related practices of social communication on the internet, was still dominated by Microsoft's MSN-space and open chat rooms.

discussed online risk. However, they often described their parents' moral agency in this area as being an overreaction to moral panics in the media.

Do's and Don'ts

In the survey both parents and children were asked if they, respectively, imposed and experienced restrictive rules concerning internet use. A set of restrictive mediating techniques, ranging from the use of chat language, through the amount of time that could be spent online to the sites they were permitted to visit online, was presented to the respondents (see Figure 2.1 and Table 2.1). The answers to these questions provided an interesting insight into parents' perspective on and perceptions of what is allowable on the internet, although the ideas about acceptability were not necessarily grounded in moral values. Furthermore, the discrepancy between the parents' and the children's answers sheds light on how the sense of what is permitted and what is not, sometimes strongly diverged.

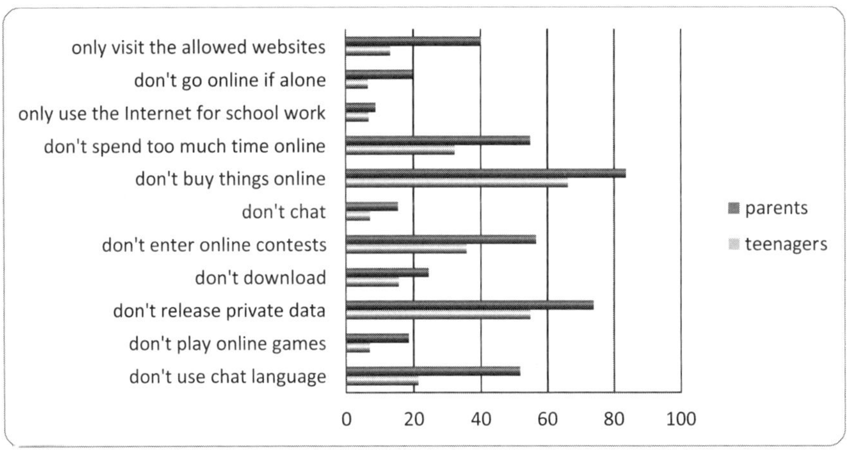

Figure 2.1 Restrictive rules parents impose versus restrictive rules as felt by young people

Obviously, as in other studies (Livingstone and Bober, 2006), parents outnumbered young people in all areas, i.e. they reported more often than teenagers that they applied restrictive mediation techniques, but the discrepancy between parents and children was in some fields much wider than in other. This is something that is instructive for two reasons. First, it showed that in four cases the gap between parents and children exceeded 20%. 51.7% of the parents reported that they prohibited their children from use chat language in non-chat situations, whereas only 21.4% of the teenagers stated they had to deal with this restrictive rule. 40.1% of the parents said they restricted their children's access to websites, whereas only 13.3% of children perceived this to be a disciplinary technique. 54.9% of the parents responded that they restrictively mediated the time spent online, whereas only 32.3% of the children said this was something that their parents imposed. And 56.6% of the parents stated that they forbid their children to enter online contests, whereas 35.8% of the teenagers reported they were not allowed to do this.

The restrictive rule related to the use of chat language showed the widest gap between parents and young people (30.3%). This is an interesting case, as it seems to represent one of the new, or at least distinct, ethical issues that James et al. (2009) is referring to. In the interviews and informal talks we had with the teenagers, it transpired that the use of language is a very important matter in young people's everyday life. Due to the increased and intense use of communication technologies and the prominence of mediated communication in interpersonal relationships (friendship, love life), young people's semantic experiences, the impact of the language and wording that they use, have become central to their day-to-day life. Moreover, mediated communication, through computer and mobile phone, plays a key role in processes of identity construction. As they grow up, they pick and choose words and expressions to tag photos, to communicate with friends and sweethearts, and to present themselves on their profile sites (e.g. Subrahmanyam and Smahel, 2011).

This is one of the domains where the moral reflexivity of young people was very much felt. Although they also told us less fine stories, they equally showed a strong concern about the authenticity, truthfulness and appropriateness of communication. For example, they would admit that they once broke off with their girl- or boyfriend by means of a text or an IM message, but at the same time elaborated their thoughts on the distinction between internet-mediated communication and face-to-face communication in terms of being true to oneself and to the other. So, rather than considering language as a toolbox, which one has to use in a proper grammatical and linguistic way, they saw language as an instrument of their inner self and the often-turbulent feelings that went together with growing up. Hence, parents' (and teachers') rules about the corruption of language passed them by to a considerable extent, as this so-called chat language constituted their identity. In one of the focus groups both teenagers and parents delegated this language problem to schools and teachers in particular. However, the generation gap between young people and adults again clearly manifested itself during the discussion, since teenagers considered that this was only a serious problem in formal educational contexts ('yes, students ought to know how to write correctly'), whereas parents saw it as a general decline of young people's linguistic feelings, including in informal contexts.

Second, although there was a divergence between parents and children as regards all restrictive rules, it nevertheless appeared that the top five do's and don'ts that parents passed on to their children corresponded to the top five that children perceived to be the rules they learnt at home (see Table 2.1). From this point of view, parental socialisation seemed to be influencing what young people are aware of. The restrictive rules that parents imposed the most, and of which children were most conscious, concerned online shopping ('Don't buy things online'), protecting one's privacy ('Don't release private data about yourself and us'), entering online contests, spending time on the internet and using chat language in non-chat situations. So, the internet mediation teenagers that experienced at home was most often framed in terms of financial risks, privacy issues, internet dependency, and the degeneration of language, and they were aware of this, although to a lesser extent than their parents would want them to be.

Interestingly, though, the order of the other six restrictive rules differed slightly, which made us assume that here common practices within the peer culture and related moral values were more influential. What struck us most was young people's relative 'ignorance' of parents' attempts to regulate the exposure and access of their children to online content. For parents this was the sixth most important rule they applied at home; young people put it in seventh place. Quite a significant group of teenagers closed the eyes to parental instructions about which websites one was allowed to visit and which not. Also the rule that they were not allowed to go online if they were alone at home, was most certainly not perceived as a general rule among teenagers. This is an interesting observation as it underlines the schizophrenia of modern risk society. On the one hand, parents prefer to keep their children in the safety of the home; however, they are often still at work or on their way home when their children get back home, so even there they cannot guarantee full surveillance. 19.7% of parents said that they do not want their children to go online when they are alone at home. On the other hand, when children are coming back to their place, they want to extend the public spaces of peer culture from which their parents are pulling them. Hence, going online is the trade-off between caring parents and teenagers that try to construct and claim a space of their own.

Triangulating these quantitative data with the interviews we had with parents and children, it is clear that public discourses, i.e. media discourses, on the risks and dangers of the internet, had a subtle effect on the answers of parents. As harmful web content is an old concern (Wartella and Jennings, 2000), as compulsive internet behaviour is often linked to excessive online time consumption (Ponte et al., 2009), and online contests bear financial risks, it came as no surprise that parents showed a strong involvement with and concern about these aspects of internet use. At the same time, both the busy nature of everyday and working life in particular (73.8% of the parental interviewees – mostly mothers – and 87.4% of their partners had a full-time job), and the increased privatisation of family life related to improved material life conditions (e.g. the proliferation of media, rooms and spaces for each family member) prevented parents from taking their role as guardian of their children's online safety and well-being as seriously as they are expected to in today's discourses on good parenting (Smedts, 2008).

Lastly, in the interviews, the young people themselves made it clear that they considered their parents' worries about their going online too long or playing too many online games to be simply everyday nagging, from parents who did not really show an interest in their online activities, let themselves be led by the moral panics, or even did them wrong by forbidding them to meet, albeit in a virtual way,

Table 2.1 Restrictive rules parents impose versus restrictive rules as felt by young people (in %)

Teenagers		Parents	
Don't buy things online	66.2	Don't buy things online	83.6
Don't release private data about yourself and us	54.9	Don't release private data about yourself and us	74.0
Don't enter online contests	35.8	Don't enter online contests	56.6
Don't spend too much time online	32.3	Don't spend too much time online	54.9
Don't use chat language	21.4	Don't use chat language	51.7
Don't download	15.6	Only visit the allowed websites	40.1
Only visit the allowed websites	13.3	Don't download	24.5
Don't chat	7.1	Don't go online if you are alone at home	19.7
Don't play online games	7.0	Don't play online games	18.6
Only use the Internet for school work	6.8	Don't chat	15.5
Don't go online if you are alone at home	6.6	Only use the Internet for school work	8.8

their friends. Probably the fact that these two restrictive rules in particular were perceived as being part of the everydayness of nagging parents, created a certain fatigue among young people, and is assumedly one explanation for the gap.

Young People's Assessment of Adult Moral Guidance

One of the criticisms and complaints young people expressed in the interviews was about the rather narrow interpretation that both parents and teachers gave to mediation of the internet. Obviously, as always in people's accounts and experiences of their everyday life, there was a lot of ambiguity in their perceptions and expectations of adults' role in their internet education. One the one hand, they got annoyed by the restrictive approach of both their parents and teachers, which pre-eminently appeared in regulations about how much time they were allowed to spend online and to play games, which content and communication they were not allowed to engage with, and which applications they were not allowed to use at school. On the other hand, especially in their stories about school, violating these rules was part of their everyday negotiation with and sometimes resistance to the disciplinary school system. As some young people told us, installing and playing games on school computers against their teachers' will made them feel too clever for their teachers, and produced the self-perception of being more competent than their IT-instructors.

Furthermore, when discussing the internet habits of younger siblings or children in their surroundings, they strongly advocated a more restrictive approach than they had encountered when they were young. In particular, they expressed strong concerns about the lack of moral guidance from the parents and teachers about how (not) to communicate with others and how (not) to present oneself on the internet. For example, in discussing an imaginary situation in which a ten-years-old boy disclosed himself completely on his personal webpage, teenagers wondered if parents should allow such young children to go online unaccompanied.

Another related ambiguity we noticed in the young people's answers concerned the resonance of moral panics about the internet in their parents' and teachers' supervision. As stated above, they expressed critical opinions about adults' susceptibility to panicky media coverage of teenagers and the internet. In particular, adult discourses about internet dependency, compulsive internet behaviour (gaming especially) and sexual risks (e.g. paedophiles, pornography) were often disclaimed as being exaggerated and unworldly, as the teenagers did not consider themselves constantly exposed to these dangers. Yet, in the focus group discussions on potential internet-related risks and how to cope with them, they often reproduced these very discourses and applied them to vulnerable others (i.e. younger children, or young people in a psychologically weaker position). In this way, we heard young people advocating disciplinary mediating techniques and rather conservative sets of moral values when confronted with risk scenarios. Especially when they referred to their younger siblings or other younger kids they knew, their recommendations echoed those of their parents.

The need for stronger moral guidance from adults was expressed with respect to forms of internet behaviour that could be labelled as being compulsive, addictive or excessive. Although teenagers often criticised their parents' obsession with the amount of time they spent online and disapproved of the fact that they often limited their internet access, they also described how young people could lose control of the technology of the internet. In particular a disproportionate use of the internet, either in the context of gaming or communicative chat practices, was considered as a significantly dangerous situation in which their parents and teachers ought to intervene. In the focus group discussions about the risks of the internet, the old fear of 'technology taking over' clearly resonated. This is actually an old moral value about technology, expressing a deep distrust of a world ruled by machines. All the respondents we talked to distanced themselves from compulsive internet users, and in the survey 72.8% stated that they could easily do without the internet for a few days. The belief that non-internet-mediated social life was more meaningful than virtual, internet-enabled social action and interaction, showed itself manifestly in the fact that 80% of the young respondents did not go along with the proposition that they preferred online to offline conversations. In the focus groups teenagers strongly condemned others when they showed this kind of behaviour, as this boy stated: *I find it disgustful that all these people are always on MSN, without coming out. I sometimes find this irritating.* Equally they suggested that possible imbalances between offline and online life should be delegated to the sphere of adult moral activity, and they proposed quite restrictive and intrusive forms of surveillance, both from parents and governments, to prevent 'addicted' children going online.

In communicative situations where young people disclosed and shared intimate information to and with each other, a strong belief in peer-driven morality was present. As the focus groups and interviews made clear to us, an ethic of reciprocity guided the online sociality among friends. They were very aware of the semantic risks of different ways of saying things, and about the thin line between the sayable and unsayable in online settings. However, the moral issues and dilemmas related to such daily communication were not considered as something in which adults could and should play a guiding role. Rather they saw this as their personal and intimate terrain that involved training and exploring peer-to-peer manners, social conventions and definitions about privacy, trust and confidence. Unless the social communication among peers deteriorated into forms of cyber-harassment, they did not ascribe adults, and parents in particular, an active role. However, the knowledge that parents were in the background or on the sidelines was a reassuring thought.

Wanted: Moral Philosophers

Using and triangulating a multitude of data, we explored the so-called moral gap between adults and young people. Confronted with considerable ambiguity and complexity, three ideas emerged from this exploration.

First, as parents are increasingly made aware of their moral responsibility regarding young people's internet usage, they continuously pass on to their children ideas about what are good and bad modes of engagement with the internet, both through restrictive regulation, which is a type of power assertion, and through induction, pre-eminently built on particular cases and the conversation, deliberation and reasoning that they encourage (Brody and Schaffer, 1982: 36). Although teenagers sometimes criticised their parents' surveillance and dissociated themselves from their parents' moral panics, they nevertheless showed that they attached great importance to their parents' role as moral philosophers. In other words, we felt a strong respect and preference for and – assumedly – need for adult moral reasoning that transcends day-to-day restrictive rules, and, as Brody and Schaffer (1982: 58) argue, is 'slightly more sophisticated than their own'.

Second, although we noticed a gap between what parents told their children (not) to do, and what children perceived they were (not) allowed to do on the internet, in peer-to-peer conversations parents were often in the background, sometimes silently, but nevertheless prominently. In young people's everyday conversations about their life, they went on about their parents' rules and anxieties about, for example, language corruption or excessive chat sessions. On the face of it, they appeared to express the wide gap there is between 'us' (peers) and 'them' (parents), yet at the same time in complaining about their parents, they also shared, circulated and reproduced their parents' views and opinions within the peer group. So adults were not absent. However, the other important agent of adolescent socialisation, i.e. teachers, played only a marginal role in their descriptions. The internet, both as a technology and as a cultural form, was considered to be an area where teachers themselves have lessons to learn. As Thomson and Holland (2002: 107) note, young people do not automatically invest teachers with moral authority, but watch them closely to see if they are worthy of it.

Third, whereas the young people in our study and in others as well (Livingstone et al., 2010) like to present themselves as competent internet users and enjoy assisting or feeling cleverer than their parents in solving internet problems, they also made it clear that they only saw themselves as internet brokers (Grossbart et al., 2002) in terms of functional and active literacy[5] (Buckingham, 2003). When it came to moral literacy, and especially when confronted with ethical questions that sharply impinged upon their personal identity, young people turned to lessons learned from adults in composing a toolkit for dealing with the social and cultural meaning of the internet, even if they imagined themselves among peers.

References

Arnett, J. J. (1995), 'Adolescents' uses of media for self-socialization', *Journal of Youth and Adolescence,* 24 (5), 519–533.

Bauman, Z. (1994), *Postmodern Ethics* (Oxford: Blackwell).

Bauwens, J., Pauwels, C., Lobet-Maris, C., Poullet, Y. and Walrave, M. (2009), *Cyberteens, Cyberrisks, Cybertools: Tieners en ICT, Risico's en Opportuniteiten [Cyberteens, Cyberrisks, Cybertools: Teenagers and ICT, Risks and Opportunities]* (Gent: Academia Press).

Bauwens, J. and Vleugels, C. (forthcoming), 'The social value of young people's digital creativity', in Walrave, M. et al. (eds), *e-Youth: Balancing Between Opportunities and Risks* (Frankfurt am Main: Peter Lang).

Batat, W. (2008), 'Exploring adolescent development skills through Internet usage: A study of French 11–15 year olds', *International Journal of Consumer Studies,* 32, 374–381.

5 For more information about literacy see also Chapters 3, 4, 7, 8, 9 and the conclusion of this volume.

Brody, G. H. and Schaffer, D. R. (1982), ‘Contributions of parents and peers to children’s moral socialization’, *Developmental Review,* 2 (1), 31–75.

Buckingham, D. (2003), *Media Education: Literacy, Learning, and Contemporary Culture.* (Cambridge: Polity Press).

Buckingham, D. (2006), ‘Is there a digital generation?’, in Buckingham, D. and Willett, R. (eds), *Digital Generations: Children, Young People, and New Media* (Mahwah: Lawrence Erlbaum).

De Haan, J., van’t Hof, C., and van Est, R. (2006), ‘De digitale generatie’, in de Haan, J. and ’t Hof, C. (eds), *Jaarboek ICT en Samenleving 2006: De digitale generatie* (Amsterdam: Boom).

Drotner, K. (2000), ‘Difference and diversity: Trends in young Danes’ media uses’, *Media, Culture & Society,* 22, 149–166.

Eastin, M.S., Greenberg, B.S. and Hofschire, L. (2006), ‘Parenting the Internet’, *Journal of Communication,* 56, 486–504.

Erikson, E. (1968), *Identity: Youth and Crisis* (New York: Norton).

Fabes, R.A., Kupanoff, K., Carlo, G. and Laible, D. (1999), ‘Early adolescence and prosocial/moral behaviour I: The role of individual processes’, *Journal of Early Adolescence,* 19 (1), 5–16.

Furedi, F. (2001), *Paranoid Parenting: Abandon Your Anxieties and be a Good Parent* (London: Allen Lane/ The Penguin Press).

Grossbart, S., McConnell Hughes, S., Pryor, S. and Yost, A. (2002), ‘Socialization aspects of parents, children, and the Intemet’, *Advances in Consumer Research,* 29, 66–70.

James, C., Davis, K., Flores, A. Francis, J.M., Pettingill, L., Rundle, M. and Gardner, H., (2009), *Young People, Ethics, and the New Digital Media: A Synthesis from the GoodPlay Project* [John D. and Catherine T. MacArthur Foundation Reports on Digital Media and Learning] (Massachusetts: MIT Press).

Jenkins, H. (2008), ‘Media literacy: Who needs it?’, in Willoughby, T. and Wood, E. (eds), *Children’s Learning in a Digital World* (Malden, MA: Blackwell).

Lévy, P. (1998), *Becoming Virtual: Reality in the Digital Age* (New York: Plenum Trade).

Lister, M., Dovey, J., Giddings, S., Grant, I. and Kelly, K. (2003), *New Media: A Critical Introduction* (London: Routledge).

Livingstone, S. and Bober, M. (2005), *UK Children Go Online. Final report of key project Findings. A Research report from the UK Children Go Online project* (London: Media@LSE). Available at: < www.psychology.pl/download/ Livingstone_ Bober _ 2005 _ UK.pdf>.

Livingstone, S. and Bober, M. (2006), ‘Regulating the internet at home: Contrasting the perspectives of children and parents’, in Buckingham, D. and Willett, R. (eds), *Digital Generations: Children, Young People and New Media* (Mahwah, N.J.: Lawrence Erlbaum).

Livingstone, S., Haddon, L., Görzig, A. and Olafsson, K. (2010), *Risks and Safety on the Internet: The Perspective of European Children.* Initial Findings. EU Kids Online. (London: LSE).

Livingstone, S. and Helsper, E. (2008), 'Parental mediation of children's internet use', *Journal of Broadcasting & Electronic Media,* 52 (4), 581–599.
Meyrowitz, J. (1984), 'The adultlike child and the childlike adult: Socialization in an electronic age', *Daedalus,* 113 (3), 19–48.
Moores, S. (1993), *Interpreting Audiences: The Ethnography of Media Consumption.* (London etc.: Sage).
Padilla-Walker, L. M., McNamara Barry, C., Carroll, J.S., Madsen, S.D. and Nelson, L.J. (2008), 'Looking on the bright side: The role of identity status and gender on positive orientations during emerging adulthood', *Journal of Adolescence,* 31 (4), 451–467.
Palfrey, J. and Gasser, U. (2008), *Born Digital: Understanding the First Generation of Digital Natives* (New York: Basic Books).
Pasquier, D. (2005), *Cultures Lycéennes, la Tyrannie de la Majorité* (Paris: Editions Autrement).
Paus-Hasebrink, I., Ponte, C., Duerager, A. and Bauwens, J. (forthcoming), 'Similarities and differences across children', in Livingstone, S. and Haddon, L. and Görzig, A. (eds), *Children, Risk and Safety Online: Research and Policy Challenges in Comparative Perspective* (Bristol: The Policy Press).
Ponte, C., Bauwens, J and Mascheroni, G. (2009), 'Children and the internet in the news: Agency, voices and agendas', in Livingstone, S. and Haddon, L. (eds), *Kids Online: Opportunities and Risks for Children* (Bristol: The Policy Press).
Smedts, G. (2008), 'Parenting and the art of being a parent', in Smeyers, P. and Depaepe, M. (eds), *Educational Research: the Educationalization of Social Problems* (New York, Dordrecht, Heidelberg, London: Springer).
Stevenson, N. (2002), *Understanding Media Cultures: Social Theory and Mass Communication* (London etc.: Sage).
Subrahmanyam, K. and Smahel, D. (2011), *Digital Youth: The Role of Media in Development.* (New York, Dordrecht, Heidelberg, London: Springer).
Thomson, R. and Holland, J. (2002), 'Young people, social change and the negotiation of moral authority, *Children & Society,* 16, 103–115.
Turkle, S. (1995), *Life on the Screen. Identity in the Age of the Internet* (New York: Simon & Schuster Paperbacks).
Turkle, S. (2005), *The Second Self: Computers and the Human Spirit* [Twentieth Anniversary Edition] (Cambridge: The MIT Press).
Valentine, G. and Holloway, S.L. (2002), 'Cyberkids? Exploring children's identities and social networks in on-line and off-line worlds', *Annals of the Association of American Geographers,* 92 (2): 302–319.
Walsh, D. (2004), 'Doing ethnography', in Seale, C. (ed.), *Researching Society and Culture* (London: Sage).
Wartella, E.A. and Jennings, N. (2000), 'Children and computers: New technologies – Old concerns', *The Future of Children: Children and Computer Technology,* 10 (2), 31–43.

Chapter 3
Family Dynamics and Mediation: Children, Autonomy and Control

Gustavo Cardoso, Rita Espanha and Tiago Lapa

Introduction

The image of family life around the 'electronic fireplace' would seem today to be giving way to the real and virtual socialising network made possible by new media and new information and communication technologies (Espanha et al., 2006). This is intimately related to broad and pervasive social processes such as the process of individualisation. Beck (1992) and Giddens (1991), the main theorists outlining this individualisation process, see it as an unavoidable and necessary intermediate phase consisting, first, of the disembedding of the industrial society's institutions (for in instance, the patriarchal family and the male 'breadwinner' familial model) and, second, of the re-embedding of new forms of social life, particularly within the family. This means that new forms of relationship between parents and children are emerging in the daily lives of families. Nowadays, individuals and families have the opportunity or are forced (by changes in social structure and society as a whole) to live biographies that deviate from traditional patterns: they experience 'do-it-yourself biographies' or 'reflexive biographies', which brings uncertainty in terms of choices and social roles. In this case, the reflexive element consists above all in the confrontation with the other, for instance, in the confrontation between parents and their children.

We can also apply the notion of individualisation to the social shaping of media biographies. According to Colombo and Aroldi (2003), it is in childhood that the media literacy[1] of individuals takes form, defining patterns of consumption and future habits. We might assume that contemporary children are creating their own *media biographies* in ways that are less linear and more de-contextualised, and open to choice, compared to the media biographies of their parents. The younger generations have grown up amidst changes in the field of communicational interactivity and in the context of a system of multiple producers and distributors. Young people are thus particularly susceptible to socialisation between various – competing or complementary – social and media realities. They grow up with multiple choices as far as communication, entertainment and information are

1 For more information about literacy see also Chapters 2, 4, 7, 8, 9 and the conclusion of this volume.

concerned. New skills seem to be intuitively acquired by young people dubbed as 'digital natives' by Prensky (2001) (for a critical discussion about this concept, see the introduction, Chapter 4 by Herold, Chapter 8 by Lugano and Peltonen and Chapter 10 by Loos and Mante-Meijer in this volume), skills such as how to maximise the interconnection between diverse media realities and how to operate several media resources at the same time.

The appropriation of the media and new technologies by the younger generations suggests that changes may be taking place in terms of family interaction that are related to ICTs. Buckingham (2000) and Livingstone and Bovill (2001) basically argue that, nowadays, the typical household in the western northern hemisphere is constructed by families as an alternative leisure space for young people. Parents spend more or less substantial sums of money in order to give their few children entertainment media in order to keep them occupied in the home away from an outside world perceived to be threatening. These transformations may in turn bring about new, specifically media related, conflicts – for example, over usage times and contents accessed. There is, thus, the possibility that new areas of family negotiation or tension may be emerging involving the independence of adolescents, parental authority, parents' rules and the control over the media at home (see also Chapter 1 by Haddon and Chapter 3 by Bauwens in this volume). In our chapter we will therefore aim to explore such tensions within the cultural and geographical location of Portugal. We are suggesting that the autonomy of children and the degree of control by parents in the household are increasingly being negotiated in a mediated environment. That is, we are increasingly negotiating the acceptance of a new communicational model over the previous one, networked communication over mass communication (Cardoso, 2010). Our analysis argues that in families where parents and children share a culture and practices involving networked communication as the adopted communication model, the balance between autonomy and control are increasingly built through such negotiation. In the new household of the network society we are developing the role of media, beyond providing reference groups and belonging groups, giving media the additional role as tools both for enforcing parental control and for building children's autonomy.

Juvenile Contexts in the Era of Networked Communication

From Mass to Network Communication

We believe that it is possible to demonstrate empirically that the changes witnessed in communication go beyond a simple reconfiguring of the mass communication model by adding the internet to a set of practices and representations already present. We would like to argue, instead, that while under the industrial model of development the communicational model was that of 'Mass Communication', we are now witnessing the building of a new communicational model taking place within the broader informational model of development in our societies.

Hence 'Networked Communication' is slowly, but steadily, replacing 'Mass Communication' and its communicational paradigms in our societies. Such a replacement, of Mass by Networked, occurs with different nuances in the varied cultural contexts and media systems around the world (Colombo, 1993; Castells and Himanen, 2003; Silverstone, 2006; Hesmondahlgh, 2007; Lash and Lury, 2007; Varnelis, 2008; Castells, 2009), but at the same time it retains a common set of features that give consistency to the argument that we are witnessing a global change in models of communication.

As we move from a system of media diets based on mass communication to a model based on networked communication (Cardoso, 2008) and individualised appropriation of Mass Communication, into what Castells called Self Mass Communication (2009), we are also focusing on the analysis of a world in which the user of media, increasingly, shares with corporate organisations the most prominent roles within the rising new media system (Cardoso, 2010).

Networked communication is the combined outcome of several key historical forces. One is the globalisation of communication. A second is networked mediation where mass technologies interact with interpersonal communication technologies (i.e. the viral adoption of 'self mass communication, multimedia interpersonal communication' and of 'one to many mediated communication' by large parts of the world population). And a third is the availability of choice as regards different degrees of interactivity, which, in turn, allow us to combine more active with less active ways of engaging in private and public life. Such a communicational change influences our institutions and our daily lives, including reaching the household and its actors, both parents and children.

The Changing Nature of Childhood

As pointed out by Livingstone (2002), in recent years we have witnessed a switch from the public to the private sphere in the lives of younger generations. This has, on the one hand, to do with the decline of 'street culture' and the withdrawal of young people into the home or apartment, particularly in urban contexts and, on the other, with the decline of family life spent together watching television and the emergence of 'bedroom culture'. Such questions connect with other more general ones about the meaning of being a 'child' and the wider status of the family. The new sociology of childhood dissociates the biological character of 'infancy' from the cultural construction of 'childhood' (Postman, 1983; Jenks, 1996; Prout, 2008). This opens up research to take into account several 'childhoods' across time and space. Postman's apocalyptic vision of the 'disappearance of childhood' as the adults know it[2] fits well with the notion that childhood is being transformed by mass media and more recently by new media. This perspective appeals to a

2 That is, the 'death' of the typical western childhood brought into being with the democratisation of literacy and education and its correlated production of free or leisure time, both inside and outside the home.

vision of social discontinuity regarding the lived experience of childhood, but it requires cautious scrutiny. Moreover, it provides a one-dimensional analysis of changes in childhood, as Buckingham (2000) argues, that falls into a technological determinism since it points to electronic media as a major determinant of changing children's lives.

More broadly, the continuous social construction of childhood is related to the broad process of individualisation and its implications for the family, namely the erosion of the patriarchal family and the changing affirmation of children as being autonomous beings. These changes were theoretically and methodologically acknowledged since, as Prout puts it, 'children's social relationships are worthy of study in their own right, independent of the perspective and concerns of adults and they 'are not just passive subjects of social structures and processes' (2008: 30). This stance does not imply an arbitrary separation between children and adults, since we still have to take into account obvious power and dependency relations between them.

Media and Childhood

The penetration of the media into everyday life can translate into new ways of organising pastimes, recreation and study as the use of diverse media could transforms the everyday routine of children in their usual spaces (home, school and others). The temporal and spatial organisation of media use also reflects the varying degrees of freedom that children have and is a focus of negotiation and possible conflict with parents and educators.

The media belong to what Merton (1957) calls reference groups, as opposed to belonging groups such as the family, friends or school. Accordingly, given their characteristics and powerful network of influences, the media are made up of reference agents that can contrast, complement, boost or annul the influence of belonging agents such as the family. All belonging and reference agents play very important roles but they may not always coincide. In this context, Loader (2007) draws attention to processes of cultural 'shift' amongst young people, in particular those most acquainted with the new technologies and who could constitute the leading group in a new techno-social culture. Such a cultural change, involving socialisation in a media context and in communicational spaces such as Facebook, MySpace, MSN or mobile phone text messaging, celebrates the diversity of lifestyles, dissemination and personal expression.

The notion of shift underlines the mismatch that may arise between belonging groups and reference groups. In other words, there may be discontinuities between the experiences of parents, educators and young people both in terms of the transmission of knowledge and values and in terms of the sharing of media and communicational cultures, as Prensky (2001) also suggested. Prensky (2001: 2) argues that parents and educators are, at best, 'digital immigrants', 'who speak an outdated language (that of the pre-digital age)', and 'are struggling to teach a population [the digital natives] that speaks an entirely new language'. Indeed,

Prensky reproduces Tapscott's (1998) argument in favour of drawing a clear line between generations, based on differentiated processes of media socialisation. However, Buckingham (2006) is cautious about this claim since the meanings and uses of technology vary according a range of variables beside age (see also Loos, 2011a/b, the introduction, and Chapter 10 by Loos and Mante-Meijer in this volume). Moreover, he argues that to set the boundaries of a generation is a far more complex task than to simply define it through its relationship with a particular technology or medium (2006:11).[3] Buckingham's argument does not imply that there are no boundaries or that children socialised amid new media are not creating their own meanings and uses of digital technologies. But the impacts of the appropriation of technology on the personal and family lives of children should be put into the wider context of other social developments.

Parent-Child Relationships

Techno-social changes affect children and adults alike, one way or another. On the one hand, the introduction and use of new media within households may exacerbate some of the contradictions in the condition of being 'young'. The first such contradiction derives from the transitional situation of young people between childhood and young adulthood. The use of new media as another means for young people to express their autonomy could bring the contradictions of the juvenile condition to the fore, in relation to the 'dos' and 'don'ts' and rules and controls laid down by the parents. Through their media use, young people can claim the right to autonomy, while parents and educators may identify worrying aspects of that use and once more place their children in a position of dependence. A second contradiction comes from the experience of children enjoying new areas of freedom in the wider context of financial dependence on their parents. Many young people today live under the protection of the 'welfare family' – particularly in the southern part of the European Continent. Financially dependent on their parents, they nevertheless struggle to enjoy existential independence or autonomy.

On the other hand, the very nature of the new media could lead to substantial changes in the possibilities and forms of educational mediation by parents. As Meyrowitz (1995) argues, the emergence of new media within the family brings with it new relationships of authority between parents and children. When mediating their children's use of traditional media such as radio and television parents can draw upon their own experiences of mediation when they were children, being members of the so-called 'TV generation', as Tapscott (1998) puts it, since their childhood.[4] However, we now have the paradoxical situation that, with the advent of new ICTs such as the internet, video games, mobile phone, etc., children lead the way in terms of knowledge and use of these technologies, a situation that can

3 See also the introduction of this volume.

4 See also technology generation (Sackman and Weymann, 1994: 41–43; Weymann and Sackman, 1998) in Chapter 10 by Loos and Mante-Meijer.

place the parents at a clear disadvantage. This situation could question parents' authority to exercise any mediation at all (Sala and Blanco, 2005). Many children discover and use digital innovations before their parents: ICTs are things that are part of their daily lives and activities.[5] In addition to this, children may differ from their parents in terms of their disposition and attitudes in relation to the media. According to Sala and Blanco (2005), children and adolescents perceive the internet and computers as being recreational or fun, while parents see these communication channels as complex realities linked to social status, etc. In the Rivoltella study (2006), the parents' representations tend to share a common dimension that involves a more instrumental use of the internet: stressing its role as regards information, as a communication and knowledge resource and as a work tool. Parental lack of knowledge of and attitudes to new media is, therefore, one of the key factors affecting family mediation of the media activities of young people, although it may be temporary and limited to the current moment of transition to the network society (Castells, 2002).

Furthermore, the different media cultures of parents and children may introduce elements of uncertainty in applying rules. How does one make rules for something one does not know or knows very little about? How does one discuss democratically or argue in favour of rules and regulations within the family when one does not know one's children's culture? In such a context, many rules could be seen as being unfair or misplaced by the children and so give rise to conflict.

One should also stress that these new domestic situations are taking place against a backdrop of a more comprehensive process involving a questioning of the values, symbols and authority that the traditional family represents (Beck and Beck-Gernsheim, 2002). Another process one has to bear in mind is the individualisation of free time and recreational spaces. Young peoples' rooms are an arena that reflects the individualisation and privatisation of leisure time, in which an important part of the gaining of freedom and autonomy is played out. Although not exactly a new development, the bedroom is a private retreat where a whole range of individualised media-related practices are increasingly being carried out. One cannot, however, say that the living room has become irrelevant as a common family space as far as the media use is concerned. On the contrary, it continues to be very important, despite the competition from other, more private, domestic spaces.

The bedroom is gaining in importance as a place for using the media as well as for the increasingly privatised use of a range of devices, given that each family member potentially has their own phone or mobile phone, television set and computer, etc. One can even say that the media system visible in the public space has invaded the private space of the younger generations' bedrooms. This 'from the bedroom to the world' logic may give rise to new tensions and the redrawing of the boundary between private and public, as well reconfigurations and negotiations as to what is understood by family life in the household and beyond it in the future.

5 See also Buckingham (2006: 3) in Bauwens in Chapter 2 on reverse socialisation.

New and Old Media

Given this context, our aim is to look not only at family dynamics in the broader sense of the term, but, above all, to examine the way in which the appropriation of the new media and technologies by young people could be impacting family life. The rapid increase in the number of families connected to the internet is being accompanied by an interest in understanding how the new technologies influence family relationships and the potential that ICTs have to change family life – both in terms of the playing out of traditional roles and the emergence of new areas of possible conflict. The questions we raise, however, do not mean that we uncritically accept the separation between the new and the old media. There is probably some validity to the argument that new media theorists have probably exaggerated the novelty of new technologies and the emergence of the second media era (Webster, 2001) that is, among other things, disrupting childhood. As Livingstone et al. (2007) suggest, young people as a whole may continue to be influenced more by television than by the internet. Therefore, the question arises about the extent to which new media introduce, in qualitative terms, new variables into the parent-child relationship or whether they merely constitute a quantitative addition to conventional media.

Media Parental Regulation in Portuguese Households

The Internet

The following analysis is based on a survey of Portuguese households conducted through an online questionnaire[6] that included specific questions on whether or not there were arguments and family conflicts relating to the use of various media. As argued earlier, parental regulation of new media is a very complex and burdensome task since parents are faced with new realities that most do not grasp. Tight control might be seen as inappropriate or unfair by children, especially if it breaks an increasingly general contract of 'democratic negotiation of mutual rights, trust, and responsibilities between parents and children' (Livingstone and

6 In collaboration with the main Portuguese telecom operator, Portugal Telecom (PT), CIES-IUL (Centre for Research and Studies in Sociology at the ISCTE-Lisbon University Institute) carried out a study on "Children and Young People: Their Relationship with the New Technologies and Media". The project used two methods of data gathering during the springtime of 2006. The data collection methods included a face-to-face survey in order to get a representative sample of the Portuguese population aged 9 to 18 years of age and an online survey created by CIES-IUL and hosted by PT portal SAPO. The respondents to the online survey were mainly young internet users. This survey was online for approximately one month and received a total of 1,377 responses from children between the ages of 9 to 18 years old, of which 1,353 were considered valid.

Bober, 2006; see also Chapter 1 by Haddon in this volume). Figure 3.1 shows that the most common family conflict over internet use, pointed out by just under half of the respondents, concerns the amount of time spent online. Only 18.5% of respondents stated that they had arguments with the parents over the time of the day when they are online.

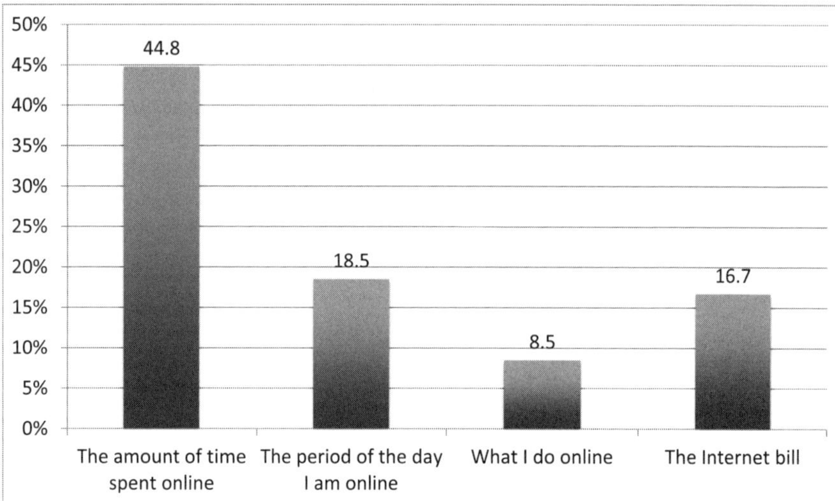

Source: PT Project (2006), Online Survey

Figure 3.1 Internet conflicts (I have had arguments with parents about ...)

Possibly mirroring the more traditional, patriarchal character of Portuguese society, compared to other European societies, our data also revealed the interesting fact that a higher percentage of girls (47.2%) than boys (42.9%) stated that they had had family arguments because of the time they spend on the internet. This might mirror an overestimation of parents of the risks girls might face in the internet, compared to the perceptions of risks that boys can face online. An equally curious finding is that the very youngest age groups (9 to 12 years old) are less likely to have arguments with their parents, concerning the amount of time spent online. Since the youngest respondents are, in general, less autonomous, parental control might be stricter, with parents perhaps blocking access to the computer or the internet and putting forward a set of rules in terms of media usage less open to discussion. The 13 to 15 age groups register a higher percentage of respondents (49,3%) who have argued with their parents about the amount of time online but the figure drops slightly for the 16 to 18 age group. This propensity for family conflicts within these ages groups concerning the time spent online might derive from negotiations with parents about their margins of freedom and autonomy. However, as regards the period of the day when children are online and what young people do when they are surfing the internet, that propensity for conflict decreases as the age of the respondent increases, probably because adolescents gain the status of being responsible individuals. This also makes sense in that younger children aged 9 to 12 are subject to greater direct parental control in terms of timing in general (meal times, time to go to bed, time to get up, etc.); in terms of space – leisure and work spaces are often more well defined for younger children – and in terms of exposure to what is perceived as inappropriate content.

Nevertheless, arguments with the parents often involve the various dimensions of internet use discussed above that are put together in a 'package' by the children. In other words, the respondents who stated they had arguments with their parents on one dimension also stated they had arguments on another dimension of internet use as well.

As one can see in Figure 3.2 below, simply asking the children what they are doing seems to be the most common form of parental supervision (38.1%), followed by the parents having a quick look at what their children are doing (36.9%). Girls seem to be subject to tighter control than boys, with 41.8% of female respondents saying their parents ask what they are doing and 40.7% of them stating their parents have a look, as opposed to 35.3% and 34% respectively for boys. Direct checking of e-mail is not common at all (0.6%) and parents also do not frequently check browser histories to see what their children have been viewing on the net (2.9%). The percentage of young people who are accompanied by their parents, i.e. sitting beside them in front of the computer, is also very small (7.1%), as is the number of children whose parents help them to surf the web (6.8%). Just over 11% stated that their parents were in the same room when they are on the internet. What is significant is the number of respondents who stated that their parents do not do anything (53.6%), although this should not be simply equated with a lack of control on the part of the parents of those respondents. This finding mainly reveals the children's perception of their parents' control or monitoring, since parents can monitor children's activities without their knowledge. That is, children might be underestimating the regulatory and monitoring practices their parents are trying to implement. Such a hypothesis is also supported by a study of British households, as suggested by Livingstone and Bober (2006). Nevertheless, as to be expected, parental control is tighter for the younger age groups: 42.5% of respondents aged 9 to 12 answered that their parents ask what they are doing and 47.5% said their parents come and have a look at what they are doing. All figures for both parental supervision and help increase for the younger age groups.

Online purchases and revealing private information are the most important actions that are forbidden (41.4% and 38.9% of cases, respectively). The third most important 'don't do' for the internet is downloading files, but only 16.1% of respondents reported that they are not allowed to do that. For all other forbidden actions the figures are lower than 10%.[7] A substantial number of the children (43.1%) answered that there are no actions they are not (explicitly) allowed to do.

7 It is a curious fact that 5% stated that they did not have their parent's permission to fill out online questionnaires, considering that the information presented herein was gathered by means of such a questionnaire; at least 5% of them disobey their parents.

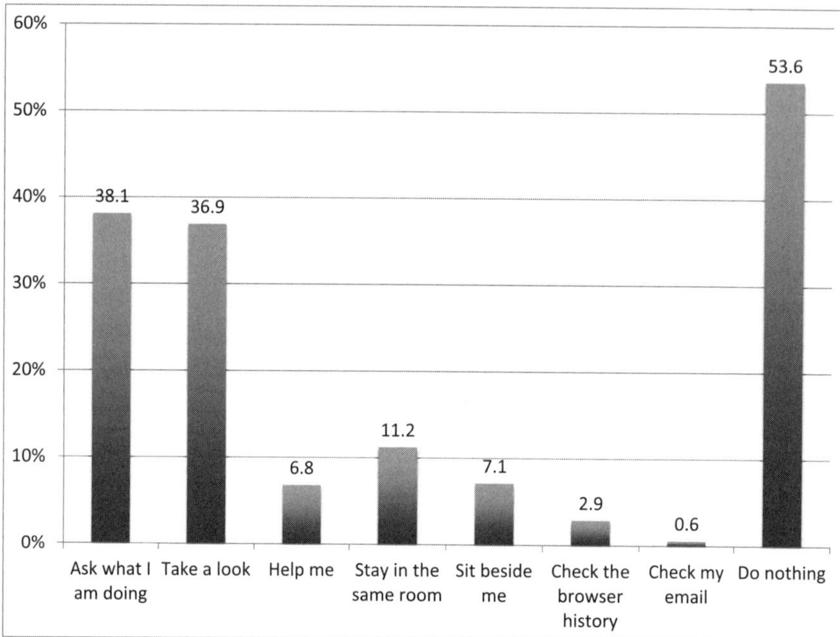

Source: PT Project (2006), Online Survey

Figure 3.2 What parents do when children are on the Internet

In the older age groups the clear trend is towards fewer restrictions. The number of respondents in the 13 to 15 age groups with no explicitly forbidden actions was 34.6%, and in the 16 to 18 age group the figure rises to 54%.

The data also show a trend whereby the internet is used more as a mechanism of punishment (12.5% of cases) than as a reward (9.3% of cases). This trend is particularly evident for girls in the 13 to 15 age groups. In the younger age group (9 to 12), the opposite is the case, with 17.5% noting that their parents use the internet as a form of reward, as opposed to 14.2% whose parents limit internet use as a form of punishment. However, one should note that most of the respondents answered that their parents do nothing. As pointed out by Livingstone and Bober (2006: 104) there are at least two difficulties that undermine parents' attempts to monitor and regulate their children's online activities. We could likewise extend these arguments to the regulation of other new media. First, parents, although socially perceived as the main guardians of their children's safety, must also manage their children's increasing demands for independence and privacy; second, we have the often greater expertise of children regarding the usage of new media.

Mobile Phone

Concerning the arguments over mobile phone use, only approximately 20% of young people answered that they had had arguments because of the time they

Table 3.1 When you are online, what things do your parents forbid you from doing?

	N	%
Online purchases	448	41.4
Frequenting chat sites	106	9.8
Giving out personal information	420	38.9
Filling out questionnaires	54	5.0
Downloading files (music, games, etc.)	174	16.1
Text messaging	39	3.6
E-mail messaging	22	2.0
Online games	80	7.4
Nothing	466	43.1

Source: PT Project (2006), Online Survey

spend on their mobile phone. One curious figure is the difference between the percentage of girls who have argued with their parents over this (27.8%) and the percentage of boys (13.5%). A few hypotheses to explain this difference can be put forward that require further scrutiny: girls are more controlled and have less autonomy than boys in a still gendered society; girls try to develop their social relationships earlier than boys hence using the mobile phone more; girls reproduce the 'caring for others' model from their mothers that is reflected in the time they spend talking to their peers over the mobile phone. Furthermore, there are more arguments over time spent using a mobile phone in the older age groups. One possible explanation for this is that older children use mobile phones more as a means of consolidating and expanding their social relationships, in line with their greater freedom, be it for chatting and exchanging views with partners, organising nights out, dates or simply conducting affairs of the heart.

What the mobile phone is used for is less a source of conflict. Only 7.7% answered that they had had conflicts with their parents because of the way they used their phone. Here there is no significant difference between boys and girls, although there is a slight tendency for girls to be more likely to get into arguments with their parents over their mobile phone. However, the youngest age group has the greatest propensity for conflict with their parents, perhaps as a result of the greater control to which they are subject.

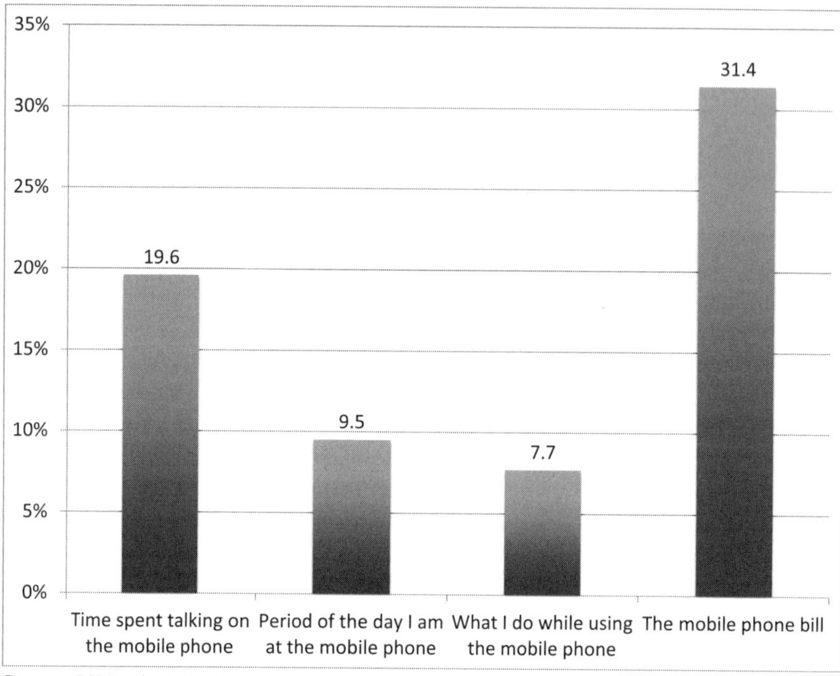

Source: PT Project (2006), Online Survey

Figure 3.3 Mobile phone conflicts (I have had arguments with parents about ...)

The amount of money spent on mobile phone use is the main topic of argument with parents for 31.4% of the young respondents. A statistical test[8] was carried out to determine to what extent arguments over mobile phone spending are related to arguments over the amount of time spent using the mobile phone; once again, a connection between the two conflicts – over spending and amount of time – was established. One can therefore say that a considerable part of the arguments about time spent on the mobile phone derives from the issue of the money being spent, particularly because a good deal of the time young people spend on their mobile phone goes unnoticed by the parents, but is revealed in the bill. Further analysis of the data reveals statistically significant connections between all types of conflicts, suggesting that when a family conflict about mobile phone use is triggered off, then frequently all dimensions of mobile phone usage are discussed: time spent phoning, the time of day in which the phone is used, what the phone is used for, and the money spent.

8 Chi-square test (sig <0.001). The Cramer's V strength of association revealed an average to strong association between the two conflicts (Cramer's V = 0.665).

Interactive Games

Approximately one-third of the young internet users have had an argument with their parents about the amount of time they spend playing video or computer games, making this the main source of conflict. Here, however, the propensity for conflict is much greater amongst boys for all the types of conflict considered: the time spent playing; the time of the day; the type of games the respondents like; and the money spent on gaming. Some 41.5% of the boys answered that they had had conflicts with their parents because of the time they spend playing games, with girls a distant 20%. In addition, 17.2% stated that they had had arguments because of the time of day they were playing and just over 10% got into arguments about the type of games they like. Only 7.5% of girls got into conflicts with their parents over the time of day they played games and as little as 4.3% said they had arguments over the type of games they liked. Younger respondents are also more likely to have arguments with their parents in the diverse areas of conflict considered in the survey but the differences between the age groups are not as big as those between boys and girls.

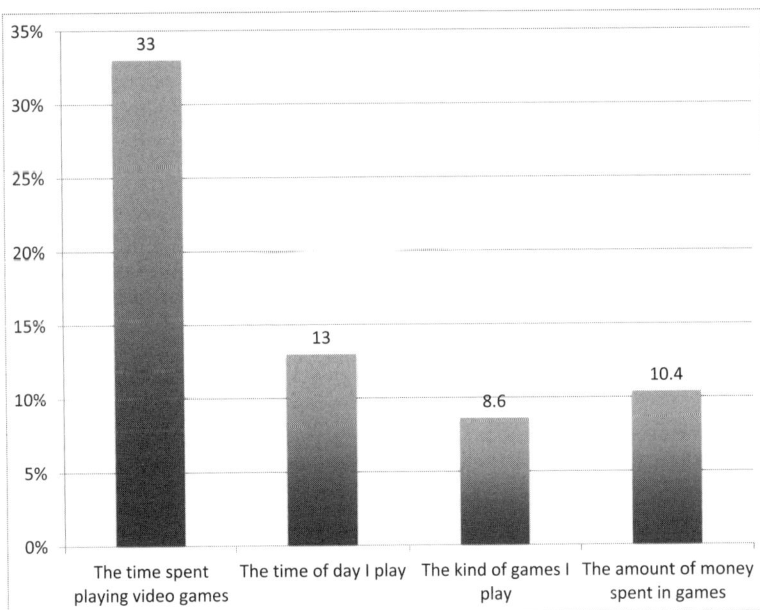

Source: PT Project (2006), Online Survey

Figure 3.4 Games conflicts (I have had arguments with parents over ...)

It is important to understand how children and youth use and appreciate different games, to what extent the games are integrated into their lives (Livingstone et al., 2001) and how changes in the media are associated with more general social developments. The cultural and social relevance of games is linked to the discussion of media and ICT skills or the info-literacy of young people and the informal ways or processes of acquiring skills within electronic games culture. Greenfield (1984) was one of the first authors to distance herself from the common-sense fear that the new media are bad educators because, for example, they instil violent behaviour in children and youths. However, new media, as cultural artefacts, do frequently develop and require complex cognitive skills learnt in an informal setting and outside the contexts of formal learning in school (Greenfield, 1984). Thus, many schoolchildren already go to school with computer skills before they receive formal instruction from teachers or educators, reinforcing the notion that younger generations are 'born taught' as far as use of the new technologies is concerned.[9]

It is thus necessary to have better knowledge of the informal learning processes and their background to avoid, as Fromme (2003) puts it, the 'media culture shock'. This metaphor draws attention to the following fact: teachers, parents and educators are, generally speaking, members of a generation that, in terms of their primary socialisation[10], grew up in a different media culture and, accordingly, have different media-related experiences than younger generations.[11] These informal media experiences not only influence private values and attitudes in relation to new media, but also have an impact on educational concepts and practices. In other words, educators tend to approach the media cultures of children and youth from with their own generational viewpoint, assuming this as the implicit norm in educational, and political, practices and discourses (Fromme, 2003).

This means that educators frequently view the media with distrust and scepticism. Electronic games, in particular, seem to appeal more immediately to children's playful nature, to an ethic that is more hedonistic, entailing immediate satisfaction, which could clash with the Weberian 'Protestant ethic' that is more present in adults, based on a more rationalised lifestyle and specific forms of self-control. Hence, specific conflicts can arise over the use of the computer, as educators may want to attract children and youths away from games and towards other computer activities and tools considered more educational and useful, such as word-processors, using encyclopaedias or other types of educational software (Leu, 1993). However, if we follow Himanen's analysis (2001), we can pose the hypothesis that, in reality, the younger generations are adopting an ethic that is different to that of their parents and that the dialectic relationship between the two ethics produces new forms of family relations mediated by the media experiences of the different family members.

Television

As far as television use is concerned, the main source of conflict with parents is over the amount of time spent watching TV (29.1% of cases). This is followed by

9 See also Prensky's digital natives earlier in this chapter.
10 See also Chapter 10 by Loos and Mante-Meijer in this volume.
11 See also technology generation (reference in footnote 4).

arguments over the time of day children and youths watch TV (14.7%) and, finally, by conflicts over the type of programmes the young respondents watch (9.1%). Girls are more likely to get into conflict with their parents over the time spent watching TV and the time of day when they watch TV. However, that situation is reversed when it comes to the type of programmes watched. The 9 to 12 age group, which has the least freedom and is subject to the most parental control, is the age group with the greatest propensity for conflict. Conflicts may be more frequent in this age group because of a continuous parent-child negotiation process in which the children seek to gain more freedom in terms of their use of media.

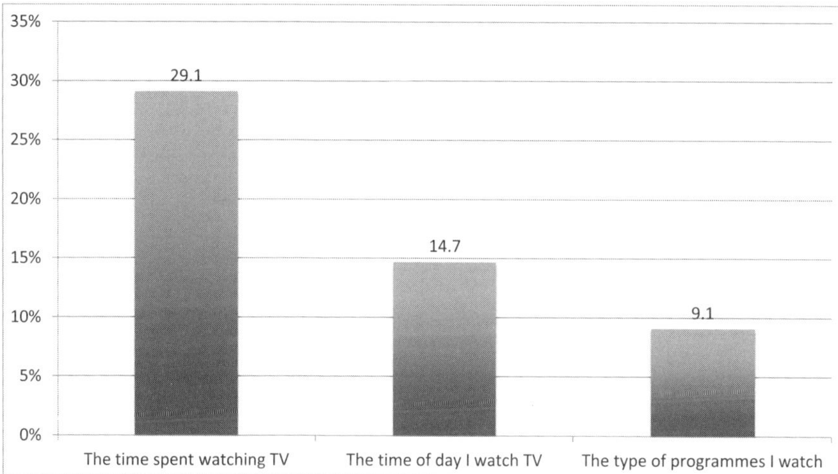

Source: PT Project (2006), Online Survey

Figure 3.5 TV conflicts (I have had arguments with parents over …)

Generally speaking, the main issues in family arguments are, without doubt, about the time and money spent, as in the case of the mobile phone. This information seems not only to apply to Portuguese society but is also in line with data gathered in other European studies (Livingstone and Bovill, 2001; Sala and Blanco, 2005). However, what is particularly relevant, both in terms of our findings and those of other studies, is the low incidence of conflicts over the contents of diverse media and the rather loose control many parents exert over said contents.

One surprising finding is that a substantial number of the children (58.9%) said they had control over what they watch on TV – even in the youngest age groups. The children's own control is only surpassed by that of the father of the family (65.3%), which is greater than that of the mother (58.3%). This may mirror the power relationships within the family but also the way in which the relationships are perceived by the respondents. Almost 31% of the children stated that their siblings also participate in deciding what programme to watch. However, one should note that not all respondents have siblings, meaning that the relative weight of siblings in deciding what is to be watched may be underestimated. What this could mean is that the decision as to what the family should watch is a process that is more negotiated and democratic between parents and children than, probably, it used to be.

Television is used more as a means of reward and punishment than the internet. Almost 28% of respondents noted that their parents use the television as a means of punishing or rewarding them. There are no significant differences between the sexes as far as this question is concerned, but there are differences between the age groups, in particular between the oldest group (16 to 18) and the rest. In the oldest group, 21.2% reported that their parents use the internet to punish or reward them, while for the 13 to 15 age group the figure rises to 35.7% and in the youngest group (9 to 12) it reaches 38.3%. In contrast to the internet, TV serves more as a means of reward (56.8% of cases) than of punishment (43.2% of cases). However, for the youngest age group the reverse is true. Nevertheless, the use of TV or of the internet as a system of punishment and rewards applies to a minority. This fits well with the claims of Giddens (1991) and Beck (1992) that the power relations within the home are shifting from a model of patriarchal authority and generational hierarchy to the more egalitarian and democratised pure relationship (see also Chapter 1 by Haddon and Chapter 2 by Bauwens in this volume). Parent-child relationships are increasingly prioritising trust and negotiation, though amid struggles and contractions, especially, in a country such as Portugal where the modernisation process still unfolds among some resilient traditional institutions and values. The nationwide face-to-face survey revealed that television is still subject to the greatest parental control. Some 40% of respondents said that their parents established rules on the time spent watching TV and 29.5% say that there were rules on the time spent playing games, which is the second most important focus of attention for parents. Time spent using the computer and the internet are less important in this respect (24.6% and 22.2% of cases respectively), perhaps reflecting the lack of access to these media for part of the Portuguese population. If one considers only those young people who are regular internet users, then television is relegated to last place as a focus of parental control rules (28.5% of cases) and the internet is clearly the most important medium (41.1% of regular internet users stated that there were rules as to the amount of time they could use the internet). There is a transfer of parental control over television to video and computer games (32.8% of cases), to the computer (36.2%) and, above all, to the internet.

Satisfaction and Support

Lastly, we analysed questions that have to do with the satisfaction level of the young respondents in relation to specific dimensions of the family dynamics. Generally speaking, the respondents are happy with the relationships within their families (see also Chapter 1 by Haddon and Chapter 2 by Bauwens in this volume). What seems to be most consensual is the young people's perception of the help they receive when a problem arises. Over 71% of them reported that they almost always receive help. But there is less consensuses amongst the respondents on the matter of the family accepting their desires to do new things and to make changes in their lifestyle. Even so, 58% of the respondents answered that their family almost always accepts their wishes. More than 60% of the children/youths interviewed also said that the family almost always discusses questions and matters of common interest and that they solve problems together with the family and also express their feelings and sentiments. One should also note that 67% of the children responding stated they were almost always happy with the time they dedicate to the family. What emerges (reinforcing the argument of Chapter 1 by Haddon in this volume) is a picture of a contemporary and more democratic family, in which feelings are expressed and paths are opened for communication and dialogue as well as conflict, be it open or latent. It is in this scenario that young people rationalise their family situation, negotiate and gain independence, manoeuvring between the permitted and the forbidden.

From Mass Mediated Control and Autonomy to Networked Parental Monitoring?

The data from the nationwide face-to-face survey and the online survey indicate a diversification of parental control on various fronts: from the TV to the mobile phone and from computer games to the internet. Studies conducted by Livingstone and Bovill (2001) generally show that the most 'controlled' media are the TV and the telephone. The data from our face-to-face survey confirms that parents exercise more control over use of the television. Even for our online interviewees, television is the means of reward/punishment more frequently used by their parents compared to the internet. However, for children better acquainted with the new technologies parental control over television consumption is being transferred to these other media. For this group, parental control over the amount of time spent on the internet is the most relevant, while control over time spent watching TV is the least relevant, behind control over the time spent on the computer and time spent playing video games. Here one can expect a future trend towards greater control of the internet, as use of the internet grows and what is now the case only for a limited group of young people becomes the norm for youth as a whole in the near future.

This diversification of parental control and rules indicates the emergence of diverse fields of negotiation between parents and children with repercussions for the organisation of family life. As the Livingstone and Bovill (2001) studies show, parents may even feel these repercussions in the way they educate, mediate and control the use of the media by their children. As far as traditional media are concerned, a large part of the control and mediation work is left to the mother, while the father is more present in relation to use of the computer and the new technologies. Our study showed that the young respondents have the idea that their fathers know better and make better use of technologies such as the computer, the internet and video games than their mothers, as these technologies are perhaps more appealing to a male audience.

One of the consequences of the ever-increasing penetration of the media into the daily life of children is the occurrence of specific family conflicts over media consumption. The online survey revealed that, for the internet, TV and video games, conflicts over the amount of time spent using the respective media are the most frequent. As far as use of the mobile phone is concerned, the main reason for conflict is the cost, which also obviously reflects the amount of time spent using the phone, but that might be less 'visible' to parents. Livingstone and Bovill (2001) throw some light on this greater significance in daily conflicts of the number of hours young people devote to the media in interviews with their parents. The parents' concerns focus on the negative effect that time spent using the media can have on school performance, family life and health, amongst other things, and not on the quality of the contents or the exposure to said contents. The most common attitude the parents have is to think that the contents do not directly affect their children. In a way, the parents develop an attitude of distributing their influence and control over contents to 'others', in two respects: it is other people's children that are affected and other people or entities should be working towards mediating or controlling the contents (the public powers, public institutions, civil society, schools, etc.).

Furthermore, there are significant associations between various types of conflict, meaning that arguments between parents and children often involve confrontations over more than one dimension of media use: time spent, time of day, activities carried out and financial cost.

One should also note that parents with a less education or with fewer skills than their children in using new technologies may adopt a more repressive style in their mediation and control. A study conducted by Mesch (2006) shows that conflicts between parents and adolescents increase in families where the adolescent is considered an expert in using the internet. This kind of conflict is all the greater the more pressure the parents are under to try to reduce adolescent's independence by controlling access to the internet and when parents show concerns or negative attitudes about internet use. Such parents constitute a group that Rivoltella (2006) has named 'anxious parents', which contrast with other types of parents: 'confident parents', who believe in their children's responsibility and for whom the media do not constitute an educational problem; 'absent parents', characterised by a 'laissez faire' attitude and the lack of mediation of their children's experiences with the media; and the 'attentive parents', who recognise that the internet offers opportunities for sensible appropriation and education. In our online survey, a large number of the young respondents claim that they know the most about the internet in their home and only 10% of them say that their father knows more. This discrepancy at the knowledge level may, on the one hand, restrict the development of 'attentive parents' and, on the other, give rise to a certain amount of confusion in the power relations in the home. The use of new technologies by young people may therefore generate anxiety and areas of uncertainty for parents as far as applying rules and performing their role of mediators is concerned. Thus, it is possible that the ranks of 'anxious parents' may be growing in families where the children are more skilled at using new technologies than their parents.

On the basis of the above one can say that new media do not merely represent a quantitative addition to family relations – they also introduce qualitative changes in the ways that parents, educators and adolescents relate to and with each other. It is clear that the influence of the media within the family is only one aspect of wider, more comprehensive social processes and the way the families react to the use of the media is influenced by those processes. The family in the early 21st century is undergoing a process of reconfiguration and negotiated democratisation between parents and children. Moreover, the contemporary family may, as Castells (2002) suggests, be facing the challenge of having to integrate characteristics of the network society – flexibility, independence, and adaptability – and networked communication (Cardoso, 2011) into the family relational structure. The question that remains is whether the family as an institution will adopt these characteristics or fight against them because they erode traditional patriarchal power. Our analysis suggests that, in families where we find a shared appropriation of networked communication, we will witness less conflict and also a more balanced management of autonomy between parents and children. Looked at the other way, in households where mass communication prevails as the communicational model shared by parents and networked communication as the one shared by children, we will witness more conflict and fewer medium used in the shared construction of autonomy. Under this latter communicational environment, parents will negotiate control and autonomy by focusing more on television rather than internet. By doing so they are enforcing control through their own communicational culture, one that sees television as the most important communicational component of one's life, while for the children that is not so clearly the case. Therefore, such children will in turn retain a higher interest in building belonging and reference groups without the need to negotiate with parents, because of a mismatch of shared communicational cultures in the household.

If a shared integration of communicational models takes place in the household, we will have a more democratic family in which power results from negotiation, because the whole family will share a same communicational environment and culture. And if the family refuses, or is unable, to adopt it, then we will see an accumulation of tensions and the rise of fractured, more distant relationships. But even if we can envisage a scenario in which families adopt network communication characteristics, it remains to be seen through what processes that could happen. One could imagine that the adaptation could take place due to the techno-social culture of the children being assimilated and appropriated by parents, educators and older generations, thus creating points of communication with the younger generations. In such a scenario we would have a model of society that is to a lesser degree referenced towards adult society, and more towards a young society. Or, in another scenario, only when a large number of internet users become parents, together with the natural generational replacement, can one expect to see the full adaptation of family life to the characteristics of the network society using a networked communicational model.

References

Aroldi, P. and Colombo, F. (2003), *La età della Tv* (Milan: VP Università).

Beck, U. (1992), *Risk Society: Towards a New Modernity* (London etc.: Sage).

Beck, U. and Beck-Gernsheim, E. (2002), *Individualization: Institutionalized Individualism and its Social and Political Consequences* (London etc.: Sage).

Buckingham, D. (2000), *After the Death of Childhood: Growing Up in the Age of Electronic Media* (Cambridge: Polity Press).

Buckingham, D. (2006), 'Is there a digital generation?', in Buckingham, D. and Willett, R. (eds), *Digital Generations: Children, Young People, and New Media* (Mahwah: Lawrence Erlbaum).

Cardoso, G. (2008), 'From mass to network communication: Communicational models and the Informational Society, *International Journal of Communication* [Online] 2:0. Available at: <http://ijoc.org/ojs/index.php/ijoc/article/view/19/178>.

Cardoso, G. (2010), 'From mass to networked communication', in Papathanassopoulos, S. (ed.), *Media Perspectives for the 21st Century* (London, New York: Routledge).

Cardoso, G. (2011), 'El nacimiento de la comunicación en red: Más allá de Internet y de los medios de comunicación de masas□, *Revista TELOS*, nº86, Madrid, Fundacion Telefónica.

Castells, M. (2002), *A Era da Informação: Economia, Sociedade e Cultura: Volume I: a Sociedade em Rede* (Lisbon: Calouste Gulbenkian Foundation).

Castells, M. (2009), *Communication Power* (New York, Oxford: Oxford University Press).

Castells, M. and Himanen, P. (2003), *The Information Society and the Welfare State: The Finnish Model* (New York, Oxford: Oxford University Press).

Colombo, F. (1993), *Le Nuove Tecnologie della Comunicazione* (Milan: Bompiani).

Espanha, R., Soares, L. and Cardoso, G. (2006), 'Do multimedia ao wireless: As dietas mediáticas dos Portugueses', in *A Sociedade em Rede: Do Conhecimento à Acção Política* (Lisbon: Colecção Debates, Ed. Imprensa Nacional – Casa da Moeda).

Fromme, J. (2003), 'Computer games as a part of children's culture', *Game Studies*, 3 (1). Available at: <http://www.gamestudies.org/0301/fromme/>.

Giddens, A. (1991), *Modernity and Self-Identity* (Cambridge: Polity Press).

Greenfeld, P. (1984), *Mind and Media: The Effects of Television, Video Games and Computers* (Cambridge, Massachusetts: Harvard University Press).

Hesmondhalgh, D. (2007), *The Cultural Industries* (London etc.: Sage).

Himanen, P. (2001), The *Hacker Ethic and the Spirit of the Information Age* (New York: Random House).

Jenks, C. (1996), *Childhood* (London, New York: Routledge).
Leu, H.R. (1993), *How Children use Computers: Study to dewitch a New Technology* (Munich: Deutsches Jugendinstitut).
Lash, S. and Lurry, C. (2007), *Global Culture Industry: The Mediation of Things* (London: Polity).
Livingstone, S. (2002), *Young People and New Media: Childhood and the Changing Media Environment* (London: Sage).
Livingstone, S. and Bovill, M. (eds) (2001), *Children and Their Changing Media Environment. A European Comparative Study* (Mahwah, NJ: Lawrence Erlbaum).
Livingstone, S. and Bober, M. (2006), 'Regulating the internet at home: Contrasting the perspectives of children and parents', in Buckingham, D. and Willett, R. (eds), *Digital Generations: Children, Young people, and New Media* (Mahwah, NJ: Lawrence Erlbaum).
Livingstone, S., Couldry, N. and Markham, T. (2007), 'Youthful steps towards civic participation: does the internet help?', in Loader, B. (ed.) *Young Citizens in the Digital Age: Political Engagement, Young People and New Media* (London, New York: Routledge).
Loader, B. (2007), 'Introduction: young citizens in the digital age', in Loader, B. (ed.) *Young Citizens in the Digital Age: Political Engagement, Young People and New Media* (London, New York: Routledge).
Loos, E.F. (2011a), 'Generational use of new media and the (ir)relevance of age', in Colombo, F. and Fortunati, L. (eds), *Broadband Society and Generational Changes* (Frankfurt am Main etc.: Peter Lang).
Loos, E.F. (2011b), 'In Search of Information on Websites: A Question of Age?', in Stephanidis, C. (ed.), *Universal Access in HCI*, Part II, HCII 2011, LNCS 6766 (Berlin, Heidelberg: Springer-Verlag).
Merowitz, J. (1985), 'No sense of place. The impact of electronic media on social behavior' (New York, Oxford: Oxford University Press).
Merton, R.K. (1957), 'Continuities in the theory of reference groups and social structure', in Merton, R.K. (ed.), *Social Theory and Social Structure* (Glencoe, IL: Free Press).
Mesch, G. (2006), 'Family characteristics and intergenerational conflicts over the Internet', *Information, Communication & Society*, 9 (4): 473–495.
Postman, N. (1983), *The Disappearance of Childhood* (London: W.H. Allen).
Prensky, M. (2001), Digital natives, digital immigrants, *On the Horizon*, 9 (5), 1–6.
Prout, A. (2008), 'Culture-nature and the construction of childhood', in Drotner, K. and Livingstone, S. (eds), *The International Handbook of Children, Media and Culture* (London etc.: Sage).
Rivoltella, P.C. (2006), *Screen Generation: Gli adolescenti e le prospettive dell'educazione nell'età dei media digitali* (Milan: V&P Università).
Sackmann, R. and Weymann, A. (1994), *Die Technisierung des Alltags. Generationen und Technische Innovationen* (Frankfurt: Campus Verlag).

Sala, X.B. and Blanco, C.S. (2005), 'Los niños y sus pantallas ¿quién será capaz de mediar', Paper presented at the 20th International Communication Congress, University of Navarra. Available at: <http://www.civertice.com/avance_resultados/cicom_bringue_sanchez.pdf>.

Silverstone, R. (2006), *Media and Morality: on the Rise of Mediapolis* (Oxford: Polity Press).

Tapscott, D. (1998), *Growing Up Digital: The Rise of the Net Generation* (New York: McGraw-Hill).

Varnelis, K. (ed.) (2008), *Networked Publics* (MIT Press, London). Weymann, A. and Sackmann, R. (1998), 'Technikgenerationen', *Literatur- und Forschungsreport Weiterbildung*, 42, 23–35.

Webster, F. (2001), *Theories of the Information Society* (London, New York: Routledge).

Weymann, A. and Sackmann, R. (1998), 'Technikgenerationen', *Literatur- und Forschungsreport Weiterbildung*, 42, 23–35.

Chapter 4
Digital Natives: Discourses of Exclusion in an Inclusive Society

David Herold

Introduction[1]

Over the past twenty years, technology has transformed the world. The speed and ease of the transmission of information, as well as its accessibility, has changed how people interact with each other. According to political and journalistic rhetoric, the world has become an information village in which people are connected to each other in a 'global network society' (Castells, 2010 [1996]). Within the boundaries of nation-states, the developments of ICTs have led to the postulation of an inclusive society, in which individuals are connected to each other and to societal institutions by overlapping ICT networks.

While politicians have often postulated that an accelerated uptake of ICTs among the population of a country means a more inclusive society, academic researchers have been more sceptical (see e.g. Selwyn, 2002; Wong et al., 2009. This chapter examines inclusivity in society through an investigation of the claims made about ICT use by university students (for a discussion of the experiences of older people, see also Chapter 5 by Hagberg, Chapter 6 by Chisnell and Redish and Chapter 7 by Schreder et al. in this volume). Against the background of the debate about so-called 'digital natives', the chapter will present the results of observations concerning the skill levels displayed by university students, and argue that, contrary to frequently made assertions, students do not display a greater affinity for ICTs. The chapter will conclude that instead of supporting the creation of an 'inclusive' society, ICTs and discourses on their use serve more to foster a growing 'exclusivity' in society for those who acquire ICT skills, running against the expectations of the 'inclusive society'.

The Digital Natives are Coming?

With increasingly easy and affordable access to ICTs, educational institutions around the world have incorporated technological elements in classrooms to enhance the learning experience of students. Online visualisations, virtual

1 This chapter is based on an unpublished paper of Herold (2009).

interactive spaces, digital storage of information, collaborative research and writing, virtual worlds or simulations, etc. are becoming *de rigueur* for lecturers at universities as well as for teachers at secondary schools.

The rationale underlying the introduction of such technology-based features into education is the assumption that young people today have grown up surrounded by and immersed in technology and so will learn better and faster if education manages to leverage their technology-based lifestyle. Students who entered universities and secondary schools since the start of the new millennium have been labelled 'digital natives' (or 'Net Gen' or 'Google Generation')[2] and it has been argued that this new group of students need more media and IT driven learning environments than the 'digital immigrants' of earlier student (and educator) generations (see e.g. Van Eck, 2006; Prensky, 2001a/b, 2007, 2009).

The internet has grown into an essential medium for communication, socialisation, and creative expression and virtual worlds like Second Life supposedly represent the future of human interaction in a globally networked world that students navigate easily, as they have grown up with the Internet. These 'digital natives' eagerly embrace tools such as Instant Messaging, social networking spaces, and massively multiplayer online games (Zhu et al., 2007: 201).

Marc Prensky, who is credited as the originator of the terms 'digital immigrants' and 'digital natives' (for a critical discussion about these concepts, see also the introduction, conclusion, Chapter 4 by Herold, Chapter 8 by Lugano and Peltonen and Chapter 10 by Loos and Mante-Meijer in this volume), has written extensively about the easy adoption of technology and the ubiquity of digital technology in young people's lives (e.g. Prensky, 2001a/b, 2004, 2005). His contention is that technology has transformed the way people live their lives and that (in education) young people today demand a fulfilment of their technological wishes as their due.

> Rather than being empowered to choose what they want (…) and to create their own personalized identity (…) – *as they are in the rest of their lives* – in school, they must eat what they are served. And what they are being served is, for the most part, stale, bland, and almost entirely stuff from the past. Yesterday's education for tomorrow's kids. (Prensky, 2005: 64 – my emphasis)

The challenge implicit (and often explicit) in Prensky's writings is that older people are ill-equipped to deal with today's younger people, who are different from preceding generations. As such, his argument – and that of many other educationalists – is based on two assumptions, the first being that older people are unable to adjust to the use of new technology, and the second that young people are so immersed in digital technology that they are unable to cope with educational methods failing to incorporate such elements. The 'classic' lecture theatre with students sitting immobile while listening to an authority figure is presented as too far removed from the life experiences of students to facilitate effective learning

2 See also Table I.1 in the introduction of this volume.

and should be abandoned in favour of newer approaches making use of the digital technologies that surround the students in their own lives.

> 93% of college students have access to the Internet. (…) Young people are highly active Internet users. For example, 60% go online to download music, 72% check email on a daily basis. 73% get information for school work, and 28% go online for instant messaging with their friends. Because of their high degree of Internet penetration and adoption the Internet is potentially an excellent medium for teaching and learning. (Lee et al., 2005)

The internet is seen as a showcase for young people's creativity and expertise in using digital technology that remains ignored by older people who are less internet-savvy and find it more difficult to deal with the flood of information available (e.g. Prensky, 2001a/b). Young people are not only amusing themselves online, but they are also creating content and working together to do so. Young people interact online to create blogs, websites, videos, etc. and thus demonstrate an array of skills that older people have to acquire through dedicated study.

> More than half of all teens who go online create content for the internet. (…) They report having done one or more of the following content- creating activities: create a blog; create a personal webpage; create a webpage for school, a friend, or an organization; share original content they created themselves online; or remix content found online into a new creation . (Lenhart and Madden, 2005: 1)

In some studies, young people were shown to be so used to technology, that it had faded into the background for them, as 'they don't think in terms of technology; they think in terms of the activity technology enables' (Oblinger and Oblinger, 2005: 2.10). Their lives revolve around the use of technology changing it from being a set of tools consciously used by 'digital immigrants' to a way of life used subconsciously and routinely.

> A junior at the university, Eric wakes up and peers at his PC to see how many instant messages (IMs) arrived while he slept. Several attempts to reach him are visible on the screen, along with various postings to the blog he's been following. After a quick trip to the shower, he pulls up an eclectic mix of news, weather, and sports on the home page he customized using Yahoo. He then logs on to his campus account. A reminder pops up indicating that there will be a quiz in sociology today; another reminder lets him know that a lab report needs to be e-mailed to his chemistry professor by midnight. After a few quick IMs with friends he pulls up a wiki to review progress a teammate has made on a project they're doing for their computer science class. He downloads yesterday's chemistry lecture to his laptop; he'll review it while he sits with a group of students in the student union working on other projects. (Oblinger and Oblinger, 2005: 2.1)

Connected to these descriptions of the lives of the 'Net Gen' are claims made about the cognitive and intellectual consequences of the constant and simultaneous immersion into multiple audio-visual data and information streams. They are supposed to be 'able to intuitively use a variety of IT devices and navigate the Internet. (…) they are comfortable using technology without an instruction manual (…) more visually literate than previous generations (…) able to weave together images, text, and sound in a natural way.' (Oblinger and Oblinger, 2005: 2.5)

> Net Geners have become some of the most technologically adept members of society. Our cell phones often serve as Web browsers, digital phones, and game consoles. We keep our schedules and addresses in Palm Pilots and our music in MP3 players. We program our televisions to record movies while we watch a game on another channel. We strive to stay ahead of the technology curve in ways that often exhaust older generations. (…) We are a generation of learners by exploration (…), we tend to learn things ourselves, to experiment with new technology until we get it right, and to build by touch rather than tutorial. (Windham, 2005: 5.6)[3]

Information Literacy of Young People: Fact or Fiction?

The existence of the 'Net Geners', or 'Google Generation', or 'digital natives' seems to be beyond doubt, and indeed anyone working with young people between 15 and 25 can easily assemble a working definition of this group that includes an increased use of technological gadgets, e.g. smart phone, X-Box, PS3, iPad, etc., a reliance on the internet for information and as a communications platform, a tendency to network with a large number of people online, familiarity with Facebook, Twitter, YouTube, Flickr, blogging services, social networking sites, etc. This Chapter does not question the increased use of technology by large numbers of young people. Based on my experiences teaching at university level for over 10 years, students' lives and studies include far more networked technology than those of students during the 1990s.

This chapter argues, instead, that the increase in availability and usability of technology has not led to a greater 'proficiency' in the use of technology. The existence of technology does not automatically lead to a proficiency of its users – even if the users grow up with it (see also Chapter 9 by Van Deursen in this volume). The almost general assumption that proficiency is acquired by 'osmosis' instead of through a dedicated learning process is in fact hiding a lack of even basic competencies in the use of computers or other networked technologies. This lack of concern over the acquisition of basic computing skills is leading not to a more inclusive, but a more exclusive society, in which the technologically skilled lead the unskilled masses.

3 See also Roberts (2005: 3.1).

While many publications rely mostly on 'generally known', or 'universally observable' phenomena, or on self-observation and evaluation (Rikhye et al., 2009), studies that focus specifically on the level of competence in computer users among the 'digital natives' have come to the conclusion that the 'digital generation' is often anything but.

> Our quantitative data show that, in general, students say they have the skills they need. The qualitative data suggest a slightly different picture. Students have very basic office suite skills as well as e-mail and basic Websurfing skills. Moving beyond basic activities is problematic. It appears that they do not recognize the enhanced functionality of the applications they own and use. The comparative literature on student IT skill self-assessment suggests that students overrate their skills; freshmen overrate their skills more than seniors, and men overrate their skills more than women (Kvavik, 2005: 7.7).

Students today *think* they know a lot about the internet, about technology, etc. while direct studies or tests of that ability show they do not (Kolikant, 2010). In fact, many educators who planned to rely on the use of technology in their own classes, found their students' skill levels insufficient for university level studies, and they had to teach students basic IT skills in addition to their subject matter.

> We expected students to already possess good IT skills to support their learning. What we found was that many necessary skills had to be learned at the college or university and that the motivation for doing so was very much tied to the requirements of the curriculum. Similarly, the students in our survey had not gained the necessary skills to use technology in support of academic work outside the classroom. We found a significant need for further training in the use of information technology in support of learning and problem-solving skills. (Kvavik, 2005: 7.17)

Rowlands and Fieldhouse (2008) came to the conclusion that there was little evidence to suggest any increase in the level of technological skills of young users. They pointed out that there was a lot of hype about the assumed increase in skills, but that almost no research had been done to back up the claims made about young people. They summarised their findings, by concluding that:

> research into how children and young people become competent in using the internet and other research tools is patchy but some consistent themes are beginning to emerge: (…) *information literacy of young people, has not improved* with the widening access to technology (… ;) internet research shows that the speed of young people's web searching means that *little time is spent in evaluating information*, either for relevance, accuracy or authority (… ;) *young people have a poor understanding of their information needs* and thus find it difficult to develop effective search strategies (…), *young people find it*

> *difficult to assess the relevance of the materials* presented and often print off pages with no more than a perfunctory glance at them (… ;) *young people have unsophisticated mental maps of what the internet is*, often failing to appreciate that it is a collection of networked resources from different providers. (Rowlands and Fieldhouse, 2008: 12 – my emphasis)

There are clearly identifiable problems that today's students have when using technology. These problems stem from a lack of education about basic technological skills that previous 'generations' of students acquired when they 'immigrated' into the 'digital age'. The next part of this chapter will present data gathered during the teaching of several undergraduate courses using the online 3D world 'Second Life' for tutorials and requiring students to give PowerPoint-supported presentations as well as to submit course assignments as Microsoft Word documents via email. My own background as a teenager of the 1980s when 'Hackers' were heroes, computers had to be mastered, networking was complicated, etc. and the fact that the internet is my research area, means that my own computing skills are more extensive and deeper than those of all but a very small number of my students – and I do spend more time online than any of them. I have taught Microsoft Excel and Access, as well as Java Programming, and worked on my first computer program when I was 13 years old. Who then *really* belongs to the 'digital generation' and can be called a 'digital native' (see also Waycott et al., 2010); and what does this mean in the context of discourses on the 'inclusive society'?

Babes in the Wood

The data presented here are based solely on two undergraduate courses run repeatedly between January 2008 and April 2011 at the Hong Kong Polytechnic University, one on Urban Popular Culture and one on Media Studies, with 160 students per academic year. The 3D online world 'Second Life' was used for student tutorials, the setting of tasks and graded assignments, and as an optional space for student presentations (as opposed to 'real-life' presentations using PowerPoint). Second Life was also used to undertake field trips, as well as for the students to interact with people outside of Hong Kong on media-related assigned tasks.

The classes were generally successful and the students provided mostly positive feedback about the intensive use of a virtual environment to support the 'real-life' lectures. Student comments suggested that the virtual tutorials made lecture topics more accessible. Some students additionally reported that they had profited from their interactions within Second Life as they themselves had never left Hong Kong.

Despite the success of the classes, though, the reliance on technological skills for the tutorials and the grading of students highlighted a number of problems that students had with the use of computers. Some of the students had to be taught basic computing skills, while almost all of the students initially struggled with the computing demands of the courses, despite extensive help. Students were *not* able to acquire the necessary skills by themselves. They were mostly neither willing nor able to become proficient in their use of standard software packages. Many had rarely used a computer outside a classroom before, and some students did not own a computer and relied instead on the computer labs for their IT needs. As a result, many students found the courses difficult, and successive iterations of the courses included increasing amounts of guidance on the use of computers, the internet, and technology in general to address the problems that emerged. For the sake of clarity, I have loosely grouped these problems under four separate headings, although there is some overlap between the categories.

Tech Problems

During presentations, most of the students displayed at least some lack of knowledge about the technical issues in using a computer to give a presentation to a group of people. Students were given the choice of either using their own notebook computers for their presentation or using the lecturer's computer. In both cases, I had to set up the computers for the students in over 90% of the cases, as students were unable to find the right connector to plug the projector's VGA cable into, and had to be asked whether or not they needed Audio for their presentation, in which case, I also had to plug their computer into the audio system in the class rooms.

Despite frequent reminders during lectures and tutorials before the start of the presentation sessions, none of the students followed my advice to download any internet files they needed before they gave their presentation. Almost a third of the presentations lost marks because their computer's wireless connection broke down during the presentation and prevented them from giving their presentation as planned.

Many presentations suffered from a mishandling of audio-visual files, both at the technical as well as at a software-control level. Students often brought files to the presentation without knowing the filetype or with which application the file could be opened. The System settings on their own computers were often inappropriate for presentations as well, as the system levels for Sounds, Brightness, Contrast, Video mirroring, etc. were often set up wrongly. During over 10% of the presentations, I had to intervene at some point to fix problems with System settings so as not to fail a group of students.

Despite the obvious problems of some of the presenting groups, though, other students who were present during these presentations did *not* learn from the mistakes of their fellow students or from the solutions I provided or the comments I gave at the end of each presentation session. During the presentation sessions throughout the three years discussed here, none of the groups presenting later learned from the mistakes of earlier groups, and I would have to point out the same problems each week. The students simply refused to learn the skills necessary to achieve a higher grade even at this most basic technical level.

Software-Learning Problems

In their use of software, most students displayed a lack of interest in learning anything beyond the skills they needed to complete their immediate tasks. Despite, for example, having to use Microsoft Word for all their university work over 90% of the students were unable to comply with stated requirements about font size, page margins, line and paragraph spacing, etc. None of the students showed any awareness of the need or the possibility to resize, crop, or position pictures of Second Life used in their Word documents to illustrate their points. Even handing out a sample assignment containing all the formatting requirements and the progressive simplification of the requirements did nothing to improve the results produced by the students.

Over a third of the students were not aware what the green or red lines under words or sentences in Microsoft Word meant, (i.e. grammar and spelling mistakes), and in five cases students approached me to tell me that their version of Microsoft Word did not contain a spell checker and that they could therefore not be expected to correct their spelling mistakes. In none of these cases did it help to encourage the student to peruse the Microsoft help system, nor did the students learn from a direct demonstration – instead they seemed to expect the lecturer to repeat his assistance for each assignment.

Although students were aware that I was online more often than they were and despite all warnings they were given, both verbally and in writing, on average about 5% of the students attempted to plagiarise in written assignments by copying materials from websites. While this is not in itself a 'software-learning' problem, the ineptitude of the students involved meant that their attempts at plagiarism were given away by their refusal to learn more about the software they were using. Students attempted to plagiarise by copying-and-pasting text from web pages into their assignments. They were not aware enough of the way Microsoft Word copies such text, though, and in 80% of the plagiarism cases hovering over the text with the mouse showed hyperlinks to other web pages that had been copied and pasted into the Word document by the unsuspecting student – who then always expressed surprise that I had caught him/her. In about half the cases, the plagiarism was even more obvious as the student had not been able to adjust the font or the font size (or in four cases the colour) of the copied text, which made the plagiarism visible at first glance.

More worrying than this serious lack of basic knowledge about Microsoft Word, though, was the repeatedly demonstrated unwillingness to learn any of the skills that they were so obviously missing. Students were given detailed handouts on how to produce their graded output, and almost 10% of the students requested and were provided with additional one-on-one tuition in my office, but there was little to no improvement in the computer skill levels of students during the course of an academic term. Students would, for instance, be taught how to download video clips from YouTube, but be unable to use this skill a week later. Students were, for example, given handouts and told that Second Life avatars could only be moved using the keyboard, but in every tutorial I would find at least one or two students who were simply clicking their mouse at the screen and complaining about the lack of movement of their avatar. As the delivery of proper tutorials depended on all students acquiring of at least some Second Life skills, this caused me to question, repeatedly, the need and the value of using computers for tutorials. The tutorials and lectures were designed to support and complement each other, yet the lack of sufficient computing skills among a majority of students and the unwillingness to learn such skills displayed by over a third of them made this very difficult and required the introduction of increasing numbers of small graded tasks and assignments designed not only to demonstrate lecture contents, but also to facilitate student learning of ICT skills.

Data-Usage Problems

A third area of problems that emerged in particular during the Introduction to the Media Studies course, were data usage problems. Students were often completely unaware of the public nature of most of the internet and of the damage they could do to themselves or to others through some of their online postings – and this despite a huge scandal involving several Hong Kong movie stars and singers in early 2008 during which a lot of their private photos and videos depicting sexual intercourse ended up on the internet and the offline media.

None of the students had read the user agreements for Facebook or Flickr giving these sites the full commercial rights to anything posted to their sites by users, although almost all of the students indicated having user accounts at one, or the other, or at both of these sites. When presented with evidence that a photo posted on Flickr had ended up as an advertisement for Virgin Mobile in Australia most of the students reacted with shocked disbelief. In discussions about public and private spheres and the internet, not one of the students knew anything about recent international developments to control internet traffic better, or about the right (and increasingly duty) of employers and universities/schools to check all contents transmitted or received on their networks. Except for two students in 2007/2008, students did not know that employers could easily google for information about potential or current employees and base their hiring or promotion decisions on the results of their search.

Despite a case in late 2007 involving the videoing of a lecturer at the university and the subsequent posting of the video clip to an online video-sharing site and the consequences this had for both the lecturer and the student involved, students on the Media Studies course insisted that the internet was only 'fun' and they were simply 'playing' online, and that as a result nothing on the internet would or should have consequences in 'real' life.

Again, it is less the ignorance of the students that is worrying, but rather their naivety in assuming that they do not even need such knowledge, or that it does not apply to them. More than two-thirds of all the students stated that they had at least one blog on which they posted their thoughts, photos, wild ideas, jokes, etc. Given the majority of students' wilful ignorance of their own lack of privacy online, this creates a huge potential for abuse and raises the question whether these students are really 'digital natives' at home in the 'digital forest' or just innocent 'babes lost in the wood' of technology. The evidence of the courses I have run during the past three years suggests the latter – especially while there are still many highly skilled predators in those woods.

Critical Awareness Problems

A final area of problems I want to mention here that goes beyond the immediate use of the internet, is the lack of critical awareness in the vast majority of the students of the so-called 'Google Generation'. Almost none of the students demonstrated the ability to maintain a critical distance from media sources, and therefore they were unable to evaluate sources and as a result misused them frequently.

Over 80% of the students in my courses based their assignments and presentations on three sources or less, usually the top hits produced by their Google searches on the topic. The unsuitability of the source materials was often ignored, and the information provided by them treated as unbiased, objective statements. Except for a very few students, they treated the information provided by academic articles, research reports, political manifestoes, advertising statements, etc. as sources of equal reliability, and except for two student papers never questioned their statements. In one presentation, for example, the students used the 'depictions of the truth' in several Pepsi advertisements as the basis for their evaluation of the reliability of statements made in a Coca-Cola advertising campaign.

The majority of students were unable to judge the suitability of their own language in assignments or during Second Life tasks, as well, and more than 10% of the students had difficulties finishing some of the tasks in the virtual environment, as they were seen as extremely rude by other users of the virtual environment who subsequently refused to interact with them. This lack of awareness of themselves, their own beliefs, and their surroundings also caused problems for students during presentations, e.g. when about 10% of students praised the level of gender equality in Hong Kong stating that men and women had achieved equal status in Hong Kong as women could now get their Filipina maids to do all the housework. Similarly, during two separate presentations on the integration of immigrants into Hong Kong, I was told about a 'man from India' who was able to 'sing like a Hong Konger' and who 'speaks fluent Cantonese' – facts that surprised many of the students. On closer inspection it emerged, though, that the family of this 'man from India' had come to Hong Kong over a hundred years ago, and that he himself had been born and raised in Hong Kong, and that Cantonese was his first language. I had to stop four more presentations early because of highly inappropriate statements made by the presenters (two because of racism, and one each because of sexism and political propaganda) – all based on an inept use of improper source materials.

The lack of awareness that students displayed towards their own presentations and assignments extended to those of others as well. During the first round of presentations, I had included a small element of mutual grading in the presentations in order to encourage students to listen to and learn from each other and to improve their critical skills. This turned out to be a complete failure, though. In all the cases, students were either unable to make any statements about the quality of the presentation, or used inappropriate language unjustly to attack the presenters. The evaluation of presentations seemed purely based on personal likes and dislikes, rather than on the actual presentation observed.

In addition to this lack of judgment displayed by students, they also continuously displayed a lack of awareness, and even of curiosity about websites, software tools, news, etc. unless 'everyone' they knew used them. Of the almost 500 students I introduced to the 3D online world Second Life between 2008 and 2011, only two had had an account with Second Life before attending the course, and only 5 had previously heard of Second Life. On feedback forms, around 10% of the students stated that they thought Second Life could never succeed in Hong Kong, because *nobody in Hong Kong uses it*, i.e. it was not fashionable enough among young people in Hong Kong, especially when compared to online *games* (e.g. World of Warcraft, or a range of Taiwanese, Japanese, and Korean role-playing games) to be attractive to them or their friends. This was despite their own admission that many of them regularly played the similar computer game 'The Sims', most of them had at least one blog, and a Facebook profile, and a significant number were actively posting photos and videos on Flickr and YouTube. Students who were more active online restricted their activities to sites that were well-known and popular in Hong Kong (either local or localised) and refrained from further exploration (see Jones and Healing, 2010 for similar observations on a 'collective agency' among students). Within Second Life, over 90% of the students stated that they only used Second Life to fulfil the requirements of the course and did not explore the virtual environment further, even though a majority expressed fascination with the possibilities and the size of the virtual world. For the purposes of the course this meant that instead of acting as an additional motivator for students, I had to design tasks to motivate students to use Second Life in addition to my routine course preparation.

Evaluation

In general, my experiences with the 'information literacy'[4] of students belonging to the 'Google Generation' suggest that their attitudes and skill levels ill-equip them for their lives as 'digital natives'. In stark contrast to previous generations of students, the 'digital natives' do *not* seem to be interested in the acquisition

4 For more information about literacy see also Chapters 2, 3, 7, 8, 9 and the conclusion of this volume.

and retention of knowledge about the tools they use, instead most students almost randomly access streams of information only to collate and then to re-arrange the data-flow in order to package it as educational output, such as assignments, PowerPoint presentations, etc. The individual user, i.e. the student, has become interchangeable and has almost no input into the end product, nor does he/she retain much of a memory of the end product or the tools employed to produce it once it has been submitted or presented (see also Margaryan et al., 2011).

Instead of combining and contrasting a range of information sources, in order to arrive at their own position, the information that is the easiest to access is used to produce an output. This often leads to single-sourced, or sequentially multi-sourced educational outputs across a whole group of students and an inability to deal with mutually contradictory source materials. The students of the 'digital generation' show demonstrable weaknesses in their ability to evaluate sources, to form, express, and defend their own opinions appropriately, and to judge other people's opinions and arguments, when compared to students on similar courses from the same backgrounds of just ten years earlier.

The lack of skills and their inability and unwillingness to acquire necessary skills is masked by an increased use of ever more powerful, but also ever more easy to use, tools that allow students to produce superficially acceptable results with a minimum of effort or expertise. The consequence of this growing reliance on barely understood tools provided by expert others is not the growth of an all-inclusive, networked society, but rather of an ever more *exclusive* society controlled by experts who lead those babes who can afford it through the woods of the digital network that are becoming less and less familiar to the 'digital natives' except as background on their guided tours. Public speeches have turned into PowerPoint presentations, the Internet has turned into Google, information and help have turned into Wikipedia, etc. a development mirrored by the Tech industry's push for the replacement of the broad network browser approach with the narrowly focused 'there's an app for that' approach that has begun to move to computers with the 'Lion' release of Apple's Mac OS X operating system in 2011.

Exclusive Society

Ironically, both sides in the debates around the abilities of the 'digital generation' are less concerned with the creation or emergence of an 'inclusive' society, and focus more on discourses of 'exclusivity'. While those claiming high levels of technical skills among the 'digital generation' emphasise the exclusion of older people from crucial new developments in society, critics of the notion – me included – talk more about the (self)exclusion of young people from an increasingly digital society through their lack of knowledge and skills.

Both sides of this discussion insist that a certain level of technological skills and knowledge are necessary to become a part of today's society, and both sides agree that large segments of the population do not possess these skills. While their views of who is part of society and who is excluded differ, both sides seem to think that the knowledge and skills gap experienced by large parts of the population is unbridgeable and will have to be accepted.

Older people are supposedly no longer able to acquire the technological skills necessary in today's world, and lecturers and teachers are almost expected to have problems setting up a projector or a PowerPoint presentation. Young people, however, seem to use technology as a natural part of their lives, while not being interested in actually mastering the tools they are using, and which are made available to them by multi-national corporations. For these corporations the creation and provision of such tools is a for-profit operation, for example, Microsoft's .Net and Hotmail services, Yahoo's webportal and Email services, Google's Search Engine, Documents, Calendar, Email, etc., or Apple's attempts at limiting the user's access to information and tools to a list of approved applications (see, for example, Mackinnon, 2008a/b, for a discussion of the implications of a reliance on such 'benevolent dictators').

The available data from both sides suggest very strongly that there are serious problems with current approaches to an inclusive society based on the amount of usage of computer networks. According to these data, the vast majority of people are unable to employ currently available technologies in an appropriate manner. Additionally, they are also presented as unwilling and/or unable to acquire the skills and the knowledge necessary for the situation to improve, which means that educational programmes will be unable to easily 'fix' the situation. Instead of there being two distinct groups of people, the 'digital immigrants' and the 'digital natives' – or the 'more experienced' and the 'naïve youngsters', though, it seems more appropriate to talk about different levels of technological expertise combined with specific attitudes towards technology (and a measure of one's disposable income and spare time) that determine how 'included' an individual is in today's 'inclusive society' (see also Bennett and Maton, 2010; Jones et al., 2010).

Taking such a scale of levels into account, the 'inclusive society' that the internet seemed to promise during the past 20 years is beginning to look more and more like an 'exclusive club' with similar rankings and insignia as, for example, the Freemasons – see the different certifications available from the European Computer Driving Licence Foundation (http://www.ecdl.org/programmes/index.jsp). Within this exclusive club, knowledge, skills, and access determine one's rank and level of inclusion, and an unmarried, (former) Hacker in his 40s with a lot of spare time and a good salary, living in a large city in the USA with fast broadband access will always be 'more included' than a secondary teacher in his 50s, married with two children, living in a rural area of northern England who has to surf the internet on an old computer over a dial-up connection (or even all the people who have never used a computer before).

Maybe it would be helpful to re-evaluate current definitions of the 'inclusive society' and to re-think its aims and goals in order to come to a new perspective on how to achieve such an inclusive society with or without a reliance on technology to provide the impetus and the networking tools for people to become closer to each other. As this chapter has shown, neither younger nor older people can be assumed to have the necessary skills to be part of an inclusive, networked society. If a majority of the people living in a society fail to meet the criteria for inclusion, then who does this 'inclusive' society really include? Can a societal model that excludes far more people than it includes still be called an 'inclusive society'? Is an 'inclusive society' simply a society that collects the highest common denominators in technological skills, so as to include the largest possible number or people? Or, is an 'inclusive society' merely definable through the creation of a set of certifications of skill levels that determine the level of one's inclusion in society?

References

Bennett, S. and Maton, K. (2010), 'Beyond the "digital natives" debate: Towards a more nuanced understanding of students' technology experiences', *Journal of Computer Assisted Learning,* 26 (5), 321–331.

Castells, M. (2010 [1996]), *The Rise of The Network Society* [Second edition with a new preface] (Malden and Oxford: Wiley-Blackwell).

Herold, D. (2009), 'Digital Na(t)ives? – Observing students in eLearning environments', research paper presented at the COST Action, 298 conference *The Good, the Bad and the Challenging*, Copenhagen, 13–15 May 2009.

Jones, C. and Healing, G. (2010), 'Net generation students: agency and choice and the new technologies', *Journal of Computer Assisted Learning,* 26 (5), 344–356.

Jones, C., Ramanau, R., Cross, S. and Healing, G. (2010), 'Net generation or digital natives: Is there a distinct new generation entering university?', *Computers & Education,* 54 (3), 722–732.

Kolikant, Y. B.-D. (2010), 'Digital natives, better learners? Students' beliefs about how the internet influenced their ability to learn', *Computers in Human Behavior,* 26 (6), 1384–1391.

Kvavik, R.B. (2005), 'Convenience, communications, and control: How students use technology', in Oblinger, D.G. and Oblinger, J.L. (eds), *Educating the Net Generation* (Boulder, Washington D.C.: Educause).

Lee, M.K.O., Cheung, C.M.K. and Chen Z. (2005), 'Acceptance of Internet-based learning medium: the role of extrinsic and intrinsic motivation', *Information & Management*, 42 (8), 1095.

Lenhart, A. and Madden, M. (2005), 'Teen Content Creators and Consumers: More than half of online teens have created content for the internet; and most teen downloaders think that getting free music files is easy to do.' Pew Internet & American Life Project (Washington D.C.: Pew Internet & American Life Project).

Mackinnon, R. (2008a), 'Silicon Valley's benevolent dictatorship'. Conversation (30.07.2008). Available at: <http://rconversation.blogs.com/rconversation/2008/ 07/silicon-valleys.html> (accessed 31.01.2011).

Mackinnon, R. (2008b), 'The Web's benevolent dictators' conversation (02/12/2008). Available at: <http://rconversation.blogs.com/rconversation/2008/12/the-webs-benevo. html> (accessed 31.01.2011).

Margaryan, A., Littlejohn, A. and Vojt, G. (2011), 'Are digital natives a myth or reality? University students' use of digital technologies', *Computers & Education,* 56 (2), 429–440.

Oblinger, D.G. and Oblinger, J.L. (2005), *Educating the Net Generation* (Boulder, Washington D.C.: Educause).

Prensky, M. (2001a), 'Digital natives, digital immigrants', *On the Horizon*, 9 (5), 1–6.

Prensky, M. (2001b), 'Digital natives, digital immigrants, part II: Do they really think differently', *On the Horizon*, 9 (6), 1–6.

Prensky, M. (2004), 'The emerging online life of the digital native: What they do differently because of technology, and how they do it'. Available at: <http:// www. marc prensky.com/writing/Prensky-The_Emerging_online_life_of_ the_digital_native-3.pdf> (accessed 23.03.2011).

Prensky, M. (2005), 'Engage me or enrage me': What today's learners demand', *Educause Review*, 40 (5), 60–64.

Prensky, M. (2007), *Digital Game-Based Learning* (St. Paul, Minnesota: Paragon House).

Prensky, M. (2009), 'Sapiens digital: From digital immigrants and digital natives to digital wisdom', *Innovate*, 5 (3).

Rikhye, R., Cook, S. and Berge, Z. L. (2009), 'Digital natives vs. digital immigrants: Myth or reality?', *International Journal of Instructional Technology and Distance Learning,* 6 (2), 3–10.

Roberts, G. R. (2005), 'Technology and learning expectations of the Net Generation', in Oblinger, D.G. and Oblinger, J.L. (eds), *Educating the Net Generation* (Boulder, Washington D.C.: Educause).

Rowlands I. and Fieldhouse, M. (2008), *Information Behaviour of the Researcher of the Future: A Ciber Briefing Paper* (London: University College London).

Selwyn, N. (2002). 'E-stablishing and inclusive society? Technology, social exclusion and UK government policy making', *Journal of Social Policy,* 31 (1), 1–20.

Van Eck, R. (2006), 'Digital game-based learning: It's not just the digital natives who are restless', *Educause Review*, 41 (2), 16–30.

Waycott, J., Bennett, S., Kennedy, G., Dalgarno, B. and Gray, K. (2010), 'Digital divides? Student and staff perceptions of information and communication technologies', *Computers & Education,* 54 (4), 1202–1211.

Windham, C. (2005), 'The student's perspective. Educating the Net Generation', in Oblinger, D.G. and Oblinger, J.L. (eds) *Educating the Net Generation* (Boulder, Washington D.C.: Educause).

Wong, Y.C., Fung, J.Y.C., Law, C.K., Lam, J.C.Y. and Lee, V.W.P. (2009), 'Tackling the digital divide', *British Journal of Social Work,* 39 (4), 754–767.

Zhu, Q., Wang, T. and Jia, Y. (2007), 'Second Life: A new platform for education', in Liu, H., Hu, B., Zheng, X. and Zhang, H. (eds), Proceedings of the 2007 1st International Symposium on Information Technologies and Applications in Education (ISITAE2007) – November 23–25, 2007 – Kunming, P.R. China (Picataway, New Jersey: IEEE Press).

PART II
Barrier Free Information for Older People

Chapter 5
Being the Oldest Old in a Shifting Technology Landscape

Jan-Erik Hagberg

Introduction

This chapter is about the oldest old. They are the people who are eighty, ninety or one hundred years old, have lived long, and have few remaining years to live. They are the people who have the longest experience of changes in society and have faced innumerable shifts in everyday technology throughout their life course; the people, who have adjusted to change after change in the technology landscape (see also Hagberg, 2004); the people who have literally experienced tuning a valve radio, washing their laundry in tubs, storing provisions in larders, ice boxes and cellars, doing mathematical calculations with a slide ruler, writing with a steel pencil after it has been dipped in an inkpot, travelling by train pulled by a steam engine, and even making local telephone calls via an operator. Such experiences have long since been amalgamated in memories of how life was when they were a child, went to school, began a working career and raised a family.

The skills and abilities that the old people have developed since those times are exclusively connected to the generation to which they belong. The experiences are seldom or never repeated today, except perhaps at meetings of veterans clubs for preserving old technology or when the local museum assembles their collection of household and leisure items from the first half of the last century. In their memories are also recollections of long periods of how life was without things that have now become necessary and natural; days without television, computers, powered screwdrivers and mobile phones. Such a long life leaves impressions on the old persons' homes. The things that are on display there have been collected at different times and represent different 'generations' of everyday technology. Many items are never or seldom used or even seen, but have their specific place.

At their advanced age, the oldest old live in the same technology landscape as everyone else, a landscape that seems to change at an accelerating pace and where the development of information and communication technologies (ICTs) alter the practices of daily life. Or do they actually live there? Perhaps most of them dwell in remote areas of that landscape where the latest technology has not yet reached? Or, perhaps old people deliberately avoid new technology? Perhaps they prefer, as long as possible, to manage with the well known and with what they already have? And if so, is refusal a possible way of acting? Or put differently, is it possibly for an individual to stand aside from technology's fast flow of new products, systems and applications because of his or her high age. Is that way of acting perhaps a right that one has as an old person?

Old people's self-chosen or imposed relation to new and old technology highlights several scientific, ethical and political questions. One basic scientific difficulty when trying to understand what it means to be old, is to be able to distinguish between the consequences of age in itself and generational belonging. This difference is obviously significant when considering the future. Will, for example, the digital divide disappear when new generations become the oldest old? Equally important is how you look at technology and technology development. What kinds of problems can be solved by technology development? In what ways can individuals make their own decisions about what to use or what to reject? It is so easy to be seduced, see the beauty and possibilities in the newest technology but forget the cost it can have in demands on resources in money, people and time.

I will try to outline in what ways the oldest generation differs from younger generations, and what those differences could mean for how technology is used (see also Chapter 7 by Schreder et al. in this volume) and how one looks at the importance of technology in one's life. There are many opinions about these matters. My approach is to build both on theories of ageing and theories of the social and cultural meanings of technology. This combination is seldom considered. At the end of the chapter, I will take up the moral dimensions associated with how everyday technology is being transformed at such a fast rate. This means seeing technology's double nature – its Janus Face. When old people's lives are scrutinised, it becomes obvious that new technologies can both complicate and simplify everyday life, and both impoverish and enrich our lives.

Concepts and Theoretical Approaches

Some of the concepts that I use require clarification. My focus is on everyday technology. This consists of technical objects related to daily chores at home, or used during free time or to move about and to communicate with others. I separate technical objects, in accordance with Mitcham, into artefacts and technical systems (Mitcham, 1994). The artefacts are of many kinds: things, household equipment, tools and appliances. The systems are essentially supply systems connected to the home – for electricity, water and sanitation, and information and communication. As a collective term, I use an individual's *material room*. The concept *technology landscape* refers to the technology objects existing in the surrounding community. In the background of my discussion is the fact that everyday technology, after having been relatively stable for some decades, is about to be changed fundamentally. A driving force is digitalisation. This has revived the dream of the smart home, a home with ambient intelligence that can adapt to the user's intentions and actions, and from where you can interact with anybody via new media.

How old people want and are able to have the opportunities to meet new technology is one area where differences are obscured by stereotypes about "how the elderly are" (Nilsson, 2008). The importance of where and how you live, your economic conditions, the knowledge you have, and whether you are a man or a woman are neglected. I am both trying to uncover general conditions, which in principle are valid for all old people's interaction with technology, and understand the differences that exist among the elderly. My discussion is based on the elderly's own perspective. It is their experiences, actions and life-world, in the phenomenological sense that count (Schutz, 1999). Accordingly, I agree with some of the key points of critical gerontology whose purpose is to explore various dimensions of elderly life, describe the variations, and show that ageing has different consequences and thus different meanings for different groups of older people (Phillipson, 1998).

Furthermore, I take as my starting point a techno-sociological tradition in which technology is understood as socially constructed and embedded in cultural values without ignoring the compelling nature of its material character (Latour, 1993; Hård and Jamison, 2005). I focus on four dimensions of that tradition.

1. The development and diffusion of new technologies is an outcome of alliances between different agencies/actors (Pinch et al., 1987).
2. Artefacts and systems are bearers of norms and values, and prescribe certain ways of action. These are not given but changed and maintained in use (Latour, 1993, 2005).
3. New artefacts and systems have to take over space in an existing technology landscape. This means that the old technology must be examined if we want to understand how the new is being appropriated (Silverstone and Hirsch, 1992).
4. The importance of technology cannot be limited to its functions. It also always has a social and emotional significance for the user. Technology in use mediates actions and values (Ihde and Selinger, 2003).

I am primarily interested in the second, third and fourth dimensions. I will not develop the first dimension further in this text. However, one can observe that in recent years clusters of different actors – commercial, political and research oriented – have emerged. These actors interact and compete in complex ways in the development of technologies (e.g. information and communication systems) that can be used in the care of the elderly, but also by old people as a support in their everyday life. Technologies for the elderly and for the care of the old have become both a matter of industrial growth and of finding solutions to the feared economic and social problems associated with an ageing society (Swedish Government 2010; EU (Cordis), 2011).

Data Collection

The empirical grounds for parts of the chapter are taken from qualitative studies of the elderly's living and accommodation conditions and their use of technology. These studies have been conducted in the city of Norrköping, and in Ydre, a rural community in Östergötland, which is a province in the southern part of Sweden. Norrköping has an industrial heritage originally based on the existence of many textile factories, closed now for four decades. Ydre is one of the smallest rural districts in Sweden. People there have lived, and to a large extend still live, by farming and forestry. The material reported in this chapter consists of interviews with eighty men and women aged 55 to 95 years, conducted in the period 2006–2010 (Hagberg, 2008; 2011; Larsson, 2009). Five different, but coordinated, studies have been made, three in Norrköping and two in Ydre. In two of the studies in Norrköping the participants were interviewed on three occasions. One of the studies in Ydre included only single men living alone who had never been married (14 participants). In addition to the interviews a survey was carried out where all the elderly inhabitants in Ydre aged 65 to 99 years (100 individuals) answered a questionnaire that had been sent to them by post.

The participants in the studies have been selected mainly with the help of the local pensioners' associations, which have provided lists of members, and by samples drawn from the national register. In all the interviews questions were asked about the participants' life course, with a special focus on their housing career and their use of every day technology during different phases of their life. The goal was to reconstruct their techno-biography. A set of value-oriented questions were posed (e.g. attitudes towards technology, being an elderly or old person, thoughts about the future). This part of the material was analysed by a grounded theory based approach. For this chapter results coming from the oldest participants in the different studies (30 participants) have been used. One limitation when trying to generalise from this research is that it is based on interviews mainly with people who have had blue-collar jobs or worked in services.

Who Are the Oldest Old?

The concept of the oldest old is rather vague. Ambiguity exists as it is nearly impossible to define in years when an individual passes the borderline between being just elderly or old to becoming one of the oldest old. There is a qualitative line, which we can all imagine; the oldest old are socially and culturally marked out. The discourse about the oldest in society is replicated in films, books and popular magazines, but also in politics. Perhaps one can say that the oldest old are a small minority who can be recognised by their habits, looks, clothes, family conditions, circle of friends and how their home is decorated and equipped. If, for the sake of argument, we set an age limit it must be based on the conditions in Sweden, the country in which I live. In Sweden there are about 250000 people who are 85 years or older. They constitute 2.5 per cent of the population (Statistics Sweden, 2011). Two thirds of them are women. Less than 2000 are aged 100 years or more.

One reason to limit the group to 85 years or older (85+) is that it has been shown in several empirical studies that most people in their late eighties have or are considering changing their daily routines and social interactions with reference to their advanced age (Dunér and Nordström, 2005; Larsson et al., 2009). The changes have a clear direction. One reduces activities, does fewer things at the same time, and plans the day carefully to achieve what one thinks is most important.

Half of those who are 85 years or older manage well on their own in their own home, one quarter have home-care help, and one quarter live permanently in a residential nursing home (National Board of Health and Welfare, 2006). Consequently, we can see three categories of old people who depend differently on help and support from their surroundings, and are thereby differently exposed to demands to accept new technology or adjust to a changed technology environment. We can see them as that – three different groups, but from the individuals' own perspective it is merely a set of phases in the ageing process. For a long time one lives in one's own home and manages well. Perhaps one has some help from a relative or a friend and in most cases a security alarm has been installed in the apartment. Thereafter follows a period when one must receive organised help to manage the daily chores. Perhaps the apartment is adjusted to the needs of an old person and some more alarms are installed. The demand that you should age in place and stay put as long as possible is strong in accordance with the dominant elderly care policy. But evidently, for some, the unavoidable occurs; one has to move to an old people's home or an assisted living facility. It will be the last dwelling, and to that place one brings a sample of personal things, perhaps some furniture, a radio, the television set, the telephone, some paintings and items that evoke memories. The small flat or room that is said to be your new home is embedded in a totally different material environment, and is described as an institution (Nord, 2011).

To be Old and Belong to an Old Generation

To draw attention to the oldest old means that *biological age* as well as *social age* (or *age position*) and *generation identity* emerge as critical factors in the individual's interaction with technology and with those changes in daily life implied by new technology. We thus have to handle three factors that, combined, distinguish the oldest old from others. I will deal briefly with their importance for how old people alter their use of technology, but will not separate the three factors completely.

Biological age must of course always be looked at in connection with a specific individual's interests, abilities, social and economic resources. The variation between old people is large, perhaps even larger than in the case of younger age groups (Schroots et al., 1999).[1] But most of the old are constantly reminded of their advanced age by deteriorating health, diminishing strength and a thinner circle of friends. It becomes harder to keep up activities that you have been used to doing for a long time. One effect of the reduced space of action is that tools and systems, which can compensate for impaired abilities, become essential. By adopting assistive technology the person may, hopefully, be able to continue to be active, participate in society, and be independent. Technology becomes an enhancement of the ageing body (Kielhofner and Tham, 2002).

Research on how and to what extent technology can compensate for lost or reduced abilities is extensive. An influential theoretical and practical 'school' goes under the label 'person-environment fit model'. In this, old people's well-being is seen as a consequence of how well one can adjust to changes in the surrounding physical environment, for example when a technology you are used to is replaced by a new and unproven form (Lawton and Nahemow, 1973; Wahl and Weisman, 2003). At present there are high expectations of coming breakthroughs in supportive technology that will utilise new insights from the cognitive and psychology sciences (Rogers and Fisk, 2010).

Age position indicates a person's social age. The expectations on how one should live one's life during different phases of the life course are strong. Within life course theory there is a special interest in transitions or turning points that make the individual change fundamental aspects of her existence (Giele and Elder jr, 1998). To be considered by others as being old can be such a turning point. I have, in another context, used the term the *ageing turn* to describe the redirection of life that takes place. The ageing turn means that high age *in itself* becomes an argument for the individual herself to reconsider her situation, or for important peers around to suggest changes. One is expected to alter essential habits, for example to stop driving a car, to stop riding your bike, to stay inside your home in the evenings, not to learn about the internet, and to get a walker to support mobility. Such changes have an emotional and symbolic significance for the individual and will affect the individual's self esteem (Chapman, 2005).

The things, the technical objects, which are added or given up as consequences of ageing become age markers. The walker is an interesting example. Initially, there is, particularly among older men, a reluctance to use a walker because it is a sign of frailty. Getting used to the walker is hard and takes some time. Those who nevertheless begin to use the walker re-evaluate it and soon begin to see it as an ally. In an experienced user's hands, it can even signal that here comes a person who certainly is old, but who takes her place in the shop, on the bus or in the neighbourhood (Wressle and Samuelsson, 2006). One of our informants, a man of 85 years of age said: *The person who invented the walker should have been awarded the Nobel Prize*. Domesticating the walker is a process that includes an ageing turn; one accepts that one has become old and that others see one as being old.

1 See also 'aged heterogeneity' by Dannefer (1988: 360) in the introduction of this volume.

A key issue in the discussion of the ageing society concerns the consequences of large generational cohorts entering this phase of higher age.[2] The coming generations of elderly and old, the baby boomers born in the 1940s and 1950s, have been ascribed with other characteristics than the previous generation: more leisure-oriented, more demanding, with better resources and perhaps even with a more positive attitude towards life. With their retirement they reach the third age, a phase in life when the individual is supposed to be active, without being limited by work or responsibility for children. There are even expectations that the 'new elderly' will enter the next stage, the fourth age, with an unbroken lust for activities. The trait of the fourth age is, otherwise, that diminishing abilities connected to the ageing process reduce the individual's power to act.[3] The question is then if the new elderly and those becoming the oldest old will be able to postpone or hinder the transition to the fourth age.

New technology is supposed to go hand in hand with the ambitious 'new old' as it is seen as having the potential to abolish established limits. Perhaps, with smart homes and individually tuned intelligent communications systems, one will be able to be active in society regardless of age. Sometimes it is even argued, in a post-modern spirit, that age will become irrelevant in the digital and virtual world; the 'new old' will have the opportunity to choose from among a repertoire of lifestyles and identities (Featherstone, 1995; Castells, 2000). In an even more spectacular vision the individual will merge with technology into a new entity, a techno-body (Haraway, 1991); an age-free potent creature from science fiction culture will be materialised. This is undeniably a fascinating thought for every true baby boomer born in the 1940s (which this author happens to be).

The dream of another old age may be enticing, but in the real world the implacable logic of biological ageing will not make an exception for the next generations of old people. The fourth age is waiting around the corner. Hopefully, social and medical improvements will increase life span even further, but that is all.

The idea that there is a third and a fourth age has faced criticism in gerontology. The criticism is that activity is set up both as a major goal and as a key criterion to determine if an individual is ageing well or not (Chapman, 2005). Against the activity theory stands the theory of disengagement, which says that old people, as a natural part of their ageing, withdraw from society and limit their social networks. Moreover, on the societal level old people are marginalised as a consequence of the inescapable transition of power and responsibility between older and younger generations (Corsten, 1999).

However, this essentially functionalistic theory is strongly criticised as well. One reason is that it gives legitimacy to an image of old people as weak and in need of support; the old are those who are 'outside'. If, for example, disengagement theory is the concept informing the development of a particular technology it will

2 See also the introduction and the conclusion of this volume for more information about generational cohorts.

3 See Laslett (1991).

almost inevitably be designed *for* the elderly, not with or by them. Our empirical results support, as we have seen above, the hypothesis that there is a qualitative leap, an ageing turn, which can be observed in how the individual approaches new technologies during the later part of the life course. However, there is no support for the conclusion that an old person would lose her interest in her right to decide which technologies she wants to appropriate and learn to use and from which she will abstain. The guiding principle is more one of deciding what is important when one has realised that life will soon be over.

Every generation will, of course, shape how its own life in old age will be. However, my third age-dimension, *generation identity*, is about something more. What I refer to is that people who belong to the same generation have experienced unique events at the same age.[4] They have collective memories, and strong impressions of how life was before (Eyreman and Turner, 1998; Godfrey et al., 2004). When old, their view on life is influenced by such events and memories.

The present generation of the oldest old in Sweden was, according to my definition, born between 1905 and 1926. It may seem a long time span but there are good reasons to see them as one generation. The domestic and other everyday technology was, for instance, rather stable during the first three decades of the century, with one important exception – the cities were electrified and households were able to replace paraffin lamps with electric light. In this generation's collective memory, the main elements are that when one was young most families were poor, material standards were low, housing conditions were bad and the technology landscape changed slowly. When this generations' members became adults, married and settled down, wider society changed at an accelerated pace – electricity became common, even in the countryside, the family gathered round the radio in the evenings, and so did the whole nation when important events took place, refrigerators were installed in kitchens, and the washing machine changed women's domestic work. Many moved to modern, light apartments in the suburbs of expanding cities. Telephones were installed, and in 1958, the year when the football World Cup was played in Sweden and the national team lost the final against Brazil, a television set could be found in most living rooms. Later on, many could afford a car. It was used during holidays or perhaps on Sundays to take trips with children and old parents. When the generation became middle-aged, IKEA opened its first large store. Up till then, one was used to keeping what one had bought, but IKEA made the way for new attitudes to how a home should be decorated; 'use, wear out, and throw away' became the motto from the late 60s onwards. IKEA was one of the signs that the consumer society had arrived (Wahl and Mollenkopf, 2003; Hagberg, 2008).

When the members of this generation became pensioners they experienced how many service functions were computerised, and they saw the breakthroughs of the home computer, the mobile phone, the internet and the growing access to

4 See also 'technology generation' (Sackman and Weymann, 1994: 41-43; Weymann and Sackman, 1998) in Chapter 10 by Loos and Mante-Meijer.

media in the home. Somewhere in this part of their life course was a borderline. Up until then they had followed the stream and adopted most new objects and systems that were introduced. Some of them were early adopters (Rogers, 1995), the first to have a new car or a colour television set. But the vast majority waited and bought the new things only when they had become common. Now, when the members of this generation are in their later years, most have adopted a pragmatic standpoint. One does not start using any new technology without being sure that its usefulness is greater then the effort it takes to learn to use it (Selwyn et al., 2003). Many of the oldest old that we have interviewed are worried and critical. One of the women, in her late eighties, says: *One wonders if it will happen as much during the next 60 years. We, who are now seventy, eighty, ninety years old, all these people, will not manage (...).* Another woman, also in her late eighties, says that everyday technology has become far too complicated: *I feel a resistance to certain things (...) it moves too fast. One cannot keep up with things. It is because one is at this age, I suppose (...) One wonders where everything will end up. Perhaps our children [when they are old] will sit, saying that everything moves too quickly. But I wonder if there can be so much more [technology] (...).*

One of the men supposes that the interviewer will think he is a boring devil as he is so critical of new technology: It just keeps accelerating more and more. Now it's so very fast. You can see it in things you buy, which quickly become out-dated (...). My dad told me how things had developed during his life and at that time one could not believe that progress would be so fast (...) He experienced the first radio and I experienced the first television broadcasts.

That "everything" nowadays changes too fast and that it is hard to follow is a recurring theme. Digitalisation in itself seems to be critical. When computers became common in working life our oldest informants had already retired and they saw no reason to learn to use one. Later on, many have, of course, addressed their lack of knowledge by getting help from relatives or by participating in courses about ICTs arranged by pensioners' organisations. But it is as if computers and the internet are definitely outside the realm of the oldest old (Findahl, 2010). Mobile phones, however, are closer to old peoples' needs. Few of the oldest old use one but a relatively large number in their eighties do. However, their pattern of use is different from that of younger people; the mobile is seen as a form of security, an extra alarm in case something happens.

Some have found ways around their exclusion from ICTs. One common solution is to get help from children and grandchildren. This ranges from getting support with installing a computer and solving technical problems, to learning to communicate with their grandchildren through the internet and using the computer to order services, or just to see what their grandchildren can do with a computer, and thus get a picture of what a computer in the home can be used for. This is often part of an extensive exchange of products and services between the generations. One of the women, more than 80 years old, says: *We have a computer, actually. We took it over from our son-in-law. He got it through his job and would get a new one (...) We got it in exchange for a lawnmower, which we did not need anymore.*

The frequent mention of children and grandchildren raises the question of how old people who lack these kinds of family ties manage to appropriate new technology. Only one of the fifteen old, single men without children living in a rural area that we interviewed had a computer. One of them says: *So it is, but the older you get, the less you feel forced to have this kind of modernity. I never even think about it, that I don't have a computer. The main thing is that you are busy during the day, and don't just sit there and stare.*

The rural-dwelling men give several arguments. One can imagine that they are used to having to defend their position: the internet is unnecessary and offers nothing for those who are old, you cannot keep up. But the mobile phone has a field of application among these old rural-dwelling men; they take it with them when they are fishing, hunting or just walking in the woods.

To defend one's decisions as regards how to use everyday technology is a common theme in the interviews. The pressure to follow the expansion of ICTs is difficult. Mobile phones, computers in the home, and access to the internet are on their way to being included in the collection of technological objects that every household is expected to possess and that are seen as obvious – what David Riesman in a classical text in the sixties coined *The standard package* (Riesman, 1993 [1964]: 111–117).

Objects that are now being included in the standard package are loaded with symbolic meaning; they mark differences between those who have and those who do not. In the long run it is nearly impossible to manage without such technology. It is *defining* in the respect that it regulates how service functions in society should be organised and accessible. The oldest old live with the tension caused by relying on one's traditional way of acting yet knowing, or suspecting, that one must change one's habits and adjust to the new demands.

The Importance of the New

We can interpret old people's resistance to new technology as being a consequence of the fact that most of them belong to groups in which knowledge and practical experiences of the new are limited. Technology is mainly developed by younger people, and new things are first used by them. For instance, for a long time mobile phones have been difficult to use for old people due to their small buttons and unclear display. In the light of the above interpretation, the issue of old people lagging behind becomes a question of information, education and persuasion (Hagberg et al., 2007). However, it is also possible to interpret the resistance as a consequence of emotional and existential reasons linked to high age.

The rapid turnover of technological objects in daily life is driven by the attraction and desire for the new. Campbell (1992) has defined various different meanings of the concept 'the new'. One can allude first to what is fresh and newly made; second, to what is improved in comparison with what already exists; third, to what is genuinely new, (i.e. something that previously was impossible or unknown) (Campbell, 1992). Campbell argues that the first dimension is a strong driving force for modern consumerism as commercial actors glorify new products and at the same time erode the value of existing ones. To be willing to discard what we have we must see it as worn out or useless. Old people seem to be more resistant to this kind of depreciation of their existing possessions. The second dimension, that the new is qualitatively better, also does not seem to be an important argument for old people. The third dimension is more complex. That which is genuinely new cannot be compared to something similar that one has or had earlier. Its value depends on its relevance and usability for the user. In such an evaluation, age and experience is critical, which implies that the differences between different generations could be large. Campbell (1992: 55) sees a pattern: objects that are interesting for one generation seem to be irrelevant or strange for the preceding generation.

Several conditions can cause generation and age differences. John Vincent argues that older people have fewer possibilities to express and accentuate identities by inserting new objects in their everyday life, simply by virtue of having a longer history of consumption. One already has a well-filled apartment and storage rooms. What has been acquired previously influences what can be acquired later, and new things may not be noticed or may be considered too deviant if one already has many items. So the choices are influenced by what fits stylistically or technically (Vincent, 2003). The latter limitation tends to be more important as new products increasingly imply access to certain technology systems.

There are also limitations that are a consequence of the individual's age and position in the life course. Products that are expensive and will last long are less meaningful late in life. To buy a house or a car can be seen as an unnecessarily large investment. A more psychological restriction could be called *anticipatory ageing*. The individual considers, then makes decisions that are meaningful only in a certain situation in life. These could be about adjusting one's living situation and technological holdings to fit in with supposed lesser mobility, diminishing abilities or need of care and help. Old people, especially those with limited economic means, tend to see even the purchase of small and regular things for the household as unnecessary and indefensible as such things will outlive the old people themselves. A pair of new winter shoes, a modern coat, new spectacles or a flat screen television become symbols. Restrictions of this kind are not entirely a consequence of the old person's own preferences, life view and experiences. They are also inserted in their social relations to others. Relatives expect, for instance, that their older relatives will have a certain consumption pattern and lifestyle (Vincent, 2003: 121–128).

The understanding that the older are less disposed than the younger to renew their material room can now be more accurately stated. First, old people have a higher threshold before they see the technical objects they use or own as worn out. They tend to keep what they have and refrain from appropriating new, but approximately equivalent, objects. They are also more motivated to repair what is broken. Second, old people are less inclined to see changes in everyday technology as improvements, and therefore they tend to keep earlier models or versions longer than the young. Third, genuine new objects are seldom connected to activities that old people are engaged in, which leads to a low interest in and lack of knowledge about the new objects that are spreading throughout society. Of course, there are also some old people who appreciate the new greatly and, using Campbell's term, are *neofili*. One of our informants, an urban-dwelling old man, had obtained new technology objects throughout his life. He tells us: *I have always been obsessed with new things and extremely interested in technical gadgets (...). On the whole I have welcomed all new technology. Occasionally I have rejected some, things that have been just trash. But most have been exceptional.* This man's home is full of the most modern objects of today; two television sets, DVD-players, coffee machines, digital cameras and computers. He hopes to continue to acquire the newest things when he has become really old. But he is well aware that he is an exception. Most others of his generation, according to him, argue with themselves along the following lines: *Shall we buy a new television set? But they have so many features and gadgets. We've got our old one. The remote control (...) you have to bang it in the table first, but it works anyhow!*

To Arrange One's Life as an Old Person

Several different generational and age grounded factors can, as we have seen, contribute to a better understanding of old people's relations to their material rooms. Usually the questions arise from the assumption that how one meets the new is the most interesting issue. But if we widen the perspective it becomes quite clear that several conditions in old people's life rather draw attention in the opposite direction – what should one do with all the things one has owned for a long time.

The meaning of things and technical objects for old people has hardly been researched at all. The few empirical studies which have been published imply, however, that many old people experience a more intense nearness to their material room. When an old person reduces her activities the way she sees things and technical objects in her home changes; some become more important, some unnecessary, and some have an altered meaning. Certain things become less important as tools for action and more important as objects for reflection (Kohli, 1988: 338). Some of the things you have can take on a strong emotional and symbolic meaning as they make you remember occasions and persons. They become hooks for the memory and offer perspectives on who you are and have been. They represent a storyline in the old person's reminiscences (Chapman, 2006; Peace et al., 2006).

For some old (but not for all) it becomes urgent to sort out their material room, both as a way to simplify the daily life and as a way to prepare oneself for the fact that life will soon be over. One wants to discard one's possessions by giving them away or otherwise disposing of them. It is a process of *household disbandment* or, using a French expression, *casser maison* (Marcoux, 2001; Ekerdt et al., 2004).

The individual selects which objects have significance and which do not. But *casser maison* can also be understood as an attempt to influence the circumstances after your own death with the intention of making it easier for your relatives to make the estate inventory, or to reassure yourself about how your belongings will be distributed among them.

In their answers, the old people we interview clearly mentioned that they were striving to reduce their material room. Several underlined the fact that much of what they own is unused and will be even more so in the future. This applies to much of the household equipment but also to many things associated with their long gone leisure interests – photo equipment, record collections, the sewing machine, the boat, and garden tools. It is a kind of burden from which one wants to be free.

The limited research implies, clearly, that during late ageing, the individual's material room gains a reinforced significance for identity, reflections, and relations to others, in the first place to close relatives and friends. One strategy is to discard all of the things that one considers less important. Another strategy is to arrange one's possessions as a preparation for the fact that life is about to end, and another one is to avoid renewing one's material room by not accepting new things or appropriating new technology.

There are of course many reasons for an old person to reconsider the content of her material room as her ageing advances. For example one may plan to move to a smaller apartment, one's partner passes away or one wants to live a more sustainable life. But the changes that I have discussed here are more deep-rooted as they have to do with the biological age as well as the phase in the life course and the expectations and demands of peers and relatives. The considerations are socially relevant and negotiated with others. We have noted the double nature of this negotiation. When an old person has decided to abstain from new technology, be it the internet, a laptop or a mobile phone, she has to defend her position. When the same old person wants to continue to use something she has mastered for a long time, be it the car, the bike or the sailing boat, she must argue for that right (Hagberg, 2008; Larsson et al., 2009). In some studies it has been observed that older women tend to finish driving earlier than men, a behaviour that can make the woman isolated or dependent on others. They risk becoming 'stranded widows' (Siren and Hakamies-Blomqvist, 2006; Levin and Dukic, 2007).

Old People on the Outskirts of the Technology Landscape

In my discussion so far, I have assumed that old people relate in the same way to their own ageing and to the norms of how old people should behave. However, the differences between old people are naturally large, depending on personal traits, interests and conditions. Within gerontology the importance of social differences has been underlined. A growing polarisation has been observed. Some groups of old people are developing a stronger position, they live in attractive areas of cities, have good opportunities to choose their housing conditions and thereby how their material room will be arranged and decorated. Other groups have few possibilities to make such choices; they live and must remain in areas in the cities or the countryside that are impoverished (Phillipson, 2007). From my perspective we can conclude that some old people age in dynamic areas of the technology landscape where there are many early adopters of new technology or services, including them. Others age in stagnating areas where the infrastructure tends to be eroded; here, they are excluded (Mattsson, 2010).

There is a dividing line between the growing cities and their urban surroundings and genuine rural areas. In certain areas in the countryside of Sweden, especially in the northern part of the country, there are almost only elderly and old people left. They are heavily dependent on the car. Looking rationally (and from the outside) at their situation, they ought to benefit greatly from the capacity of ICTs to bridge geographical distances. However, it is an irony that in the places where they live the conditions for using modern communication technology are the worst: broadband networks are not accessible, the coverage for mobile phones is patchy, and the old telephone lines are being phased out.

The differences that exist lead to compelling questions about old people's abilty to decide about their material room during their ageing according to their own needs and interests. We have concluded that many of the oldest old are either unable or unwilling to appropriate new ICTs and want to, or must, rely on older systems. Particularly during the last part of the life course many strive to reduce their use of technology and simplify their material room. The first moral question is whether the oldest old should have the right to be outside, to keep their habits and routines, and not have to learn new practices. And if so, how should the individual's independence be upheld? The second moral question is how the oldest old who want, but are unable to use, new technology, can be supported. I would argue that an individual who has lived a long life and gone through all the phases of the life course but the very last, has a special right to have access to technology that is crucial for her participation, independence and mobility in society. Obviously ICTs and how that conglomerate of agencies and applications will develop are of critical importance.

Many that debate the problems of the coming ageing society tone down the ways in which old people are excluded from new technology in the belief that the exclusion is a consequence of the generation to which they belong. The next generation of old people, one supposes, will see things differently. In one regard, this is right. Many more in the coming generations will use ICTs in the form we know it today.

However, the digital divide will then run through other parts of the technology landscape. Other systems will be spreading, from which old people at that time will be estranged.[5] The ageing turn, which is inscribed in the biological and social logic of ageing and in the understanding of that life will soon be over, will also be a reality for the coming oldest old.

5 See also the introduction of this volume.

The Janus face of technology is that it takes and it gives. It creates the new and destroys and undermines the old. It redistributes between generations. It can enforce the antagonism between young and old. It can be a part of the discrimination against old people. It can bridge age differences and abolish the consequences of age. One face of the God Janus looks in the direction of the future. His other face looks back, into the past.

References

Campbell, C. (1992), 'The desire for the new: Its nature and social location as presented in theories of fashion and modern consumerism', in Silverstone, R. and Hirsch, E. (eds), *Consuming Technologies: Media and Information in Domestic Spaces* (London, New York: Routledge).

Castells, M. (2000), *Informationsåldern: ekonomi, samhälle och kultur* (Göteborg: Daidalos).

Chapman, S.A. (2005), 'Theorizing about aging well: Constructing a narrative', *Canadian Journal on Aging*, 24 (1), 9–18.

Chapman, S.A. (2006), 'A "new materialist" lens on aging well: Special things in later life', *Journal of Aging Studies,* 20 (3), 207–216.

Corsten, M. (1999), 'The time of generations', *Time & Society*, 8 (2), 249–272.

Dannefer, D. (1988), 'What's in a name? An account of the neglect of variability in the study of aging', in Birren, J.E. and Bengtson, V.L. (eds), *Emergent Theories of Aging* (New York: Springer).

Dunér, A. and Nordström, M. (2005), 'Intentions and strategies among elderly people: Coping in everyday life', *Journal of Aging Studies,* 19 (4), 437–451.

Ekerdt, D.J., Sergeant, J. F., Dingel, M. and Bowen, M.E. (2004), 'Household disbandment in later life', *The Journals of Gerontology, Series B: Psychological Sciences and Social Sciences*, 59 (5), 265–273.

EU (Cordis) (2011), ICT – Information and Communication Technologies Work Programme 2011–121. Available at: <http://ftp.cordis.europa.eu/pub/fp7/ict/docs/ict-wp-2011-12_en.pdf> (accessed 15.01.2011).

Eyreman, R.T. and Turner, B.S. (1998), 'Outline of a theory of generations', *European Journal of Sociology,* 1 (1), 91–106.

Featherstone, M. (1995), 'Post-bodies, aging and virtual reality', in Featherstone, M. and Wernick, A. (eds), *Images of Aging: Cultural Representations of Later Life* (London, New York: Routledge).

Findahl, O. (2010), *Svenskarna och Internet. 2010* (Hudiksvall: World Internet Institute).

Giele, J.Z. and Elder jr, G.H. (1998), 'Life course research: Development of a field', in Giele, J.Z. and Elder jr, G.H. (eds), *Methods of Life Course Resarch. Qualitative and Quantitative Approaches* (London etc.: Sage).

Godfrey, M., Townsend, J. and Denby, T. (2004), *Building a Good Life for Older People in Local Communities. The Experience of Ageing in Time and Place* (York: Joseph Rowntree Foundation).

Hagberg, J.-E. (2004), 'Old people, new and old artefacts: Technology for later life', in Öberg, B.-M., Närvänen, A.-L., Näsman, E. and Olson, E. (eds), *Changing Worlds and the Ageing Subject: Dimensions in the Study of Ageing and Later Life* (Aldershot: Ashgate).

Hagberg, J.-E. (2008), *Livet genom tekniklandskapet. Livslopp, åldrande och vardagens förändring. [The life through the technology landscape. Life course and ageing in a changing everyday life]*. Skrifter från NISAL, Vol. 2008, 1 (Linköping: Linköpings universitet).

Hagberg, J.-E. (2011), *Åldrande på landsbygden. Att leva som äldre i Ydre,* Skrifter från NISAL, Vol 2011, 1 (Linköping: Linköpings universitet).

Haraway, D. (1991), 'A cyborg manifesto: Science, technology and socialist feminism in the late twentieth century', in Haraway, D. (ed.), *Simians, Cyborgs and Women: The Reinvention of Nature,* (London: Free Association Books).

Hagberg, J.-E., Burdick, D.C. and Sunkoy Kwon (eds) (2007), 'Gerotechnology: Research and practice in technology and aging – A textbook and reference for multiple disciplines' [Book review], *Ageing & Society, 27*, 1, 171–172.

Hård, M. and Jamison, A. (2005), *Hubris and Hybrids: A Cultural History of Technology and Science* (London, New York: Routledge).

Ihde, D. and Selinger, E. (2003), *Chasing technoscience: matrix for materiality* (Bloomington, Ind.: Indiana University Press).

Kielhofner, G. and Tham, K. (2002), 'Performance capacity and the lived body, in Kielhofner, G. (ed.), *Model of Human Occupation Theory and application* (Baltimore: Lippincott Williams & Wilkins).

Kohli, M. (1988), 'Ageing as a challenge for sociological theory', *Ageing and Society* (8), 367–394.

Larsson, Å. (2009), *Everyday life amongst the oldest old: descriptions of doings and possession and use of technology* (Norrköping: Department of Social and Welfare Studies, Linköping University).

Larsson, Å., Haglund, L. and Hagberg, J.-E. (2009), 'Doing everyday life: Experiences of the oldest old', *Scandinavian Journal of Occupational Therapy,* 16 (2), 99–109.

Laslett, P. (1991), *A Fresh Map of Life: The Emergence of the Third Age* (Cambridge, Massachusetts: Harvard University Press).

Latour, B. (1993), *We have never been modern* (New York, London: Harvester Wheatsheaf).

Latour, B. (2005), *Reassembling the Social: An Introduction to Actor-Network-Theory* (New York, Oxford: Oxford University Press).

Lawton, M.P. and Nahemow, L. (1973), 'Ecology and the aging process', in Eisoderofer, C. and Lawton, M.P. (eds), *Psychology of Adult Development and Aging* (Washington, DC: American Psychological).

Levin, L. and Dukic, T. (2007), *Äldre i transportsystemet: mobilitet, design och träningsproblematik* (Linköping: VTI).
Marcoux, J.S. (2001), 'The "casser maison" ritual: Constructing the self by emptying the home', *Journal of Material Culture*, 6 (2), 213–235.
Mattsson, K. (2010), *Landet utanför: ett reportage om Sverige bortom storstaden* (Stockholm: Leopard).
Mitcham, C. (1994), *Thinking through Technology. The Path between Engineering and Philosophy* (Chicago: University of Chicago Press).
National Board of Health and Welfare (2006), Care and services to elderly persons 2006, *Statistics – Social Welfare* (Stockholm: Official Statistics of Sweden).
Nilsson, M. (2008), *Våra äldre: om konstruktioner av äldre i offentligheten* (Linköping: Institutionen för samhälls- och välfärdsstudier, Linköpings universitet).
Nord, C. (2011), 'Architectural space as a moulding factor of care practices and resident privacy in assisted living', *Ageing & Society* (Prepublish. 1 doi:10.1017/ S0144686X 1000 1248) , 1–19.
Peace, S.M., Kellaher, L.A. and Holland, C. (2006), *Environment and Identity in Later Life* (Maidenhead: Open University Press).
Phillipson, C. (1998), *Reconstructing Old Age: New Agendas in Social Theory and Practice* (London etc.: Sage).
Phillipson, C. (2007), 'The "elected" and the "excluded": Sociological perspectives on the experience of place and community in old age', *Ageing & Society,* 27 (03), 321–342.
Pinch, T.J., Hughes, T.P. and Bijker, W.E. (1987), *The Social Construction of Technological Systems: New Directions in the Sociology and History of Technology* (Cambridge, Mass.: MIT Press).
Riesman, D. (1993 [1964]), *Abundance for what?, and other Essays* (London: Chatto & Windus).
Rogers, E.M. (1995), *Diffusion of Innovations* (New York, NY: Free Press).
Rogers, W.A. and Fisk, A.D. (2010), 'Towards a psychological science of advanced technology design for older adults', *The Journals of Gerontology Series B: Psychological Sciences and Social Sciences,* 65 B (6), 645–653.
Sackmann, R. and Weymann, A. (1994), *Die Technisierung des Alltags. Generationen und Technische Innovationen* (Frankfurt: Campus Verlag).
Schroots, J.J.F., Fernández-Ballesteros, R. and Rudinger, G. (1999), 'Introduction – Aging in Europe: Perspectives and prospects', in Schroots, J.J.F., Fernández-Ballesteros, R. and Rudinger, G. (eds), *Aging in Europe. Biomedical and Health Research*, 17 (Amsterdam: IOS Press).
Schutz, A. (1999), *Den sociala världens fenomenologi* (Göteborg: Daidalos).
Selwyn, N., Gorard, S., Furlong, J. and Madden, L. (2003), 'Older adults' use of information and communications technology in everyday life', *Ageing and Society,* 23, 561–582.
Silverstone, R. and Hirsch, E. (1992), *Consuming Technologies. Media and Information in Domestic Spaces* (London, New York: Routledge).

Siren, A. and Hakamies-Blomqvist, L. (2006), 'Does gendered driving create gendered mobility? Community-related mobility in Finnish women and men aged 65+', *Transportation Research Part F-Traffic Psychology and Behaviour,* 9 (5), 374–382.

Statistics Sweden (2011), Statistic database, population. Available at: <http://www.ssd.scb.se/databaser/makro/start.asp> (accessed 15.05.2011).

Swedish Government (2010), Government's Budget Bill for the year 2011. Health and Social Care. Available at: http://www.sweden.gov.se/content/1 /c6/15/33/07/ 715be3dc.pdf. (accessed 06.06.2011).

Vincent, J. (2003), *Old Age* (London, New York: Routledge).

Wahl, H.-W. and Mollenkopf, H. (2003), 'Impact of everyday technology in the home environment on older adults', in Charness, N. and Schaie, K.W. (eds), *Impact of technology on successful aging* (New York: Springer).

Wahl, H.W. and Weisman, G.D. (2003), 'Environmental gerontology at the beginning of the new millennium: Reflections on its historical, empirical, and theoretical development', *Gerontologist,* 43 (5), 616–627.

Weymann, A. and Sackmann, R. (1998), 'Technikgenerationen', *Literatur- und Forschungsreport Weiterbildung*, 42, 23–35.

Wressle, E. and Samuelsson, K. (2006), *Brukares tillfredställelse med rollatorn och dess betydelse i dagligt liv* (Stockholm: The Swedish Institute of Assistive Technology).

Chapter 6
Modelling Older Adults for Website Design

Dana Chisnell and Janice (Ginny) Redish

Introduction

In this chapter, we present research and practical guidelines for designing for older adults[1]. In particular, we present a model for understanding diversity among older adults and provide heuristics for inclusive designs that help this age group. There are at least six reasons for paying attention to and including older adults when designing products and services:

- Older adults are a large and growing group.
- Older adults have money.
- Many older adults are online – and that number is growing.
- Age affects us all.
- Designing for older adults helps everyone.
- Older adults want useful and usable technology.

Advances in medicine, nutrition, and technology make it easier to live longer, healthier lives. Every wave of older adults is living longer and remaining active longer than their parents. For example, between 1900 and 1994, the number of people aged 65 and older in the United States increased by a factor of 11, from 3 million to 33 million. That was almost four times faster growth than the rest of the U.S. population (U.S. Census Bureau, 2009). All the major forecasters of population growth and ageing agree that this trend will continue for decades. The U.S. Census Bureau projects that the number of Americans 65 and older will more than double by 2050 to 80 million (U.S. Census Bureau, 2009). By 2050, in the U.S., average life expectancy will be 89–94 years for women and 83–86 years for men (Cox, 2009). This trend is worldwide. Asia, especially, will see a dramatic increase in the number of older adults, going from nearly 400 million in 2009 to 1.24 billion in 2050. Even today, life expectancy around the world is well into the 70s and 80s: in 2010, in Europe, women could expect to live to be 82, men to be 76. In Japan, life

1 Different sources use different ages defining for older adults. Some of our sources (Bernard et al., 2001; Coyne and Nielsen, 2002; Kantner and Rosenbaum, 2003; Bailey et al., 2004; Chadwick-Dias et al., 2004b) consider age 60 or age 65 to be the defining point for older adults. The primary organization of older adults in the United States, AARP, invites everyone to join at the age of 50.

expectancies in 2010 were 86 for women and 79 for men. Tables 6.1 and 6.2 give us numbers and percentages of older adults throughout the world in 2009 and 2050.

Table 6.1 Population over age 60 (thousands)

	2009	2050
Africa	53,770	212,763
Asia	399,881	1,236,103
Europe	158,503	236,426
Latin America	57,039	186,036
Northern America	62,744	124,671
Oceania	5,338	12,246

Source: United Nations Department of Economic and Social Affairs (*www.unpopulation.org*)

Table 6.2 Percentage of people 60+ within the total population

	2009	2050
Africa	5	11
Asia	10	24
Europe	22	34
Latin America	10	26
Northern America	18	28
Oceania	15	24

Source: United Nations Department of Economic and Social Affairs (*www.unpopulation.org*)

In the U.S., grandparents buy an estimated $2,000,000,000,000 worth of goods and services of which $52,000,000,000 goes toward goods and services for grandkids (Francese, 2009). For Great Britain, the claim has been made that people over 65 own assets worth £2.300,000,000,000 (Kirkup, 2010). And the comparable figure for the whole of Europe is over €3,000,000,000,000 (Ageing Well Network, undated). Some of this wealth comes from a lifetime of saving and investing, but it also results from lower spending. Older adults usually no longer have children to support. Many have paid off the mortgage on their homes. In many countries they have government-sponsored pensions and medical coverage. Thus, they may have greatly reduced household expenses and more discretionary income to spend.

Characterising Today's Older Adults

Today's older adults tend to be more discriminating, sceptical, and analytical than today's younger adults. They tend to be less tolerant of sloppy, uninformed, or inconsistent design. They also tend to read more. In usability testing with older adults, we often sense an attitude of "if they wrote it, I should read it". But when they find pages that are less dense, with shorter paragraphs, common words, questions and answers, and lists and tables, they prefer all these hallmarks of clear web writing, just as younger adults do.

Older Adults Are Diverse

Although many researchers and designers act as if older adults form a single, uniform group, clearly that is not the case (see also the concept of 'aged heterogeneity' – Dannefer, 1988 and Bouma, 2000: 71). The group may include an 80-year-old marathon runner and a 60-year-old with symptoms of dementia. Yes, older adults are different from younger adults, but there are also many differences among older adults that are worth exploring here.

Older Adults Span Several Generations

If everyone over 50 is an 'older adult', we are using that phrase for five to six decades worth of birth dates. In the U.S. people aged 50–100+ are generally grouped into three generations:

- GI Generation (born in 1934 or earlier)
- Silent Generation (born 1935–1946)
- Baby Boomers (born 1946–1964)

Clearly, they are different from each other (Rainie, 2010). But also, clearly, the first and third of those generations are much too broad. From one end to the other of the 18-year span of Baby Boomers, we find very different experiences, needs, habits, thoughts, and beliefs. Baby Boomers born in 1946 came of age in the mid-1960s, while those born in 1964 came of age in the early 1980s. In every part of the world, the 1960s and the 1980s were vastly different eras – culturally, politically, and economically. For example, in the U.S., in the 1960s, if you were male, you could be drafted into the military to serve in Vietnam. By the 1980s, military service was entirely voluntary and was open to women as well as men.

Age: More – and Less – than a Number

Even among people of exactly the same chronological age, we find great differences. One 75-year-old may bicycle 15 miles a day, teach a class, and craft parts for antique clocks; while another needs a walker, is forgetful, and should not be driving. Yes, typically, eyesight degrades, hearing may get worse, and short-term memory becomes less reliable. But not for everyone and not at the same age (Bouma, 2000: 71). Older adults with diabetes may have more serious vision problems than their contemporaries. Older adults who take medication for high blood pressure or high cholesterol may suffer more short-term memory loss than their contemporaries. Older adults with arthritis may lose motor skills and fine coordination more rapidly than their contemporaries. Generalisations about limitations and disabilities faced by older adults will not work when designing new media and technologies. What we need are good designs for all with the flexibility to adjust to a wide variety of needs.

Older Adults Online

> In 2009, in the United States, 70% of people age 50–64 and 38% of people age 65 and older were online (Rainie, 2010). As the generations move on, these percentages will surely increase. The oldest old may still be learning to use computers as retirees. But many Baby Boomers have used computers and other technology at work. People born in the 1970s, 80s, and 90s have grown up with technology playing a role in all facets of their lives. They will all be online as older adults. Even today's older adults use the internet for many of the same tasks as younger people. They send messages, do research, post statuses, shop, buy, send, store, blog, and play games. Moreover, the percentage of U.S. Internet users aged 50 and older who use social media nearly doubled just from 2009 to 2010, from 22% to 42% (Madden, 2010). A different source reports that in 2009, 36% of U.S. Internet users aged 63–75 used social media, and 90% of them were on Facebook (Van Grove, 2010). In fact, people over 50 are the fastest growing segment on Facebook (Kafka, 2011).

Age-Related Problems

Some of the issues that today's older adults have with computers will disappear as today's younger people age. Technological savviness and comfort will be less important to worry about as people who have grown up with the technology become tomorrow's older adults. But other issues are related to the process of ageing. The changes that ageing brings – in hearing, in vision, in attention, in memory, in mobility, and more – will not go away (see also Czaja and Jacko, 2009; Loos and Mante-Meijer, 2009: 38–39; Bouma, 2000). Everyone who lives long enough experiences the symptoms of ageing to a greater or lesser degree, and some of those limitations are relevant for how we design. For example, years ago, when rotary dial telephones were new, a generation of older users was probably uncomfortable with that new technology while the then-current younger cohort embraced it eagerly. And that same old / young, hesitant / eager difference probably persisted

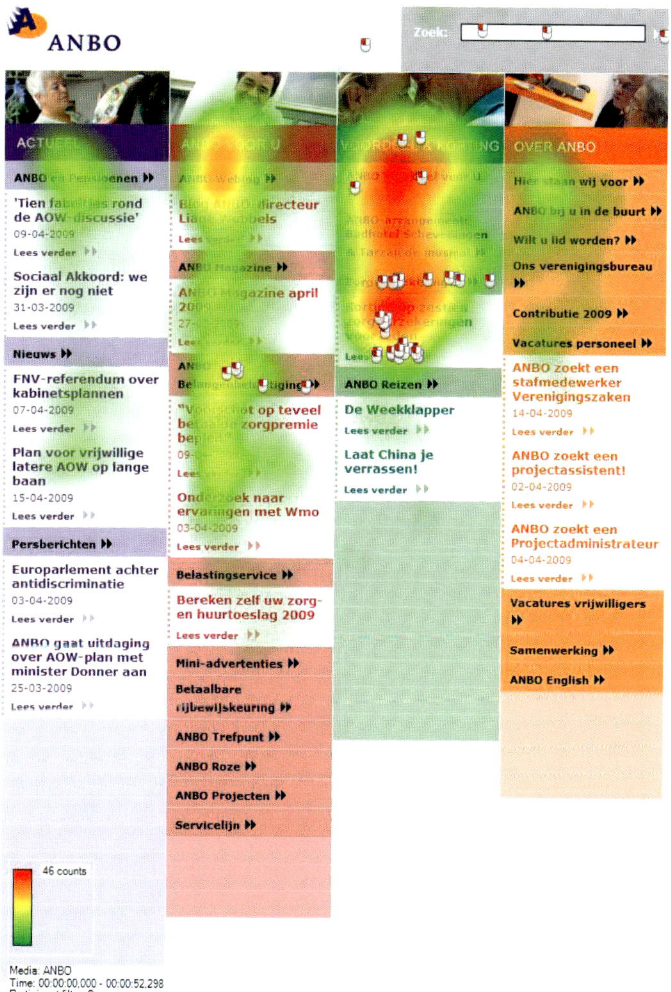

Plate 1 Heatmap of all older users

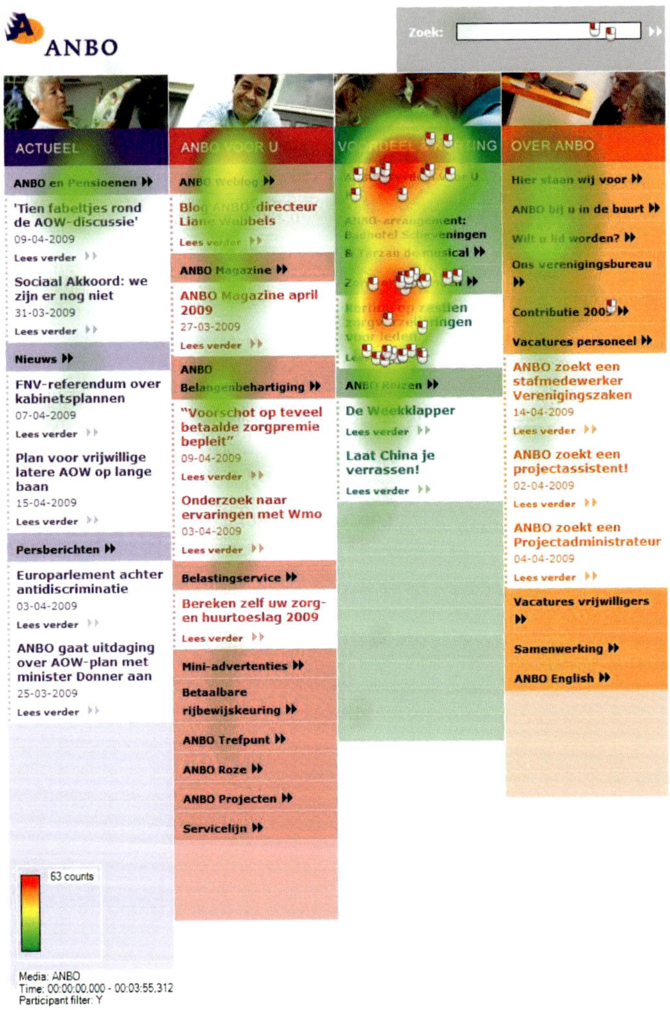

Plate 2 Heatmap of all younger users

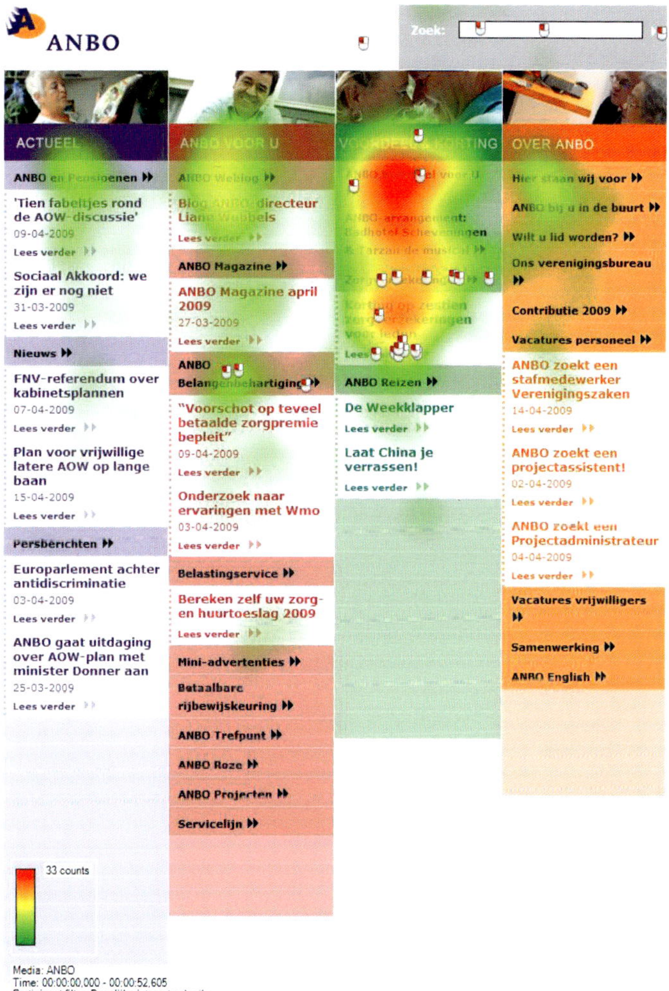

Plate 3 Heatmap of all older people using the internet daily

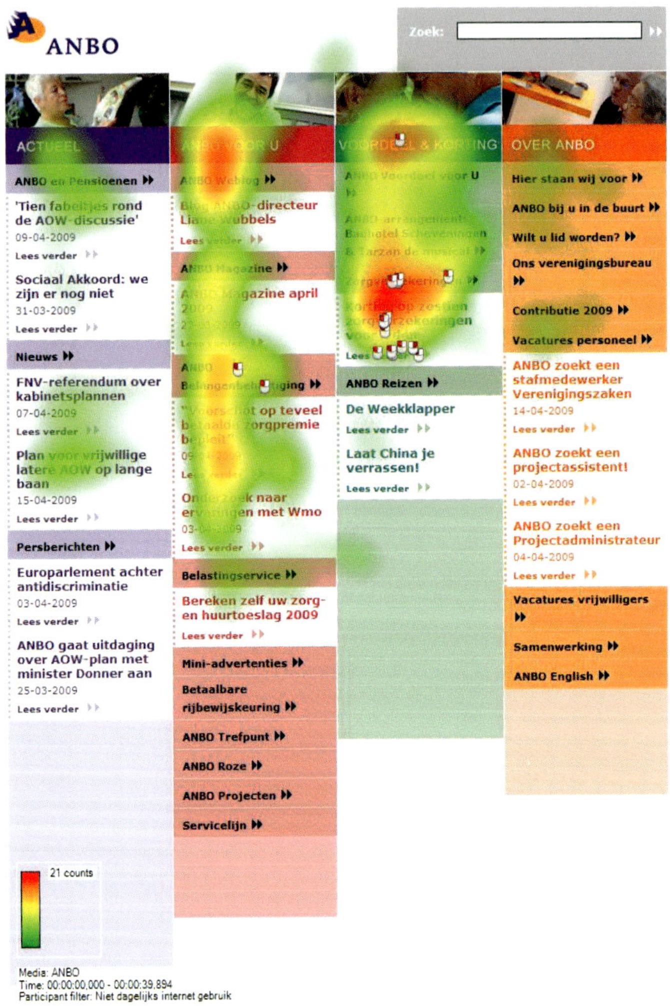

Plate 4 **Heatmap of all older people not using the internet daily**

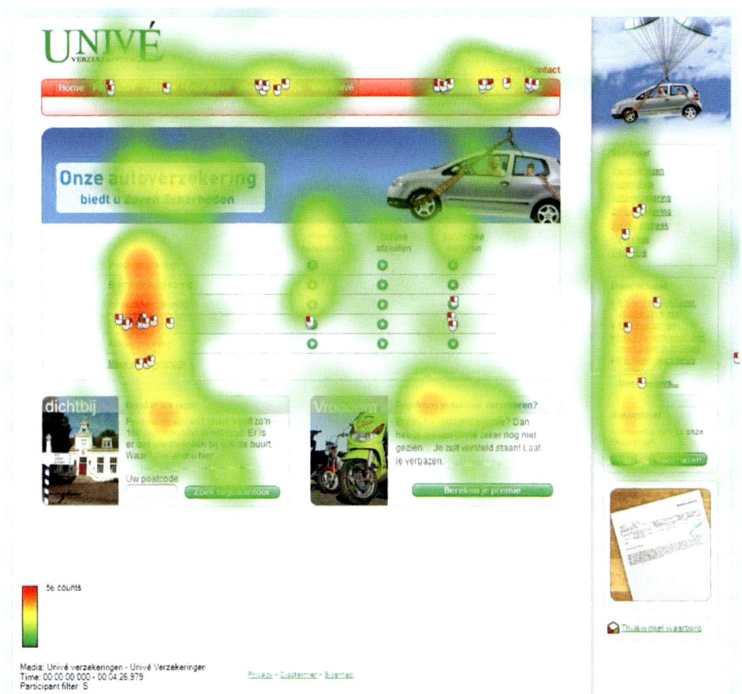

Plate 5 Heatmap of all older users

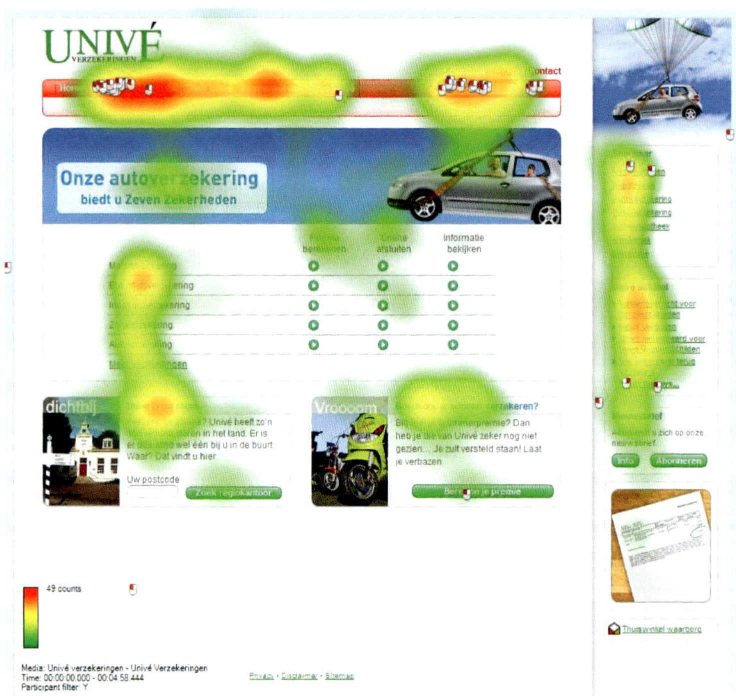

Plate 6 Heatmap of all younger users

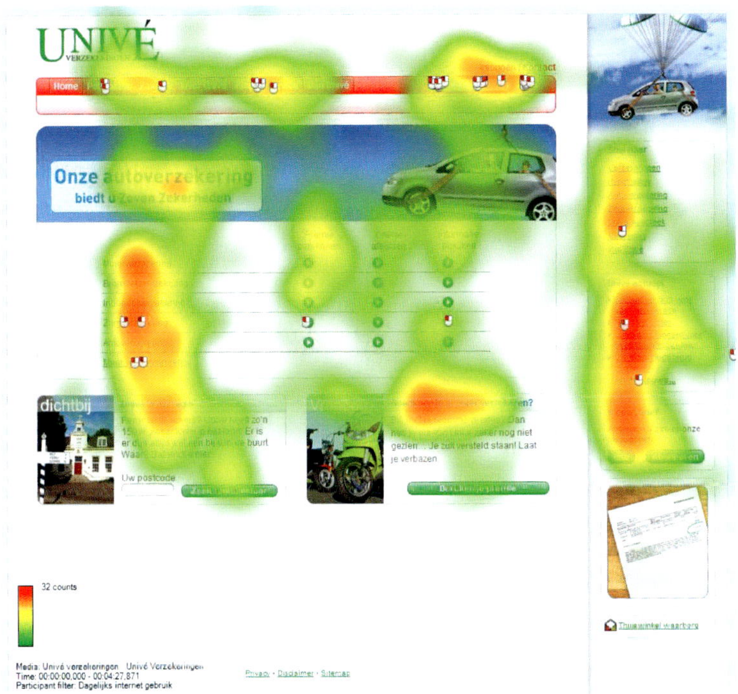

Plate 7 Heatmap of all older people using the internet daily

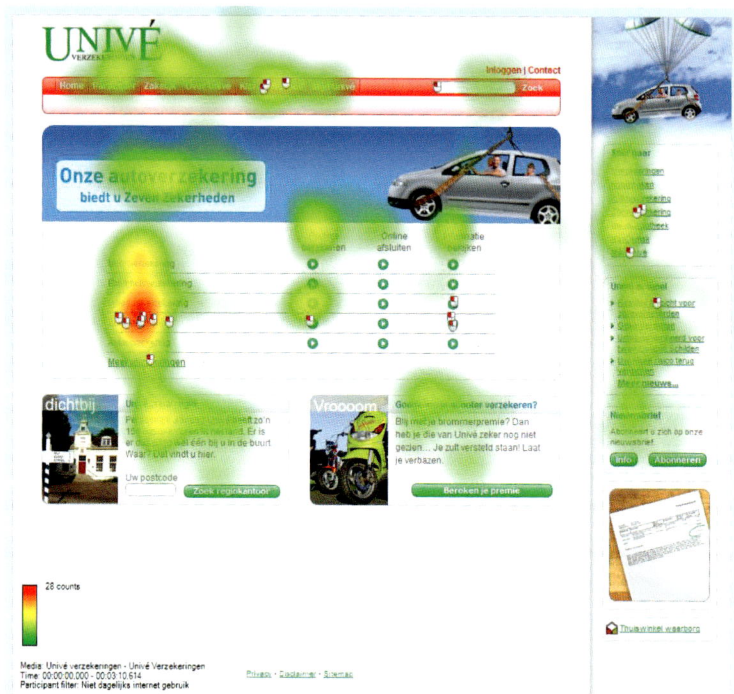

Plate 8 Heatmap of all older people not using the internet daily

through each new version of phone technology: push-button calling, early cell phones, today's smart phones. Now, however, almost everyone, regardless of age, is savvy and comfortable with the basic technology of communicating through phones. But being able to hear on the phone is still a relevant issue for many older adults who are experiencing hearing loss. It is not an issue any more of savviness or comfort, but it is an issue of what physically happens as we age.

Worldwide statistics on people living with vision problems and hearing problems are staggering:

- 285 million people are visually impaired (Lighthouse International, 2011)
- 90% of blind people are 45 or older (Thylefors et al., 1995)
- 278 million people have moderate to profound hearing impairment (WHO, 2010)
- One in three people older than 60, and half of those older than 85, have hearing loss (Cienkowski, 2003)

Ageing also slows down mental processes. In a recent study of memory, Gazzaley (2009) found that on average the older adults (ages 60–80) had more difficulty than younger adults (ages 18–30). The older adults were slower at suppressing information that was not relevant to their task. This slowing down is important; as Gazzaley (2009: 7) writes, 'how well you ignore information directly relates to how well you remember what is relevant'. Of course, not all problems affect all older adults. Many retain all their facilities well into their 90s and later (see also Bouma, 2000: 71). Stereotyping older adults as a bundle of limitations and disabilities would be a shame. But designers must consider the issues of ageing and the need for universal usability. Fortunately, universal usability is a realistic goal. Designs that help older adults work well for everyone.

Designing for Older Adults

Most technology is designed by young people, few of whom have experienced the vision, attention, memory, and other changes that ageing can bring (see also Pernice and Nielsen (2002: 4) in Chapter 10 by Loos and Mante-Meijer). And yet research shows that when you design with older adults in mind, everyone benefits. Although 'inclusive design', 'universal design', and 'design for all' (see also Stephanidis (2009: 1–2) for a discussion of these concepts) often refer to designing for disabilities, taking the perspective of generations applies here, as well (see also Haddon and Paul, 2001). As an example of a device, consider Apple's iPad. It is enormously popular with people of all ages: older adults, their children, and their grandchildren (Marsh et al., 2010). Apple sold 15 million iPads in its first 9 months. Certainly, price is not the main attraction; starting at $499 in 2010, the iPad is expensive to many consumers. But it requires little effort to start using it; the technical support is remarkable; and it lets people do what they want to do easily. As an example of a website, consider Fidelity.com. Several years ago, the usability team at Fidelity studied a cohort of older adults and a cohort of younger adults as they used the financial services website to do typical tasks. The Fidelity usability specialists then revised the website to fix the problems they saw older adults having. And they repeated the original study – again watching and listening as a cohort of older adults and a cohort of younger adults used the new site to do the same tasks. The new site helped everyone – not just the older adults (Chadwick-Dias et al., 2003).

The market is huge and ripe. As Natasha Singer pointed out in *The New York Times* on February 6, 2011, 'Devices for I've-fallen-and-I-can't-get-up catastrophes (…) represent the old business of old age. The new business of old age involves technologies and services that promote wellness, mobility, autonomy and social connectivity' (Singer, 2011). Older adults want designs that fit into their lives but that do not look like their grandmother's orthopaedic shoes.

When we discuss with our colleagues at conferences, workshops, and on social media sites why it is important to design for older adults, the collective answer is, because making designs accessible for older adults makes designs better for all users. While this is true, looking at an older adult as a collection of disabilities misses the person who wants to use a thing that is beautifully designed, regardless of limitations. For example, OXO designs kitchen utensils. The OXO company started when a husband wanted to buy a vegetable peeler that his wife, who had arthritis in her hands, could use without pain. OXO utensils have a distinctive look and feel. They are recognisable and desirable for their design and ease of use – not because they are made for old people with dexterity issues. The company has a philosophy of making products that are easy to use for the widest spectrum of users.

Looking Beyond Age: Ability, Aptitude, Attitude

We must look beyond age to understand older adults and thus to design with them in mind. In the model we developed, which we show later in this chapter, we consider three characteristics beyond age: *ability*, *aptitude*, and *attitude* (Chisnell and Redish, 2004).

Ability

In the early 21st century, the opportunity to see and use technology is even greater than in the late 20th century. However, exposure and experience (length and frequency of use) are not the same as expertise – for example, being able to identify features of a web browser or manage updates to a mobile device. Many older adults have spent many hours over long periods using just a few computer programs for a limited number of tasks. Chadwick-Dias et al. (2004a) found that web expertise – an ability defined by how much people know and understand about what they are doing – correlated with performance much better than simple exposure/experience (i.e. how often and how long they had used the technology). And expertise seems to be a function of training and cooperative learning.

Aptitude

For today's older adults training to use technology seems to be very important. Studies show that many older adults learn new technology best in collaborative situations that are task- and goal-oriented (Coyne and Nielsen, 2002; Morrell et al., 2002; Chadwick-Dias et al., 2003; Fisk et al., 2009). Perhaps we all learn best in collaborative settings, but many older adults did not have the benefit of learning to use computers and the web that way (see also Bouma 2000, 76 about the importance of 'situated learning'). They retired before these technologies became part of their work environment. Some researchers insist that providing training is the only way to make websites truly accessible and useful to older adults who have low web expertise (Morrell, et al., 2002; Czaja and Lee, 2003). Many older adults enjoy being trained to use technology; some even see it as quality time with the young people in their lives. Wright (2000) suggests that if you set up learning situations in which opportunities for errors are reduced, distractions from task goals are also reduced. In such situations, attention, memory, and recognition abilities are also better supported. Designs that include support for cognitive ability help all users navigate, interact, learn, and make decisions to achieve their goals.

Attitude

A major hindrance to gaining expertise can be the attitude with which the person faces ageing. Older adults' motivations for learning to use technology range from not wanting to be left behind to fearing that they will appear to be stupid in front of family, friends, and other learners. People who do not perceive themselves as being old are less risk-averse than people in the same age range who do consider themselves to be old. People who have 'young' attitudes are more likely to take on new challenges. Many of the older adults in our usability studies had a positive attitude about ageing and an overall positive attitude towards life (Mazur and Lee 2003; Chisnell et al., 2004). They did not perceive themselves as being old. They told us that when their parents were their age, their parents felt old, but they did not feel that they old. They expected to live longer than their parents had expected to live. (Many appeared to be younger than the ages they reported, as well.) The perception of what it means to be 'older' or 'ageing' has shifted not only for individuals but also for societies over the last 50 years.

A Model for Understanding Diversity Among Older Adults

We developed our 4As Model through our research for AARP, a U.S.-based organisation open to everyone age 50 and older (Chisnell and Redish, 2004; Chisnell et al., 2004). The model allows a nuanced approach to understanding and working with older adults and for planning, designing, and evaluating websites and other interfaces. The 4As Model uses the factors we have been discussing:

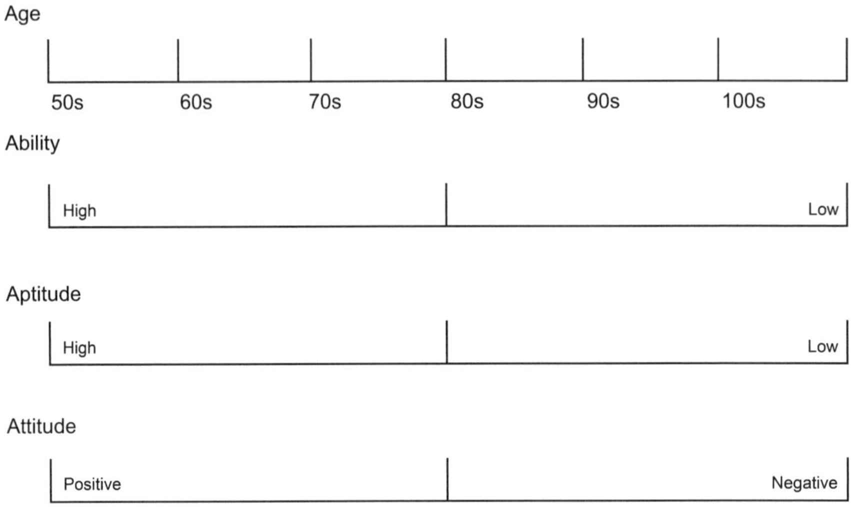

Figure 6.1 Four attributes for modelling older adults as web users

- Age – not just chronological, but taking into account life experiences
- Ability – physical and cognitive vaiation
- Aptitude – expertise with the target technology
- Attitude – outlook and risk perception

The model can be used to understand past research and to raise issues for future research.

Age – Beyond Chronology

As we mentioned, age is much more than a number. Age is both chronological and experiential. It encompasses maturity levels, life events, and experiences including the jobs the person has held over a lifetime; whether the person has served in the military; if the person has been married, widowed, or divorced; whether there were children, and if so, when they were born and how many there were; along with where the person has lived; and finally, where, when, and how much they were educated.

Ability – Physical and Cognitive Variation

Ability comprises the degree of physical and cognitive limitations or restrictions that the person experiences. Design must also take into account whether the limitations are remedied easily and inexpensively – for example, correcting vision with eyeglasses or improving hearing with a hearing aid. Designs can also be made to support people who need more assistance, from technology such as screen readers, tremor-reducing pointing devices, or wide-aim touch targets on screens (Jacko et al., 2002). Often, however, the design itself can be implemented to prevent difficulties. For example, studies show that older adults may have difficulty ignoring irrelevant information or they may be distracted by interconnected or cross-referenced links (Zaphiris et al., 2002; Lin, 2003; Gazzaley, 2009). By streamlining navigation and information architecture into 'happy paths' that echo users' goals, a design can make it more likely that both older and younger adults will reach their goals on a given website or in another type of application.

Aptitude – Expertise with the Target Technology

Rather than simply looking at the frequency and duration of exposure to technology, we found that a more relevant measure of aptitude for using technology comes from mastery and autonomy, which lead to expertise. When older adults are put in collaborative learning situations and feel that they control where they go and what they can do with a design, they develop expertise (Chadwick-Dias et al., 2003, 2004a).

Attitude – Outlook and Risk Perception

When older adults have a positive outlook, when they are forward looking, risk-taking, and open to experimenting, they often have more success with websites. But the picture is more complex. Older people who may be perceived as negative, fearful, or diffident might have a more difficult time learning to use the web, but they may also have a healthier scepticism about protecting their identity and security online than positive, risk-taking people. We can also look at this dimension as an indicator of confidence or emotional need for the support of other people (Gregor et al., 2002; Hawthorn, 2003; Kantner and Rosenbaum, 2003).

Applying the 4As Model

Design teams can use the model to determine the level of complexity that different users might tolerate, as well as how much support and training different users might need. Users on the far left of each attribute are likely to handle more complexity and need less support. Users on the far right of each attribute are likely to need less complexity and more support. We expect that teams will gather data about their users. That is, teams should conduct field research and usability studies, observing people both before beginning the design process and as those people then actually use their prototypes. In that way, teams can accumulate data about users' behaviour and performance in doing the tasks the design was created to support. Through observation, teams can also place users in the model. After studying a number of participants, clusters emerge that can be associated with task success rates.

Using data from user research and usability studies, teams can make informed trade-offs about features and functionality in a design. For example, high age is likely to require less complexity, but high aptitude allows for more complexity. Higher ability (that is, physical and mental fitness) allows for more complexity. Higher ability is likely also to correlate with lower age, but not always. Let us see how this plays out by placing a few people in the model.

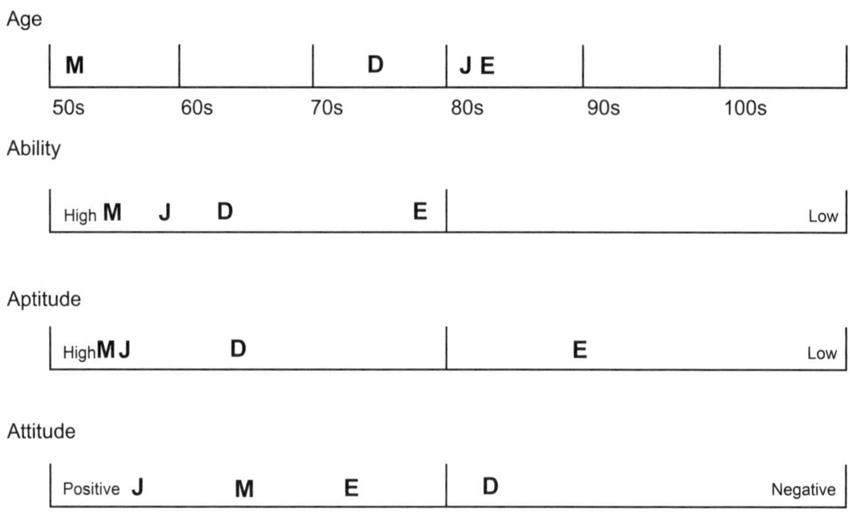

Figure 6.2 Study participants placed on the 4As Model

Introducing Four Older Adults with the 4As Model

In this example, the four letters represent different users:

- M for Matthew
- D for Duane
- J for Jim
- E for Edith.

The range of ages is wide, from the mid-50s to the early 80s. Without considering diversity, the inclination might be to assume that the oldest were the least able. But we can see on the model that this is not uniformly true. Jim, who is 82, lines up closely with Matthew who is 53 on ability and aptitude. But Matthew is less patient and less tolerant, and so appears closer to the middle on the attitude scale than Jim does. Duane is not the oldest, at 76, and he is highly functioning in ability and aptitude, but he is very cautious, almost to the point of being fearful of technology for this particular application. He has a more negative attitude than Edith, who, while very persistent, has no mastery of the technology used in the design but is experienced with other technologies. Her physical and mental fitness along with her attitude help her overcome her lack of skill.

If a team were to support all four of these users and the many other people whom these four represent, the team could assume that these users could all become reasonably proficient fairly quickly and easily, but that some might need more encouragement either in feedback from the system or though support such as practice, trials, or demonstrations.

An Example of the Model in Action

Let us say that we are developing a new photo sharing website. The idea of the website is simple: people can post photos where their friends and family can see the photos. All four of our users, Matthew, Duane, Jim, and Edith, have cameras. Matthew and Jim use their mobile phones as their primary camera. Despite their 30-year age range, all four are fairly high in ability. None has any physical or cognitive disabilities that would prevent them from interacting with a website. Three of the four have high aptitude. Let us also say that we observed that they have mastered most of the features of a web browser and are comfortable navigating online. Edith has more questions. She often gets lost among multiple browser windows. Her attitude helps her – she is very persistent; but someone new to the site might have the same kinds of questions that Edith has as she uses the site infrequently. Remember, we are focusing on behaviour here. All the users in our model have the same goal: they want to share photos with friends and family from one central location. They just happen to be older adults.

Having the data about the participants' abilities and dispositions, and looking at the model, it is clear we do not have to make an extraordinary number of accommodations in our new photo sharing website for these older adults. It might be enough to have a video demonstration that introduces the site. Matthew might not use it at all. Duane and Jim might use it once. Edith might go back to it more than once. Creating a trial mode could help users of all types. The trial mode would walk new users through their first uploads from start to finish, complete with step-by-step instructions and plenty of confirmation messages to help users be successful the first time they use the service. The trial could also instruct users how to set up contacts and share images. Users could maintain this mode after they sign up for the service, or turn it off with the click of a button. Designers can use the 4As Model as an outcome of their observations and other user research. Combining that understanding of their users with best practice heuristics, a team can turn out a design that will be useful, usable, and desirable to a wide range of users, older adults included.

We turn now to the heuristics for best practice that we have derived from research about older adults and from our own experience in watching and listening to older adults in usability tests.

Heuristics for Inclusive Designs Helping Older Adults

In our work for AARP, we developed a set of best practice design heuristics for reviewing websites from the perspective of older adults. These heuristics come from

- an extensive review of the literature on ageing and on older adults (Chisnell and Redish, 2004)
- our own studies, evaluating websites and conducting usability tests with older adults (Chisnell et al., 2004; Chisnell and Redish, 2005)

Each heuristic has a list of questions to focus our observations about websites. We are not suggesting that this is a complete set of heuristics to evaluate a website or other media. The heuristics cover the elements that the research we reviewed and conducted says are particularly needed by older adults because of the special aspects of age, ability, aptitude, and attitude that come with ageing. Many will work when applied to small, mobile devices, as well.

Although the heuristics are based on research about web design for older adults, most of the heuristics are just plain good design for everyone. Some are reminders of specific designs needed to accommodate the changes in vision, memory, and mobility common to ageing.

Interaction Design: Designing the Way Users Work with the Site

The navigation schema for a website and its information architecture are tightly bound. Both are driven by designers understanding clearly who the users are and what tasks they want to accomplish on the site. Processes represented in the navigation must match how users think of those processes. The location and labels used in navigation elements must be what the user would expect to find and also appear where the user expects to use them. In addition, the interaction must behave predictably and consistently.

1. Use conventional interaction elements

1.1 Does the site use standard treatments for links?
1.2 Is link treatment the same from section to section within the site?

2. Make it obvious what is clickable and what is not

2.1 In lists of bulleted links, are the bullets clickable?
2.2 Are command and action items presented as buttons?
2.3 Do buttons and links show that they have been clicked?
2.4 Are buttons clearly labelled?
2.5 If there is an image on a button or icon, is it relevant to the task?

2.6 Do graphic buttons avoid symbols that will be unfamiliar to older adults who have low computer and web expertise?

2.7 Is there a visible change (other than the cursor changing) when the user 'points' to something clickable with his or her mouse?

3. Make clickable items easy to target and hit

3.1 Are buttons large enough to see the image or text easily on them – at least 180 x 22 pixels?

3.2 Is the area around buttons clickable?

3.3 Is there enough space between targets to prevent hitting multiple or incorrect targets?

3.4 Do buttons and links enlarge when the rest of the text size is increased?

4. Minimise vertical scrolling; eliminate horizontal scrolling

4.1 Does the site work at the resolution that the user would typically view the site at without horizontal scrolling?

4.2 Do pop-ups and secondary windows open wide and long enough to contain the content without the need for scrolling?

4.3 For scrolling lists, for example, in the list of all the possible states:

– Are checkboxes used rather than drop-down ones (menus that drop down when requested and stay open without further action until the user closes them or chooses a menu item) or pull-down menus (menus that are pulled down and that stay available for as long as the user holds them open)?

– If not, are drop-down menus used rather than pull-down menus?

5. Ensure that the Back button behaves predictably

5.1 Does the Back button appear on the browser toolbar on every page?

5.2 Does clicking the Back button always go back to the page that the user came from?

6. Let the user stay in control

6.1 Is there no rolling text that goes by automatically?

6.2 Does the site use static menus (a click leads to another page) rather than 'walking menus' (exposing a sub-menu by hovering the mouse over the label)?

6.3 If there are 'walking menus', do they expand on a click (rather than a hover)?

6.4 Are the sub-menus timed to stay open for at least five seconds or until they are clicked?

7. Provide clear feedback on actions

7.1 Are error pages descriptive and did they provide a solution to the user?
7.2 Are confirmation pages clear?

8. Provide feedback in other modes in addition to visual

8.1 Are captioning and/or meaningful alternative text provided for images, video, and animation?
8.2 Does the site support haptic pointing devices (such as the Logitech iFeel mouse)?

Information Architecture: Organising the Content

Information architecture often involves dividing and classifying web content into categories. Our research found that older adults perform better – stay oriented within the site, find their way through sites, and are more likely to reach tasks goals successfully and efficiently – with information architectures that are broad and shallow, rather than narrow and deep.

9. Make the structure of the website as visible as possible

9.1 Does the site use a directory list format (a list of links) for listing topics (such as usa.gov does)?
9.2 Does the site use cross-references to related topics and redundant links?
9.3 Is the site hierarchy as broad and shallow as possible?

10. Clearly label content categories; assist recognition and retrieval rather than recall

10.1 Are labels descriptive enough to make it easy to predict accurately what the content will be under each topic category?
10.2 Do labels and links start with different, distinct, and relevant key words?
10.3 Is each label useful and understandable on its own?
10.4 Do labels reflect the language that older adults are familiar with?

11. Implement the shallowest possible information hierarchy

11.1 Are important, frequently needed topics and tasks closer to the surface of the website?
11.2 Are related topics and links grouped and labelled?
11.3 Do labels and category names correspond to users' tasks and goals?

11.4 Do paths through the information architecture support users' tasks and goals?
11.5 Is the path for any given task a reasonable length (2–5 clicks)?
11.6 Is the path clear of distracters and other obstacles to reaching task goals?
11.7 Are there a few, helpful cross-reference links that are related to the current task goal?
11.8 Do redundant links have the same labels?

12. Include a site map and link to it from every page

12.1 Is there a site map?
12.2 Is the site map linked from every page?
12.3 Does the site map provide a quick overview of the whole site (rather than descriptions of the top level choices, a rehash of the main navigation, or a list of every single topic on the site)?

Visual Design: Designing the Pages

Effective visual design depends on the context of the user and the context within the website. The compensation measures aimed at older adults may not work for others – or for younger audiences. For example, some colour and contrast combinations may work very well for some people with low vision but be unappealing to others. Observing users in usability tests can help resolve this apparent conflict.

13. Make pages easy to skim or scan

13.1 Are pages clean looking and well organised (versus cluttered or busy)?
13.2 Is there a clear visual 'starting point' to the page?
13.3 If pages are dense with content, is content grouped or otherwise clustered to show what is related?
13.4 Is it easy to tell what is content and what is advertising?
13.5 Do task-supporting keywords stand out?
13.6 Are images relevant to, and supportive of, the text content?
13.7 If there are videos or animated sequences, do they support specific goals or tasks?

14. Make elements on the page easy to read.

14.1 Is the default type size 12-point or larger?
– If not, is there an obvious way on the page to increase the type size?
– If not, does changing the type size in the browser enlarge all of the text?
14.2 Is the type size on pull-downs and drop-down menus the same size as the text content? Does it change when the user increases the type size?
14.3 Are headings noticeably larger than body content (18- or 24-point)?

14.4 Is sans serif type used for body content?
14.5 Are headings set in a typeface that is easy to read?
14.6 Are there visual cues to direct users' attention to important items that are in the left and right columns?

15. Visually group related topics

15.1 Is the amount of information – sparse, dense, or in between – appropriate for the audience and type of site?
15.2 Are the most important and frequently used topics, features, and functions, close to the centre of the page rather than in the far left or right margins?
15.3 Are task-related topics grouped together?
15.4 Are frequently used topics, actions, and links 'above the fold'? That is, can the user see important content without having to scroll down the page? (Bailey, et al. 2004; Chadwick-Dias et al., 2004b)

16. Make sure text and background colours contrast

16.1 Are text and interaction elements a different colour from the background (not just a different hue)?
16.2 Do the colours that are used together make information easy to see and find?
16.3 Are clickable items highlighted differently from non-clickable highlighted items?
16.4 Are multiple types of highlighting minimised on each page?

17. Use adequate white space

17.1 Are there visual cues in the layout of the page that help users know there is more content 'below the fold'?
17.2 Is there line space between clickable items? (at least 2 pixels)
17.3 Is body text broken up with appropriate and obvious headings?

Information Design: Writing and Formatting the Content

To ensure that the information in a design is effective, it is important to emphasise clear, plain language. But information design is more than that. Information design also includes features that make the content easy to skim and scan, understand, and act upon.

18. Make it easy to find things on the page quickly.

18.1 Is the amount of text minimised; is only necessary information present?
18.2 If there are introductory paragraphs, are they necessary?

18.3 Are instructions and messages easy to recognise?
18.4 Is there liberal use of headings, bulleted lists, and links to assist skimming?
18.5 Do bulleted lists have the main points and important keywords at the beginning of each item?
18.6 Do links have meaningful labels?
18.7 Are buttons labelled clearly and unambiguously?
18.8 Do button and link labels start with action words?

19. Focus the writing on audience and purpose.

19.1 Is the content written in the active voice, directed to 'you'?
19.2 Are sentences short, simple, and straightforward?
19.3 Are paragraphs short?
19.4 If humour is used, is it appropriate?
19.5 Are headings, labels, and captions descriptive of associated content?
19.6 Are conclusions and implications at the top of a body of text, with supporting content after? (i.e. an inverted pyramid)

20. Use the users' language; minimise jargon and technical terms

20.1 Does the site use words that most older adults know?
20.2 If there are technical words or jargon, are they appropriate for the level of domain expertise that the audience has?
20.3 If there are new or technical terms, does the site help users to learn what the terms mean?
20.4 Are the concepts and technical information (such as safety and effectiveness information about a prescription drugs) written in plain language?
20.5 Are instructions written in plain language?
20.6 Is the reading level appropriate for the capabilities of the audience and their literacy in the topic area? Is it easy to draw inferences and to understand the implications of text?

Reviewing these heuristics should make it clear how much of good design is just that – better design for everyone. For example, we know that most users, regardless of age, are more successful at finding information in broad, shallow information architectures than they are with deep, narrow hierarchies (Zaphiris et al., 2002; Lin, 2003). Most users perform better on websites where

- the interaction matches users' goals
- navigation and information are grouped well
- navigation elements are consistent and follow conventions (Coyne and Nielsen, 2002; Chadwick-Dias et al., 2003; Chisnell et al., 2004)
- writing is clear, straightforward, in the active voice (Gribbons, 2006).

Much of what makes good design for younger people helps older adults as well. Heuristic checklists are useful as both design guide and first evaluation of any product. But they do not replace the need to involve users at every stage of design and development.

Conclusion

Just thinking about old age as a collection of disabilities is old business. The new world of designing for older adults is about creating websites and other technology that are useful and desirable as well as accessible to the broadest range of users. Older adults are a large and growing market, increasingly online, increasingly using social media, and with money to spend. You can design with older adults in mind and still meet the needs of younger people – in fact, helping older adults makes products better for younger people, too.

Older adults as a cohort are living longer than their parents because they are healthier, and many will be affluent because they have been saving up for a lifetime – this means they have time, money, and motivation to be online.

Neither a monolithic view of older adults nor an entirely separate design for older adults is necessary. The age span is too broad. Furthermore, even among people born in the same year, we find vast differences in physical and mental health, in technological ability and aptitude; in attitude and motivation. Yes, we must pay attention to the problems that come with ageing; but we must also respect the abilities, aptitudes, and positive attitudes that many older adults bring to their use of technology. The realisation of this great diversity led us to create our multi-dimensional model and to use it for research, design, and usability activities with older adults.

Younger designers developing websites for older adults need to learn more about older adults' life experiences. For example, many older adults do not perceive themselves as being old. And so, all technology design – not just designs for older adults – should involve users. Using the 4As Model and the heuristics included in this chapter can help designers involve users and interpret what they are observing.

References

Ageing Well Network (undated), 'Wealth, power and productivity', The Business of Ageing. Available at: <http://www.businessofageing.com/www/default/index.cfm/the-silver-market/get-the-facts/ wealth-power-and-productivity/> (accessed15.03.2011).

Bailey, R., Joyani, S., Amadi, M., Changkit, M. and Harley, K. (2004), 'Older Users and the Web', *Usability University,* July 2004; jointly sponsored by General Services Administration, Health and Human Services, and AARP.

Bernard, M., Liao, C.H., and Mills, M. (2001), 'Effects of font type and size on the legibility and reading time of online text by older adults', conference paper, ACM SIGCHI 2001.

Bouma, H. (2000), 'Document and interface design for older citizens', in Westendorp, P., Jansen, C. and Punselie, R. (eds), Interface Design *& Document Design* (Amsterdam: Rodopi).

Chadwick-Dias, A. McNulty, M. and Tullis, T. (2003), 'Web usability and age: How design changes can improve performance', Proceedings of the 2003 Conference on Universal Usability, 30–37.

Chadwick-Dias, A., McNulty, M. and Tullis, T. (2004), 'Web usability and age: How design changes can improve performance', presentation at Aging by design, September 2004. Available at: <http://www.bentley.edu/events/agingbydesign2004/presentations/ tedesco_ chadwickdias_tullis_webusabilityandage.pdf>.

Chadwick-Dias, A., Tedesco, D., and Tullis, T. (2004a), 'Late breaking result papers: Older adults web usability: Is web experience the same as web expertise?', conference paper, Extended abstracts of the 2004 conference on human factors and computing systems, ACM SIGCHI 2004.

Chadwick-Dias, A., Tedesco, D., and Tullis, T. (2004b), 'Demographic differences in preferred website content', conference paper, Usability Professionals' Association Proceedings 2004.

Chisnell, D., Lee, A. and Redish, J.C. (2004), 'Recruiting and working with older participants'. Available at: <http://www.aarp.org/ olderwiserwired>.article AARP <http://www.aarp.org/olderwiserwired>.

Chisnell, D. and Redish, J.C. (2004), 'Designing web sites for older adults: A Review of recent research', report to AARP, December 2004. Available at: <http://www.aarp.org/ olderwiserwired>.

Chisnell, D. and Redish, J.C. (2005), 'Designing web sites for older adults: Expert review of usability for older adults at 50 web Sites', report to AARP, February 2005.

Cienkowski, K. M. (2003), 'Auditory aging, hearing loss', *The Journal of Self Help for Hard of Hearing People.* Available at: <http://www.hearingloss.org/magazine/mag-mayjun03.asp> (assessed 22.03.2011).

Cox, L. (2009), 'We will live longer in 2050, study predicts', ABC News Medical Unit. December 14, 2009. Available at: <http://abcnews.go.com/Health/ActiveAging/humans-live-longer-2050-scientists-predict/story?id=9330511>.

Coyne, K.P. and Nielsen, J. Web (2002), *Usability for Senior Citizens*, Report Nielsen Norman Group, April 2002.

Czaja, S.J. and Lee, C. (2003), 'Designing computer systems for older adults', in Jacko, J.A. and Sears, A. (eds), *The Human-Computer Interaction Handbook: Fundamentals, Evolving Technologies and Emerging Applications* (Mahwah, NJ: Lawrence Erlbaum Associates).

Czaja, S.J. and Lee, C. (2009), 'Information Technology and Older Adults', in Sears, A. and Jacko, J.A. (eds), *Human-Computer Interaction: Designing for Diverse Users and Domains* (Boca Raton: CRC Press).

Dannefer, D. (1988), 'What's in a name? An account of the neglect of variability in the study of ageing', in Birren, J.E. and Bengtson, V.L. (eds), *Emergent Theories of Ageing* (New York: Springer).

Fisk, A., Rogers, W., Charness, N., Czaja, S. and Sharit, J. (2009), *Designing for Older Adults: Principles and Creative Human Factors Approaches* (Boca Raton: CRC Press.).

Francese, P. (2009), The grandparent economy: A study of the population, Spending habits, and economic impact of grandparents in the United States, *Grandparents.com.* Available at: <http://www.grandparents.com/gp/home/index.html>.

Gazzaley, A. (2009), 'The aging brain, user experience' 8 (1), 10–13. Available at: <http://www.usabilityprofessionals.org/upa_publications/user_experience/past_issues/2009-1.html>.

Gregor, P., Newell, A. and Zajicek, A. (2002), 'Solutions for aging – Designing for dynamic diversity: Interfaces for older people', conference paper, Proceedings of the fifth international ACM conference on Assistive technologies. ASSETS 2002, 151–156.

Gribbons, W. (2006), 'Functional illiteracy and the aging population: Creating appropriate design support', presentation at Aging by design, October 2006. Available at: <http://www.bentley.edu/events/agingbydesign2006/documents/gribbons.ppt>.

Haddon, L. and Paul, G. (2001), 'Design in the ICT Industry: The role of users', in Coombs, R, Green, K. , Richards, A. and Walsh, V. (eds), *Technology and the Market: Demand, Users and Innovation* (Cheltenham, Camberley, Northampton: Edward Elgar Publishing).

Hawthorn, D. (2003), 'How universal is good design for older users?', conference paper, ACM SIGCAPH Computers and the Physically Handicapped, Proceedings of the 2003 conference on universal usability, Issue 73–74.

Jacko, J.A., Scott, I.U., Sainfort, F., Moloney, K.P., Kongnakorn, T., Zorich, B.S., and Emery, V.K (2002), 'Effects of multimodal feedback on the performance of older adults with normal and impaired vision, *Universal Access: Theoretical Perspectives, Practice, and Experience* (7th ERCIM International Workshop on User Interfaces for All. Paris, France, Octover 2002. Revised papers.), 3–22.

Kafka, P. (2011), 'Hey! Old people totally use the internet, too!', *All Things Digital*, February 3, 2011. Available at: <http://mediamemo.allthingsd.com/20110203/hey-old-people-totally-use-the-internet-too/>.

Kantner, L. and Rosenbaum, S. (2003), 'Usable computers for the elderly: Applying coaching experience', IPCC 2003 Proceedings (Annual Conf IEEE Professional Communication Society).

Kirkup, J. (2010), 'Baby-Boomers own half of Britain's wealth', *The Telegraph*, January 27, 2010. Available at: <http://www.telegraph.co.uk/news/politics/7085489/Baby-boomers-own-half-of-Britains-wealth.html>.

Lighthouse International (2011), 'Prevalence of vision impairment', *Statistics from the World Health Organization*, 2011, retrieved March 22, 2011. Available at: <http://www.lighthouse.org/research/statistics-on-vision-impairment/prevalence-of-vision-impairment/>.

Lin, D-Y., M. (2003) 'Hypertext for the aged: effects of text topologies.', *Computers in Human Behavior*, 19, 2, 201–209.

Loos, E.F. and Mante-Meijer, E.A. (2009), *Navigatie van ouderen en jongeren in beeld. Explorerend onderzoek naar de rol van leeftijd voor het informatiezoekgedrag van websitegebruikers* [Navigation of older and younger people. Explorative study into the role of age on website users' information search behaviour] (The Hague: Lemma).

Loos, E.F. (2011a), 'Generational use of new media and the (ir)relevance of age', in Colombo, F. and Fortunati, L. (eds), *Broadband Society and Generational Changes* (Frankfurt am Main etc.: Peter Lang).

Loos, E.F. (2011b), 'In search of information on websites: A question of age?', in Stephanidis, C. (ed.), *Universal Access in Human-Computer Interaction. Users Diversity,* HCI International 2011, LNCS 6766 (Berlin, Heidelberg, New York: Springer).

Madden, M. (2010), 'Older adults and social media: Social networking use among those ages 50 and older nearly doubled over the past year', Pew Internet and American Life Project, August 27, 2010. Available at: <http://www.pewinternet.org/Reports/2010/Older-Adults-and-Social-Media.aspx>.

Marsh, A., Ip, E., Barnard, R., Wong, Y.E. and Rejeski, W.J. (2010), 'Video animation to assess mobility in older adults', *Journal of Gerontology*, December 6, 2010.

Mazur, B. and Lee, A. (2003), 'Older, wiser, and wired', *Intercom, Society for Technical Communication.*

Morrell, R.W. (ed.) (2002), *Older Adults, Health Information and the World Wide Web* (Mahwah, NJ; Lawrence Erlbaum Associates).

Pernice, K. and Nielsen, J. (2002), *Web Usability for Senior Citizens. Design Guidelines Based on Usability Studies with People Age 65 and Older* (Fremont: Nielsen Norman Group).

Rainie, L. (2010), 'Internet, broadband, and cell phone statistics', January 5, 2010. Pew Internet and American Life Project.

Singer, N. (2011), 'The fountain of old age', *New York Times*, February 6, 2011.

Stephanidis, C. (2009), 'Universal access and design for all in the evolving information society', in Stephanidis, C. (ed.), *The Universal Access Handbook* (Boca: Raton: CRS).

Thylefors, B., Négral, A.D. Pararajasegaram, R. and Dadzie, K.Y. (1995), 'Global data on blindness', *Bulletin of the World Health Organization,* 73 (1), 115–

121. Available at: <http://www.ncbi.nlm.nih.gov/pmc/articles/PMC2486591/> (accessed 22.03.2011).

U.S. Census Bureau (2009), Population profile of the United States: The elderly population. Available at: <http://www.census.gov/population/www/pop-profile/elderpop.html> (accessed 06.02.2011).

Van Grove, J. (2010), 'Baby Boomers and seniors are flocking to Facebook', January 28, 2010, Mashable. Available at: <http://mashable.com/2010/01/28/baby-boomers-social-media/>.

WHO (2010), 'Deafness and hearing impairment', retrieved March 22, 2011 Available at: <http://www.who.int/mediacentre/factsheets/fs300/en/index.html>.

Wright, P. (2000), 'Supportive documentation for older people', in Westendorp, P., Jansen, C. and Punselie, R. (eds), *Interface Design & Document Design* (Amsterdam: Rodopi).

Zaphiris, P., Kurniawan, S.H. and Ellis, R.D. (2002), 'Age related differences and the depth vs. breadth trade off in hierarchical online information systems', in *Universal Access: Theoretical Perspectives, Practice, and Experience* (7th ERCIM International Workshop on User Interfaces for All. Paris, France, October 2002. Revised Papers.), 23–42.

Chapter 7

The Ticket Machine Challenge: Social Inclusion by Barrier-free Ticket Vending Machines

Günther Schreder, Karin Siebenhandl, Eva Mayr and Michael Smuc

Introduction[1]

In recent years, many railway stations have reduced the number and opening hours of their ticket counters and replaced them with self-service ticket vending machines. Indeed, ticket machines are now Austrian Rail's (Österreichische Bundesbahnen, ÖBB) most popular sales channel: around 67 % of all tickets sold in 2010 were purchased from a ticket machine (information provided by ÖBB, 31 January 2011). Although ticket machines offer a number of advantages for rail companies and passengers (reduced waiting times, no restrictions on opening hours), they also raise an important question: to what extent does the enforced use of these machines in some locations restrict the mobility of some groups of people? For example, only a small number of ticket machines are low enough to be used by wheelchair users. Similarly, the lack of an alternative to the touchscreen makes it impossible to be used by the blind and visually impaired. But it is not only people with serious disabilities who face barriers in using public transport systems. A study presented by Kasper and Scheiner (2002) indicates that besides health problems and loneliness, difficulties with public transport constitues the third most significant problem facing people over the age of 60. Complicated timetables, ticket machines and a lack of connections were most frequently cited as specific barriers in public transport systems. The older people who took part in a telematics project of Vienna University' a Natural Resources and Life Sciences department expressed a wish for easy-to-use technology, noting that many of the information and communication technologies currently available on the market simply do not suit their needs in terms of either design or ease-of-use. Small keys, long menus and confusing displays all make information and communication tools more difficult to use (ÉGALITÉ, 2006) – a criticism directed not just at consumer electronics products, but in particular at everyday objects like ticket machines.

ÖBB sales statistics clearly confirm the above and indicate that both elderly and disabled people use ticket machines less frequently than other groups: 63%

1 This chapter is based on an unpublished paper of Schreder et al. (2009).

of senior citizens purchase tickets from a ticket machine, while 31% opt to go to a ticket counter. ÖBB passengers under the age of 26 use ticket machines almost exclusively (91% of them do so). Holders of regular travelcards ('Vorteilscard') or family travelcards ('Familienvorteilscard') use ticket machines relatively frequently (69–74%), followed by purchases at a ticket counter (17–22%) and via the internet (4–8%). Disabled passengers make equal use of the internet (29%) and ticket machine (28%) sales channels, but also purchase tickets from conductors (24%) and at ticket counters (17%)[2]. Austrian Rail suspects that the inflexible menu structure (a consequence of its different fare options and the basis for its automated ticketing and ticket information) is the main reason why the elderly make less use of its ticket machines.

The InnoMat research project presented in this chapter seeks to identify how a new generation of ticket machines should be designed to best meet the needs of different user groups. Giving consideration to the target groups, the project team is drawing up a framework for an analysis of user requirements for inclusive design.[3]

The first step was to identify the special needs and requirements of the target groups using public transport systems based on insights from the relevant literature. The specific needs of disabled persons are mostly connected to questions of accessibility, such as the existence of voice-output for visually impaired persons or the optimal height of the hardware to allow wheelchair users the access to the machine. A similar approach can be found concerning the group of senior citizens who are often seen as persons with reduced physical and mental abilities due to their age. Relevant design aspects therefore include the contrast of screens, the size of (virtual) buttons and text, the speed of required input and so on.

As important as these factors may be, older people (but not only them) are likely to face further problems that are not identified as easily: research into ticket queues at 12 major stations in Great Britain supports this assumption. Among those who could have bought their ticket from a machine the decision to purchase at the counter was driven by a lack of confidence in using the machine as well as a lack of confidence in the ability to select a ticket (Passenger Focus, 2008). These results hint not only at the possible lack of technological skills that are necessary when using ticket vending machines but at the underlying motivational factor responsible for avoiding them as well. We will discuss the psychological concept of 'self-efficacy' that could possibly provide insights into dealing with this often neglected problem.

With regard to the specifics of the machines currently being used at Austrian railway stations, the project team chose to conduct an empirical study with interviews and observations to learn from the actual experiences of users and identify those particular elements that most frequently cause problems or hinder

2 Figures based on ÖBB sales data for 2008 (Weeks 8–30); these only includes purchases by Travelcard ('Vorteilscard') holders, a customer group which shows a bias toward ticket machine purchases (information provided by ÖBB, 28 November 2008).

3 See Stephanidis (2009: 1–2) for a discussion of this concept. See also Chapter 6.

use. In subsequent phases of the project, we intend to use our results to develop design specifications for a prototype of a new generation of ticket machines and to draw the main criteria for the evaluation phase consisting of laboratory experiments and field tests from them.

Catalogue of Accessibility Requirements

Existing research on the special needs of people with disabilities revealed a range of specific requirements that need to be met to make ticket machines accessible to the visually impaired or to wheelchair users and that should be considered in the design of a new generation of accessible ticket machines. The literature review also provided preliminary insights into the special needs of the elderly, needs which result primarily from changes in their cognitive abilities.

Austrian Federal Government figures for 2007 show that 3.9% of the Austrian population had sight problems (despite the use of visual aids), around 13% of Austrians suffered from a permanent mobility restriction and 0.6% of the population were wheelchair-bound (BMSK, 2008). The visually impaired are particularly dependent on public transport, since they cannot use private means of transport on their own (Kremser, 2008). However, 42% of the visually impaired people reported problems using public transport (BMSK, 2008). The number of people affected increases with age. Trends indicate that advances in medicine and demographic developments will lead to a further increase in the number of people with visual impairments and restricted mobility (Bühler et al., 2006; Duncan, 2006). According to Statistics Austria forecasts, the Austrian population is expected to grow strongly in size and could reach 9.52 million by the year 2050. The population will also clearly age. Currently, around 22% of the population is aged 60 or over, with this figure expected to rise to about 26% in the medium-term (2020) and exceed 30% in the long term (after 2030). Given the repeated emphasis placed in mobility and demographic studies on the influence access to mass and private transport has on the quality of life, health and happiness (Metz, 2000), the provision of barrier-free access to public transport becomes highly relevant.

Kirchmaier (2005) stresses the heterogeneity of senior citizens[4] and dismisses the notion of the 'elderly' as a sociological category. Among this group, increasing differentiation can be seen in different areas of life, since their age range spans several decades and includes several generations with different backgrounds and experiences. Consequently, different social practices, values, consumer behaviour and, of course, levels of 'technological literacy'[5] must also be assumed. Aside from this, general changes in visual and acoustic perception, motor skills and some aspects of memory and cognition are also observed as a consequence of

4 See also Dannefer (2008: 360), and Chapters 6 and 10.

5 For more information about literacy see also Chapters 2, 3, 4, 8, 9 and the conclusion of this volume.

getting older (Carmichael, 1999; Hawthorn, 2000).[6] These changes can be used to determine the basic design requirements for ticket machines suitable for use by senior citizens (see Table 7.1).

Table 7.1 Catalogue of requirements (compiled from Carmichael, 1999; Hawthorn, 2000)

User requirements	Cause
Screens must be light, high-contrast and provide an option to increase the size of any text, different colour coding should be used, and blue-green colours should be avoided.	Deficits in focusing, visual acuity, contrast and colour perception (in the blue-green spectrum).
The location of ticket machines should be carefully chosen to circumvent a risk of reflective glare and avoid rapid fluctuations in brightness.	Reduced ability to adapt to light conditions and increased sensitivity to glare.
Clear, well arranged structure without unnecessary graphics or animations; minimal, discrete indications of changes should be replaced by clear visual signs; symbols should be clear and simple, and windows should not overlap.	Slower processing of visual stimuli, a reduced ability to recognise embedded figures and an increased tendency to be distracted.
If voice output is used, preference should be given to lower frequencies.	Higher probability of not detecting signals of 2500 Hz and above.
Mechanically sounding 'synthesised voices' should be avoided, and since the elderly also tend to have problems understanding them, voice output does not appear to be a suitable primary information channel for this target group.	Background noise, incomplete messages or stress, which is compounded by a partial reduction in selective concentration ability.
Users should be given the possibility to operate ticket machines at their own pace. Long breaks between commands without the purchase process being automatically cancelled.	Reduced speed and accuracy of motor skills.
Provision of confirmatory feedback from the machine as well as easy-to-use 'Back' function.	Strong tendency to try to avoid mistakes.

Continued

6 See also Chapter 10 and Bouma (2000), Czaja and Lee (2009), Loos and Mante-Meijer (2009: 38–39) for an overview of the studies on age-related functional limitations in these areas.

Table 7.1 Concluded

Large input fields with plenty of space between these fields. Alternatively, they could be provided with buttons outside the screen.	Restricted gross and fine motor skills due to some illnesses related to higher age
Machines that provide touch-sensitive, on-screen feedback might be unsuitable.	Reduced sensitivity to touch and vibration.

The blind and the visually impaired primarily use local public transport on their own for routine journeys; they rarely travel alone to 'new destinations' (Harper and Green, 2000). It should come as no surprise that they find it difficult to use conventional ticket machines such as those in use at Austrian railway stations: ICT systems usually emphasise the visual information channel, and good interface design is basically matched to the mental models of 'normally' sighted people. Interface hardware addressing the need for multimodal input is currently not common in Europe, where systems are generally touchscreen-based (Naniopoulos, 1999). Members of the focus group held at Danube University Krems on 23 March 2009 in order to address these problems mentioned that individual solutions (like optimally designed ticket machines) will not really help this target group if the whole system is not changed – finding a ticket machine is one thing, but to complete their journey successfully, they also have to be able to negotiate their way around the station, find the right train, etc. (see also Naniopoulos, 1999; Coroama, 2006; Marin-Lamellet and Aymond, 2008). Table 7.2 shows a selection of the most important changes to conventional interface design which have to be made for a barrier-free access by impaired persons.

Technological Skills and Motivational Aspects

From the mid-90s onwards studies showed that age, gender, ethnicity, social status, education and income are the major socio-economic indicators for the societal gap that exists in the usage of digital technologies. While the discussion of the digital divide was focused on access to the internet and the necessary hardware, strategies of inclusion showed that users' lack of know-how seems to contribute to the emergence of the digital divide as well. It is argued that the rather poor usability of novel technologies combined with little or no missing experience with digital technologies in school or the workplace, as well as a lack of support by social networks lead to a reduced chance of acquiring adequate skills (Van Dijk and Hacker, 2003).

The question of so-called technological literacy (Funiok, 1998) which includes the ability to use not only computers and consumer electronics products but also everyday items like cash and ticket machines, becomes more relevant among older generations. People born before 1939, for example, did not have any opportunity

Table 7.2 Catalogue of requirements

	User requirements	Cause
Blind users	Inclusion of multimodal functions, such as: voice output for texts and instructions that automatically adapts to the background noise; use of Braille or other tactile lettering elements (e.g. on buttons outside the screens, Braille panels)	Compensation for limitations in the visual channel by using other information – primarily touch and audio inputs
	Issuing of tickets in Braille or other tactile forms of lettering, or some form of tagged ticket (similar to an online ticket) that can be put into a machine and the destination is read out	Need to provide positive feedback on the successful purchase of a ticket (Harper & Green, 2000)
	Machines should be designed with solid fronts.	Possibility of identification with a cane (ÖNORM B 1600)
	Use of audio signals and guiderails to communicate the machine's location or machines that 'speak' to people when they approach ('Welcome to the ticket machine', see Coroama, 2006; Janoschek, 2006).	Orientation and identification of the machines
	Travelcards that store details of the user's most frequent ticket purchases	Members of this target group often make the same journey (Harper and Green, 2000).
Wheelchair Users	An adequate height of screens and other interface devices must be considered (Égalité, 2006). Users have to be able to position themselves easily in front of such machines.	Conventional displays are adapted to a standing adult's average size and cannot be reached by a person sitting in a wheelchair.
	Customers should be able to stipulate trains with wheelchair access (Bühler et al., 2006).	Need for information on barrier-free trains

to learn how to use digital technologies at school or in the workplace (Sackmann and Weymann, 1994; Weymann and Sackmann, 1998).[7]

In addition to senior citizens, some other groups are also disadvantaged by the so-called 'secondary digital divide' that emerges due to reduced technological literacy (Hargittai, 2002). People with lower levels of education and members of ethnic minorities number relatively frequently among those with little experience of technology. Gender, income level and occupation are also seen as predictors of a lower level of technological literacy (Doh, 2005; Czaja et al., 2006). Whereas at first glance these results suggest that younger, educated people could generally

7 See also Chapter 10 by Loos and Mante-Meijer on 'technology generations'.

be described as technological professionals, this misleading conclusion is contradicted by the evidence provided by Herold in Chapter 4 and Van Deursen in chapter 9 of this volume – it seems that students, for example, are rather inclined to overestimate their technological skills.

Furthering opportunities for learning and acquiring skill might seem invaluable; yet a significant part of the population is still actively avoiding the use of computers and the internet. In the representative German Online Nonusers Survey (Gerhards and Mende, 2007) 72,9% of the non-users stated that they did not want to connect to the internet. A variety of reasons are listed in Figure 7.1. It should be noted that only half of the non-users (48%) rejected using a private computer partly due to financial limits, whereas the more numerous answers pointed at a lack of interest, or need or a general dislike. Van Dijk and Hacker (2003) see these results as an argument for being aware that such motivational factors also contribute to the digital usage gap.

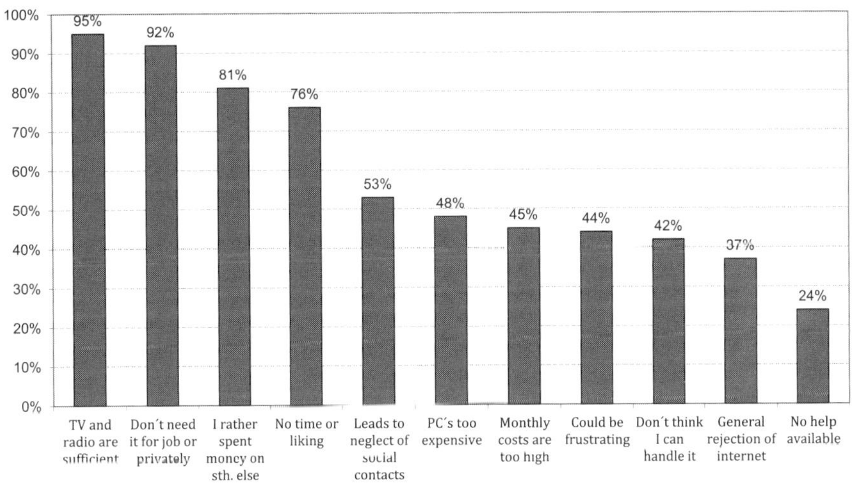

Figure 7.1 Reasons for not using the internet (based on data at Gerhards and Mende, 2007)

According to Eastin and LaRose (2000) social cognitive theory offers an alternative to the socio-economic explanations normally used when discussing the digital divide (see also Chapter 9 by Van Deursen in this volume). Self-efficacy is the belief 'in one's capabilities to organise and execute the courses of action required to produce given attainments' (Bandura, 1997: 3). People with lower self-efficacy display less motivation to engage in a task than do those with higher self-efficacy. Bandura summarises that efficacy beliefs

> (…) influence the courses of action people choose to pursue, how much effort they put forth in given endeavors, how long they will persevere in the face of

> obstacles and failures, their resilience to adversity, whether their thought patterns are self-hindering or self-aiding, how much stress and depression they experience in coping with environmental demands, and the level of accomplishments they realise (…). (Bandura, 1997: 3)

A correlation between learning to use computers and self-efficacy was demonstrated by Karavidas et al. (2005), indicating that computer self-efficacy also depends on the subjective feeling of having made progress during training.

For Czaja et al. (2006) 'computer self-efficacy'[8] was an important predictor of the use of technical devices, while being influenced by 'computer anxiety'[9] as a mediator. For persons with a low level of self-efficacy the probability of using the technology was generally reduced. Additionally, persons with a high level of computer anxiety had less experience with computers and the internet, and used these technologies for a smaller number of different activities. The combination of both resulted in the active avoidance of technological devices. As senior citizens are frequently found among the group described, the authors stressed the importance of using technology that allows senior citizens to experience success so that they are able to build up confidence in their abilities.

Struve and Wandke (2009) showed that older adults, in comparison to younger adults, have lower self-efficacy beliefs in their ability to successfully use a ticket vending machine. While they focused on developing a specific training program to enhance the user's abilities to operate the machines as well as their beliefs in their capabilities, our study also aims to answering research questions about the relation between the user's self-efficacy beliefs and the usage of the ticket vending machine: Do the users' or non-users' beliefs as to whether the can successfully buy a ticket themselves influence the purchase process? Are there any negative experiences connected to buying tickets at the machine? Furthermore the research team sought to identify those elements of the current ticket machines that have the strongest effects on users' perception of their ability to cope with them.

Empirical Study

Observations

For a period of two hours on a weekday at the railway station in Baden (Austria) and on a Friday and a Saturday at a major station in Vienna (Südbahnhof), a total of 50 people were observed as they used the ticket machines. The observers sought to identify those people who had problems using the machines. Notes were taken about how decisively they made their selection, whether they demonstrated any unusual behaviour or showed signs of nervousness, how often they corrected or

8 See also Chapter 8 by Van Deursen.
9 See also Beckers et al. (2008).

cancelled their input, and whether they actually managed to successfully purchase a ticket. The subjects were categorised into three age groups: 'young' (up to about 30 years of age), 'middle-age' (30–60) and 'old' (over 60). A sales data log file analysis was additionally carried out to support the observations and interviews.

The 50 people observed were split fairly evenly across both genders (45% men, 55% women). One third of these people were classed as 'uncertain' by two observers (inter-rater agreement: close to 100%), since, in contrast to other passengers, they did not make a clear and direct selection or had obvious problems using the machines (see Figure 7.2). Almost 70% of this group had to cancel the purchase process and start again at least once, while nearly two-thirds ultimately gave up and left the machine without purchasing a ticket. This means that the chance of successfully operating the machine can be predicted to a very high degree during the first few seconds after a person approached the machine.

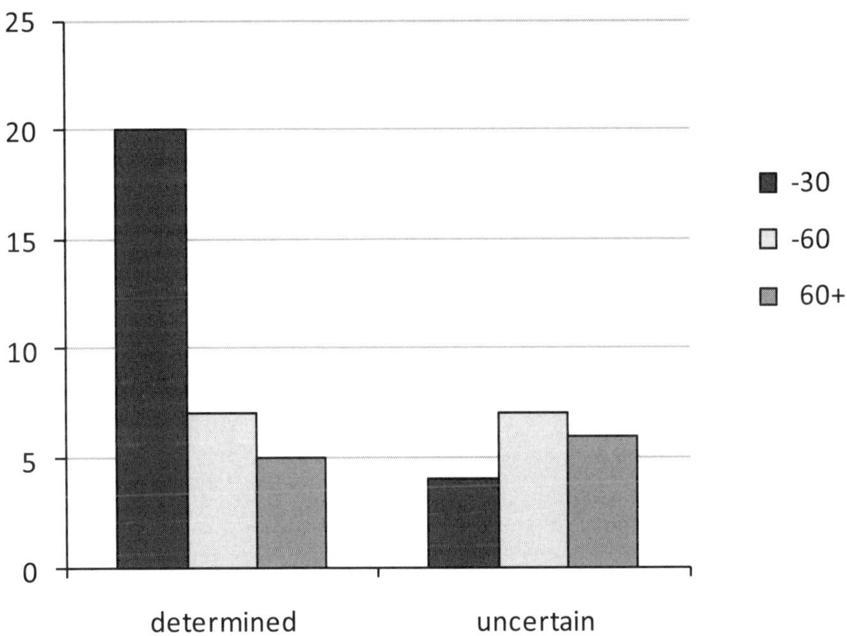

Figure 7.2 Number of determined and uncertain customers in the three different age groups

The number of young people (i.e. estimated to be under the age of 30) in the group of 'uncertain' users was very low (only four out of a total of 17). We also observed some distinctive patterns of behaviour among members of this group. They repeatedly watched other customers using the machines and frequently received assistance from their companions or other customers, e.g. those using the next machine. Also typical of this group was the length of time spent looking at

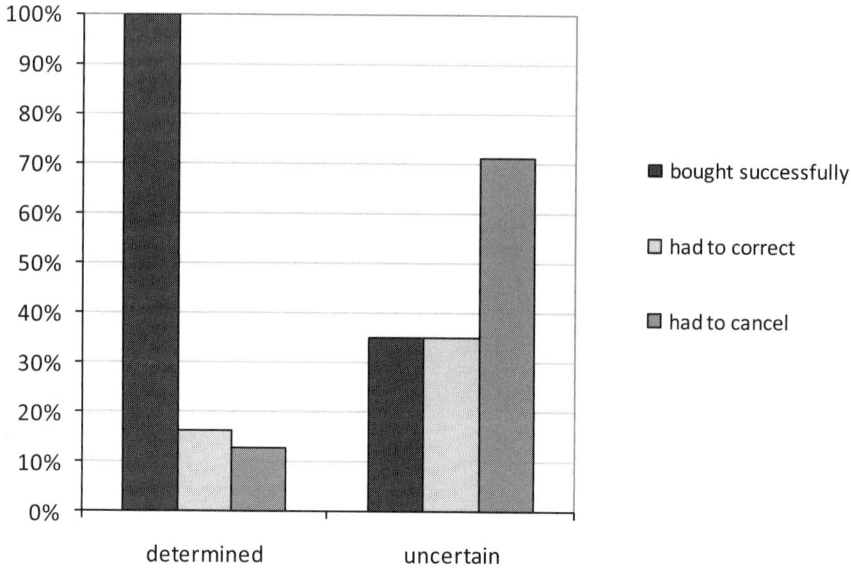

Figure 7.3 Percentage of determined and uncertain customers who bought successfully, had to correct their input at least once and had to cancel

the machines from a distance and a hesitant approach; some members of this group cancelled the purchase process and went away from the machine, only to return a short time later and try again. We also observed that they spent a particularly long time studying both the launch screen and the options screen (Figures 7.4 and 7.5).

Our analysis of the sales data log files (internal logs of an ÖBB ticket machine at Vienna Südbahnhof for the time between 06:24 and 10:56 a.m. on 14 October 2008) indicated this could be a fairly common pattern of behaviour. Of the 144 purchase processes started during this period, 61 were cancelled before completion: 54% at the launch screen, 20% at the options screen and 10 % on request for payment.

The observations suggest strong evidence for the role of uncertainty, but it remains unclear whether low self-efficacy is responsible for this behaviour. Therefore, the results were complemented by interviews with users and non-users of ticket vending machines.

Interviews

On two weekdays at the railway station in Baden and on a Friday and a Saturday at the Südbahnhof in Vienna, a total of 65 people (roughly equal numbers of men and women) from all age groups (15 to 89) were asked about their experiences, level of satisfaction and reasons for choosing/avoiding a ticket machine. The subjects were

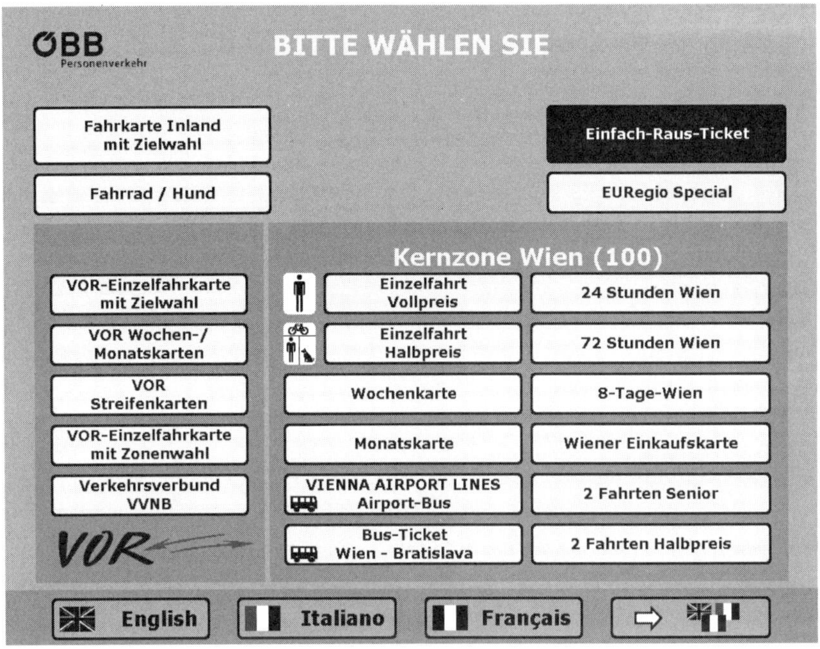

Figure 7.4 Screen shot from the ÖBB ticket vending machines: launch screen

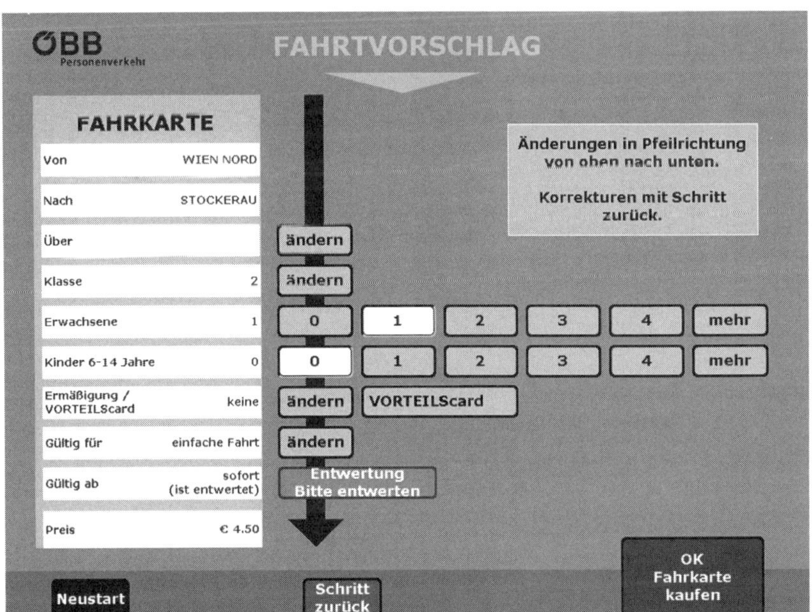

Figure 7.5 Screen shots from the ÖBB ticket vending machines: options screen

interviewed after purchasing a ticket either at the ticket counter (Group C) or from a machine (Group M). To identify their level of affinity for technology in general, the interviewees were also asked about their use of mobile phones, computers, cash machines and the internet. In addition, they were asked to make concrete suggestions for improving ticket machines.

Over half the people interviewed (59%) indicated that they used the ticket machines regularly. Only 14% of the interviewees never used the ticket machines. Overall, the level of satisfaction of the people interviewed was surprisingly high: 72% considered the machines to be 'very good' or 'good'. Only 4% of the interviewees were very unsatisfied. Nonetheless, 78% of those persons who had used a ticket machine at least once reported problems or difficulties in understanding some aspects of the purchasing process. The most common negative experiences were problems in operating machines, such as pressing the wrong keys or buying the wrong ticket, difficulties in understanding the complexity of the system, and having the impression that the machines are not always working properly. Problems with payment, such as credit cards not being accepted or wrong amounts being charged were reported as well, though less frequently (see Figure 7.6).

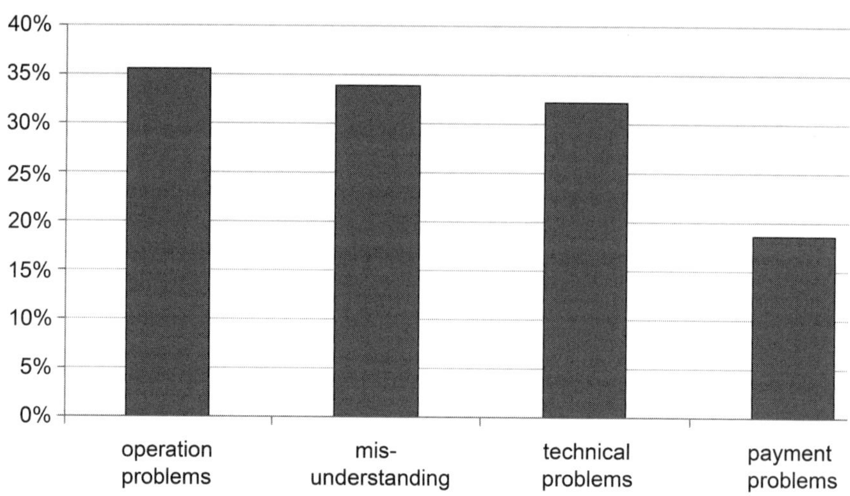

Figure 7.6 Percentage of experienced problems reported by customers

But different age groups clearly had different problems with the machines. While older passengers with little technical experience reported problems in actually operating the machines, such problems were rare among younger interviewees: the group of passengers under the age of 19 reported no problems of this kind at all.

For more information on the role of technological literacy, interviewees were asked how frequently they used the ticket vending machine and also other everyday technologies (cash machines, mobile phone, computer, the internet). The results showed that rare use of other everyday technologies is correlated to buying a ticket at the machine less often (Rho=.21, p<.05, N=64).

Qualitative analysis of the interviews showed that about two-thirds of customers who experienced operating problems or misunderstanding seemed to attribute this failure to external causes (see e.g. Weiner, 1985), which means they actually spoke of problems caused by the interface design of the device, referring to an inflexible system or an overloaded screen. The complex fare system reflected in the menus clearly often caused confusion. The interviewees mentioned a lack of clarity regarding the input of information about city limits by passengers, the zone distribution, the purchase of monthly tickets and the purchase of tickets for multiple passengers. Not all customers automatically understood the dual system of distance-based ÖBB fares and zone-based local transport association fares. They also had problems identifying the links between the two systems and the special fares on offer: At first *it took me a while to realise that I had to tell the machine that I had a travelcard – and that in this case you can't tell it how many zones you need, you have to tell it where you actually want to go.* (C4)

The remaining third interpreted their failures as a result of their know-how and some of them even said they felt helpless when facing the machine: *It just didn't work. Each time I tried I got something different.* (C17) Not surprisingly, all these customers were prone to avoid the ticket machines, two persons stated that they never used the machine again after one bad experience with it: *I once tried to buy one, but I was completely confused and got a wrong ticket.*' (C5). Negative experiences were often combined with an expression of uncertainty: some people mentioned their fear of inadvertently buying the wrong ticket: *One of my friends once even bought a ticket for a dog instead of a normal ticket* (M15) or paying more money out of ignorance: *If you ask me, the counter's better, because someone there tells you what's what. If you buy a ticket from a machine, you might pay twice as much as you had to!* (C28). This is complemented by a conviction that they would not be able to buy a ticket from a machine without help: *Nobody showed me what to do, and I don't know what I am doing. If I knew how it worked, I would try it myself.* (C21). It should be mentioned that even some of those people who used the ticket machines regularly said that they had only learned to use them with the help of other passengers, the readiness of experienced users to help other customer is accordingly high: *I sometimes help people who don't use the trains so often. I also found the machines difficult to use at first.* (M19)

Other issues mentioned by the interviewees included technical problems, long waiting times because there were not enough machines available: *Everyone arrives just before the train is due (...) there is only one machine up here and it is often busy. I don't go down there. I would put two up here* [on the platform]. (C10) as well as payment problems, e.g. malfunctioning machines not accepting a cash card or credit card, rejecting coins and banknotes or not giving out the right change.

Passengers considered speed of purchase to be an advantage of the ticket machines (36%). Other reasons for using them included lower prices (16%), but also the fact that ticket counters were either not available or were closed (15%).

The most common reasons given for going to a ticket counter instead of a machine were to get information or travel details (19%) or to purchase long distance tickets (11 %), which passengers obviously did not like to buy from machines.

Discussion

Austrian Rail is aware that the interface on its current ticket machines does not best address the needs of all target groups. In the course of the InnoMat project, numerous suggestions and technical concepts relating to an interface design that suits the needs of the visually impaired have been taken from the relevant literature. The same applies for wheelchair users and other people with restricted mobility, who currently only have access to suitable ticket machines at a few locations. However, it remains to be seen whether the members of these target groups actually consider the realisation of all these concepts necessary, or whether they place greater priority on other, in particular online, sales channels as the sales statistics suggest. Representatives of the Austrian Federation of the Blind and Partially Sighted (ÖBSV) point to the fact that Braille is only used by a rather small percentage of visually impaired people – mostly those who have been blind since childhood. Furthermore many of this target group prefer the use their own supportive equipment and software, which means accessible online ticketing may be more important than improving the ticket vending machine (personal communication, H. Onitsch, 23.03.2009).

Overall, the ticket machine users we interviewed expressed a relatively high level of satisfaction, with the vast majority of machines, assessing them to be 'very good', 'good' or at least 'satisfactory'. Our observations also revealed that a large number of users had no problems in purchasing the ticket they wanted in a very short period of time. The sales statistics analysed also indicate that younger passengers in particular far prefer this sales channel.

Some of the specific needs of the elderly discussed in this chapter (problems with text size, layout and size of keys, etc.) were not mentioned at all by the senior citizens we interviewed, indicating that – as far as the use of ticket machines is concerned – these issues are a low priority or have already been adequately resolved for this target group.

However, our observations and interviews revealed a number of serious barriers to the use of the ticket machines, above all among older and middle-aged passengers. A considerable number of users were clearly already daunted by the multiple options offered on the launch screen. The switch between approaching the ticket machines and subsequently avoiding them observed for some users could be interpreted as an expression of an 'inner approach-avoidance-conflict' (sensu Miller, e.g. Miller and Kraeling, 1952), a tendency to seek out a specific situation, combined with the simultaneous wish to avoid it because it might have negative consequences. In these age groups especially some customers had little confidence in their ability to buy a ticket at the machine successfully: when asked why they avoid the machines, they referred to bad experiences, doubt about their own abilities, and distrust of the technology. While customer's distrust was sometimes motivated by problems encountered with the machine's handling of Austrian Railway's rather complicated fare system or technical problems, it is interesting to note that some of the interviews hinted at the development of specific 'urban legends', such as knowing someone who inadvertently bought a ticket for a dog. These may indicate low self-efficacy in the context of using everyday technologies. A similar result was found in Great Britain (Passenger Focus, 2008), where elderly used the ticket machine only seldom and believed less in their own abilities.

When developing the new layout, it will be important to ensure that people who are nervous of the ticket machines or are characterised by low technological self-efficacy are given the feeling that they can master the task easily and without the help of others. As initial steps, the choice of options could be better structured and a clearer visual demarcation introduced between higher level menu elements. Another relative easy and intuitive step is to avoid computer terminology and to use everyday language instead (e.g., yes/no instead of ok/cancel).

A further barrier was encountered on the screen offering a so-called suggested route that can be partly modified by the user. An increased number of users cancelled the process on this screen, indicating that they either felt overwhelmed by the information they were asked to provide or did not succeed in changing the information in the way they wanted. This process is linked to the fare structure (which many passengers found unclear): the relevant fare has to be entered before some products can be selected. It would be worth considering whether some of these factors could be calculated automatically in the background without the need for user input.

Additionally it is necessary that the purchase process in some way resembles the passengers' cognitive scripts of this process. While a salesman at the ticket counter can easily adjust the sales process to the customers' diverse cognitive scripts, the ticket machine is not as flexible. It only meets one possible cognitive script – the programmer's. This poses a barrier to people whose cognitive scripts are not addressed. To meet their needs as well, the ticket machine's interface could be split up into two modes: a fast purchase mode and a step-by-step-mode that leads customers through the purchase process and poses only one question after the other.

Best Practice

Design examples gathered from systems currently in use in other countries provide some clues to a more user-friendly graphic design: the French ticket machines show that it is possible to reduce the number of options on the launch screen while maintaining a maximum of possible interactions (buying and exchanging tickets for national and international journeys, printing tickets bought online, see Figure 7.7).

The Austrian system displays the choices made by customers as a virtual ticket in the left part of the screen. To make changes, it is necessary to start at the top and to proceed in only one direction (see Figure 7.5). But some people tried to make

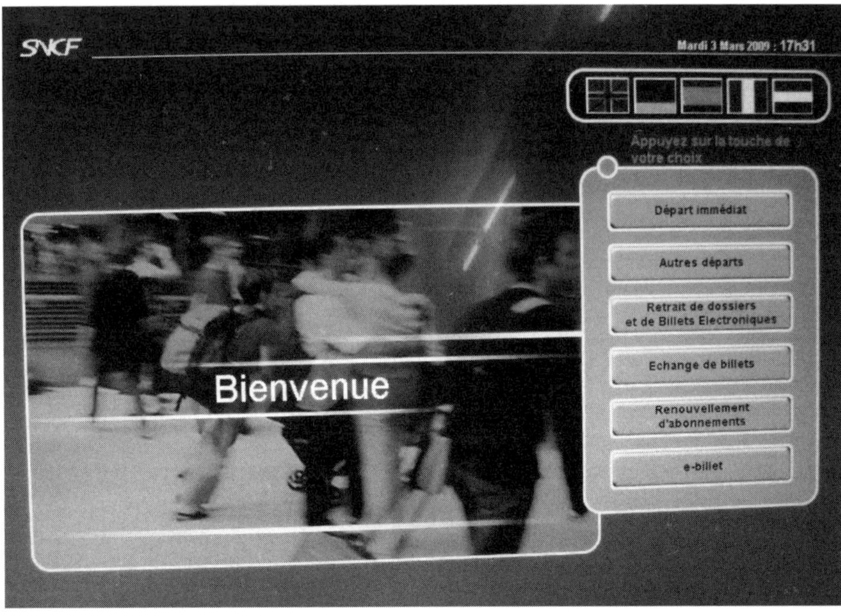

Figure 7.7 Start screen of the French ticket machines by SNCF (photograph taken by the authors, 2009)

changes by touching the left, virtual ticket area. In the Netherlands, this problem does not exist as the buttons also provide information about the choices already made and changes are possible in any order (see Figure 7.8.) A demonstration of the system is available at: <http://www.ns.nl>.

Conclusion

Shortly after we finished this study colleagues in Great Britain conducted very similar research on the ticket vending machines of different British train operating companies (Passenger Focus, 2010). They summarised the key findings from 60 interviews as following: the overall clarity and layout of the screens should be improved and the information volume on certain screens (especially the first) reduced, the programme sequence should be simplified, more and clearer information on travelling fares and restrictions should be provided and further consideration to the specific needs of disability groups should be given. Furthermore, the problem of self-efficacy as described in this chapter seems to be indicated as well:

> Importantly however, most of the respondents in this sample claimed to lack the confidence that would be required in reality to purchase the ticket selected from a TVM [ticket vending machine]. The key barriers in this respect are uncertainty

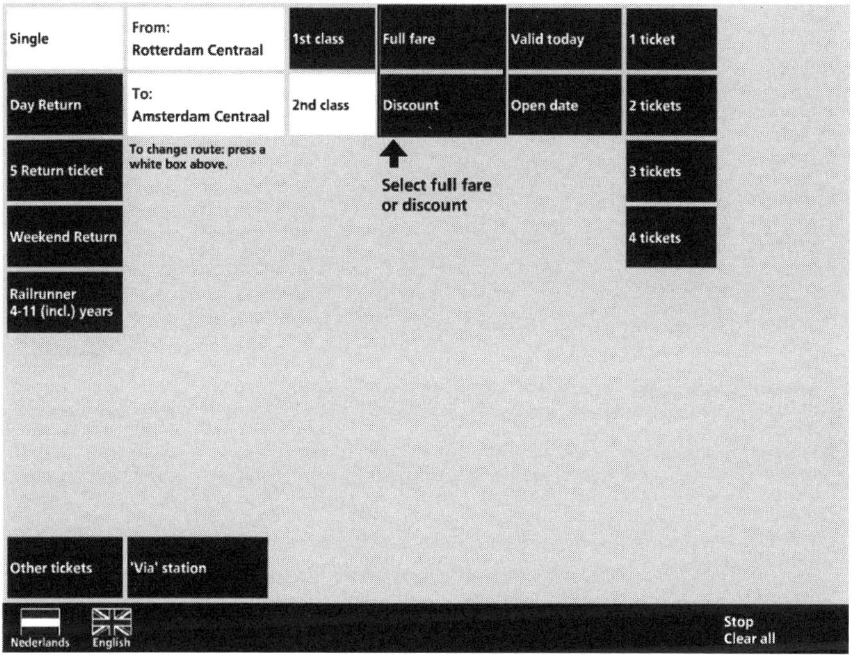

Figure 7.8 Options screen of the Netherland's ticket machines by NS (screenshot from http://www.ns.nl., 2009)

> over the validity of tickets due to timing restrictions that apply and the inability to be certain that the best fare has been achieved. (Passenger Focus, 2010: 3)

The striking similarities to our own results show that the problems encountered are not confined to Austrian ticket vending machines, but also exist with other similar systems that were built a decade ago without proper usability engineering. Another study that was motivated by the recognition of this problem was recently published by Sandes et al. (2010) who conducted an expert heuristics study on the ticket vending machines of a Taiwanese railroad company.

The improvements in the design and the usability of ticket vending machines presented in this chapter will not only help people with low technological literacy, but also ease the purchase process for all customers.[10] In addition improving the design, further measures should be taken to facilitate access for people with low self-efficacy, as the results by Karavidas et al. (2005) suggest: at-home-training, local support, information leaflets and advertisements can also reach those, who might even avoid the railway station. Struve and Wandke (2009) showed that a

10 See also the impact of improvements in the design and the usability on site's user friendliness for both older and younger people in Chapter 6 by Chisnell and Redish who refer to Johnson and Kent (2007) and Chapter 10 by Loos and Mante-Meijer.

training procedure can increase self-efficacy beliefs and reduce the number of errors in relation to ticket vending machines – for older and for younger customers. An easy-to-use system will not only facilitate access to public transport systems for people with low technological affinity, but could provide a chance to develop positive attitudes towards digital technology in general.

Many projects and ideas follow the approach of accessibility in order to support and promote the mobility of these socio-economic groups by providing accessible computer-based technologies and information services. Certainly physical barriers to access can be eliminated, but barriers like limited acceptance and limited affinity for technology still remain. In addition, failing to use everyday technology can decrease the feeling of mastery of technology in general. A tendency to avoid novel technologies and a lack of technological knowledge can build barriers that affect mobility and lifestyle. This certainly holds true for elderly people and other socio-economic groups disadvantaged in terms of the digital divide as they, especially, rely on public transport (Egalité, 2006). However, if everyday technologies can be designed to facilitate mastery and the user gains a feeling of success, self-efficacy can be increased in the long run and might also reduce the perceived barriers to using other kinds of media.

References

Bandura, A. (1997), *Self-Efficacy: The Exercise of Control* (New York: Freeman).

Beckers, J., Schmidt, H. and Wicherts, J. (2009), 'Computer anxiety in daily life', in Loos, E., Haddon, L. and Mante-Meijer, E. (eds), *The Social Dynamics of Information and Communication Technology* (Aldershot: Ashgate).

BMSK (2008), *Bericht der Bundesregierung über die Lage von Menschen mit Behinderungen in Österreich 2008* (Wien).

Bouma, H. (2000), 'Document and interface design for older citizens', in Westendorp, P., Jansen, C. and Punselie, R. (eds), *Interface Design & Document Design* (Amsterdam: Rodopi).

Bühler, C., Heck, H., Sischka, D. and Becker, J. (2006), 'BAIM – Information for people with reduced mobility in the field of public transport', *ICCHP 2006 (LNCS 4061)*, 332–328.

Carmichael, A. (1999), *Style Guide for the Design of Interactive Television Services for Elderly Viewers* (Winchester: Independent Television Commission).

Coroama, V. (2006), 'Experiences from the design of a ubiquitous computing system for the blind', paper presented at CHI 2006, Montreal.

Czaja, S.J. and Lee, C. (2003), 'Designing computer systems for older adults', in Jacko, J.A. and Sears, A. (eds), *The Human-Computer Interaction Handbook: Fundamentals, Evolving Technologies and Emerging Applications* (Mahwah, NJ: Lawrence Erlbaum).

Czaja, S.J., Charness, N., Fisk, A.D., Hertzog, C., Nair, S.N., Rogers, W.A. and Sharit, J. (2006), 'Factors predicting the use of technology: Findings from the

Center for Research and Education on Aging and Technology Enhancement (CREATE)', *Psychology and Aging*, 21 (2), 333–352.

Dannefer, D. (1988), 'What's in a name? An account of the neglect of variability in the study of aging', in Birren, J.E. and Bengtson, V.L. (eds), *Emergent Theories of Aging* (New York: Springer).

Doh, M. (2005), 'Ältere Onliner in Deutschland – Entwicklung und Prädiktoren der Internetdiffusion', in Kimpeler, S. and Baier, E. (eds), *IT-basierte Produkte und Dienste für ältere Menschen – Nutzeranforderungen und Techniktrends* (Karslruhe: Fraunhofer-Institut für System- und Innovationsforschung).

Duncan, R. (2006), 'Universal design and overview of center for universal design at North Carolina State University', *Japan Railway & Transport Review*, 45, 232–37.

Eastin, M.S. and LaRose, R. (2000), 'Internet self-efficacy and the psychology of the digital divide', *Journal of Computer-Mediated Communication*, 6 (1).

ÉGALITÉ (2006), *Equality issues in everyday life in a telematics supported field of transport* (Vienna). Available at: <https://forschung.boku.ac.at/fis/suchen.projekt_uebersicht?sprach e_in =en&ansicht_ in= &menue_id_in=300&id_in=5863> (accessed 31.01.2011).

Funiok, R. (1998), 'Ich fange erst gar nicht an, mich damit zu beschäftigen – Schwierig-keiten und Wünsche älterer Menschen gegenüber der Kommunikationstechnik. Eine generations-spezifische Fallstudie', *Literatur- und Forschungsreport Weiterbildung*, 42, 63–72.

Gerhards, M. and Mende, A. (2007), 'Offliner:2007: Zunehmend distanzierter, aber gelassener Blick aufs Internet', *Media Perspektiven,* 8, 379–392.

Hargittai, E. (2002), 'Second-level digital divide: Differences in people's online skills', *First Monday*, 7 (4), 1–20.

Harper, S., and Green, P. (2000), 'A travel flow and mobility framework for visually impaired travellers', paper presented at the International Conference on Computers Helping People with Special Needs, 289–296.

Hawthorn, D. (2000), 'Possible implications of aging for interface designers', *Interacting with Computers*, 12, 507–528.

Janoschek, D.R. (2006), 'DISA – Digitale Sprachausgabe von Fahrgastinformationen für blinde und sehbehinderte Menschen im Öffentlichen Verkehr', *Forschungsforum Mobilität für Alle – 2006: Chancengleichheit im Verkehr*, 19–21.

Johnson, R. and Kent, S. (2007), 'Designing universal access: web application for the elderly and disabled', *Cognition, Technology and Work*, 9, 209–218.

Karavidas, M., Lim, N.K. and Katsikas, S.L. (2005), 'The effects of computers on older adult users', *Computers in Human Behavior*, 21, 697–711.

Kasper, B. and Scheiner, J. (2002), *Leisure Mobility and Mobility Problems of Elderly People in Urban, Suburban and Rural Environment*, paper presented at the 42nd congress of the European Regional Science Association (ERSA), Dortmund, August, 27–31, 2002.

Kimpeler, S. and Baier, E. (eds), *IT-basierte Produkte und Dienste für ältere Menschen – Nutzeranforderungen und Techniktrends* (Karslruhe: Fraunhofer-Institut für System- und Innovationsforschung).
Kremser, M. (2008), *Sehbehinderte und blinde Menschen im öffentlichen Raum, Rückblick und Ausblick, Barrierefreie Mobilität* (Vienna).
Loos, E.F. and Mante-Meijer, E.A. (2009), 'Getting access to website health information: Does age really matter?', research paper presented at the conference Digital Media Technologies Revisited, University of the Arts, Berlin, 20–21 november 2009.
Marin-Lamellet, C. and Aymond, P. (2008), 'Combining verbal information and a tactile guidance surface: The most efficient way to guide people with visual impairment in transport stations?', *British Journal of Visual Impairment*, 26, 63–81.
Metz, D. H. (2000), 'Mobility of older people and their quality of life', *Transport Policy*, 7 (2), 149–152.
Miller, N.E. and Kraeling, D. (1952), 'Displacement: Greater generalization of approach than avoidance in a generalized approach-avoidance conflict', *Journal of Experimental Psychology*, 43 (3), 217-221.
Naniopoulos, A. (1999), 'European approaches to accessible transport systems', *Japan Railway & Transport Review*, 20, 9–13.
Passenger Focus (2008), *Buying a Ticket at the Station: Research on Ticket Machine Use – Technical Report* (London). Available at: <http://www.passengerfocus.org.uk> (accessed 28.01.2011).
Passenger Focus (2010), *Ticket Vending Machine Usability,* Report of Findings.
Sackmann, R. and Weymann, A. (1994), *Die Technisierung des Alltags. Generationen und Technische Innovationen* (Frankfurt: Campus Verlag).
Sandes, F.E., Jian, H.L., Huang, Y.P. and Huang, Y.M. (2010), 'User interface design for public kiosks: An evaluation of the Taiwan high speed rail ticket vending machine', *Journal of Information Science and Engineering,* 26, 307–321.
Schreder, G. et al. (2009), 'The ticket machine challenge? Social inclusion by barrier-free ticket vending machines', research paper presented at the COST Action 298 conference The Good, the Bad and the Challenging, Copenhagen, 13-15 May 2009.
Stephanidis, C. (2009), 'Universal access and design for all in the evolving information society', in Stephanidis, C. (ed.), *The Universal Access Handbook* (Boca: Raton: CRS).
Struve, D. and Wandke, H. (2009), 'Video modeling for training older adults to use new technologies', *ACM Transactions on Accessible Computing*, 2 (1), 1–24.
Van Dijk, J. and Hacker, K. (2003), 'The digital divide as a complex and dynamic phenomenon', *The Information Society,* 19, 315–326.
Weiner, B. (1985), 'An attributional theory of achievement motivation and emotion', *Psychological Review*, 92 (4), 548–573.
Weymann, A. and Sackmann, R. (1998), 'Technikgenerationen', *Literatur- und Forschungsreport Weiterbildung*, 42, 23–35.

PART III
Younger and Older People Using New Media: A Contrastive Analysis

Chapter 8

Building Intergenerational Bridges Between Digital Natives and Digital Immigrants: Attitudes, Motivations and Appreciation for Old and New Media

Giuseppe Lugano and Peter Peltonen

Introduction[1]

Modern western societies have taken a long leap in developing post-industrial society towards what has been labelled the information society. Nowadays in these societies Information and Communication Technologies (ICTs) such as the internet and the mobile phone represent essential instruments for managing work, social life and leisure activities. Lack of access to, competences in or motivation for using ICTs in daily life represent serious obstacles to the realisation of an inclusive society by preventing users from participating in and benefiting from the opportunities of an information society.

Being digitally literate[2] (Gilster, 1997) – being able to understand and use technologically mediated information – can be a defining factor in how different generations and groups of people manage their daily lives. For Prensky (2001) the quality of being digitally literate is a factor that differentiates between generations: he defined 'digital natives' as individuals who have always used the computer and mobile phone, and 'digital immigrants' as those who have, at a later point in their lives, migrated to digital technologies. Through the notion of digital wisdom, Prensky (2009) has recently argued that the original dichotomous position between digital natives and digital immigrants will be less marked in the near future.

In our view, the classifications of digital natives and digital immigrants make sense, and before proceeding any further, they should be more clearly understood on an empirical basis. Stoerger (2009) observed that 'age may not be the only factor to consider' because 'there are significant differences between and among

1 This chapter is based on an unpublished paper of Lugano (2009). Acknowledgement: this work was supported by a research grant from Jytte Association and by the Network for Higher Education and Innovation Research (HEINE).

2 For more information about literacy, see also Chapters 2, 3, 4, 7, 8, 9 and the conclusion of this volume.

countries'. On this premise, digital natives and digital immigrants would be better understood if analysed from the perspective of the local history and culture that create the basis for digital literacy, rather than being analysed from a global perspective. The importance of the cultural perspective is particularly important when considering the choice of the landmark year for defining who count as digital natives (see section Data and Methods).

Prensky (2001) has suggested that because of the transition to a society where young people are born to digital nativity, education institutions should 'talk the language of digital natives' and therefore move towards more 'informal learning'. But do we really need as radical a change as that in our education systems because of the existence of digital natives? Bennet and Maton (2010) have argued that we should, instead, evaluate educational and everyday contexts as different activities with different purposes. Hence, being complementary, formal and informal learning could support each other, while leaving room for more 'traditional' education. In this chapter we support this latter view and present the case of Finnish Communication Camps as an example of an informal learning experience that complements the school by promoting the development of intergenerational bridges between digital natives and digital immigrants. This promotion takes place through a range of community activities, which bring to mind the concept of a 'digital melting pot' introduced by Stoerger (2009).

The distinction between digital natives and digital immigrants remains an ongoing issue (see also Loos, 2010; the introduction, the conclusion and Chapter 3 by Cardoso et al., Chapter 5 by Harold, and Chapter 10 by Loos and Mante-Meijer in this volume). Recent research (Bennet and Maton, 2010; Jones et al., 2010) has highlighted the fact that there is not enough evidence for the existence of these two categories, at least in terms of identifying homogeneous groups. Moreover, it should also be noted that Prensky has not scientifically evaluated the new pedagogical strategies that he proposes (see also Schulmeister, 2008 and Bennett et al., 2008).

In studies of digital natives and digital immigrants one further development has involved moving the discourse claiming that these two generations are merely 'different' to a view arguing that digital natives, due to having a natural aptitude for learning with ICTs, are 'better' than digital immigrants. Prensky (2001: 3) himself has argued that 'the single biggest problem facing education today is that our digital immigrant instructors, who speak an outdated language (that of the pre-digital age), are struggling to teach a population that speaks an entirely new language'. In contrast, if the experiences and abilities of each generation had been viewed as being different but equally important, Prensky could have proposed a strategy of mutual enrichment. But by advocating that tomorrow's education systems should speak the language of digital natives, he actively asserts their superiority in the digital age. Prensky (2009) later modified his original position by rejecting this view of digital native superiority in favour of a more constructive approach that reconciles the needs and characteristics of the two generations.

Similar approaches have been proposed in other studies (Stoerger, 2009; Bennet and Maton, 2010).

In this chapter, unlike other studies in this field (Howe and Strauss, 2000; Oblinger and Oblinger, 2005; Tapscott, 1998, 2009; Palfrey and Gasser, 2008), we try to contribute to these discussions by taking an empirical approach to the debate and linking it to a specific cultural context (i.e. the Finnish one). We do that by concentrating instead on 'motivations', which in our view is the main factor differentiating between digital natives and digital immigrants. This moves beyond investigating the traditional themes of digital literacy like access and skills, and instead takes into account different motivational factors that may be influencing the perception and experience of ICTs.

In the following sections, we first illustrate the theoretical concept of 'communication capability' (Viherä, 1999; Viherä and Nurmela, 2001) and show the informal learning experiences taking place in Communication Camps (Viherä, 1999 Lugano, 2003; Lugano et al., 2006), which respectively represent the conceptual framework and the setting of the study. After presenting the methodology of the research we describe our findings by considering ten types of 'old' and 'new' media clustered into four categories: non-digital applications (e.g. letters), traditional mobile applications (e.g. phone), 1st generation of internet applications (e.g. email) and 2nd generation of internet applications (e.g. social networking sites). Finally, we consider the implications of our findings from the perspective of the ongoing debate on digital natives and digital immigrants.

Theoretical Framework: Communication Capabilities

The debate about generational differences between digital natives and digital immigrants has so far focused on their skills in perceiving, learning and using digital media in daily life. As Bennet and Maton (2010) observed, in the nineties various aspects of technology use were quantitatively assessed by considering indicators related to access to information and communication devices. When the penetration of computers and the internet was not very high, it made sense to consider schools' and households' access to digital networks, as this is a necessary condition for the development of computer skills. However, owning a computer or having access to the internet does not automatically imply being digitally literate. Once access to ICTs is widespread, it is necessary to assess their use in specific contexts, a task that requires qualitative research.

In addition to digital literacy (Gilster, 1997), educators and policy makers have also been describing and investigating various other forms of literacy (e.g. information literacy[3], information fluency, new media literacy, visual literacy, which are all well illustrated by Lorenzo and Dziubian (2006). All these terms are commonly used to refer to a set of competences that a citizen needs in order to participate actively in

3 See also Chapter 4 by Herold in this volume.

an information society. In this chapter, we adopt the less known but still powerful concept of communication capability (Viherä, 1999). This is particularly suitable for our analysis because it consists of three complementary factors, namely access to communication technology, competences needed to operate it properly and the motivation to use it to satisfy everyday needs (Figure 8.1).

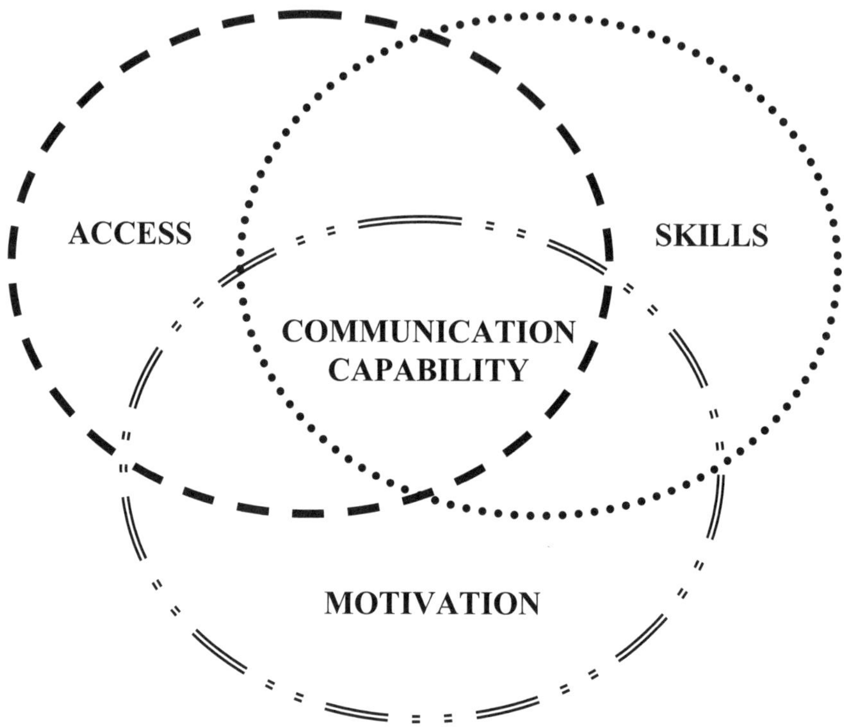

Figure 8.1 Communication capability (Viherä, 1999)

Each individual possesses a stock of communication capabilities — the potential of which can be realised only in a social environment (i.e. a community). For this reason, access, skills and motivation represent the basic dimensions of social interaction. Each of these can be operationalised in order that they can be measured quantitatively. Like Bennet and Maton (2010), Viherä (1999) also observed that access is much easier to measure than skills, while assessing motivations is conceptually harder and therefore requires more efforts to ensure its validity.
In the communication process, three basic types of problems can occur relating to lack of access, lack of competence and lack of motivation (Figure 8.2). This leads to incompatibilities when some of these three elements are present, but not others.

The first type of communication problem occurs when a group of users has adequate skills and motivation to interact, but no access. This may be due to

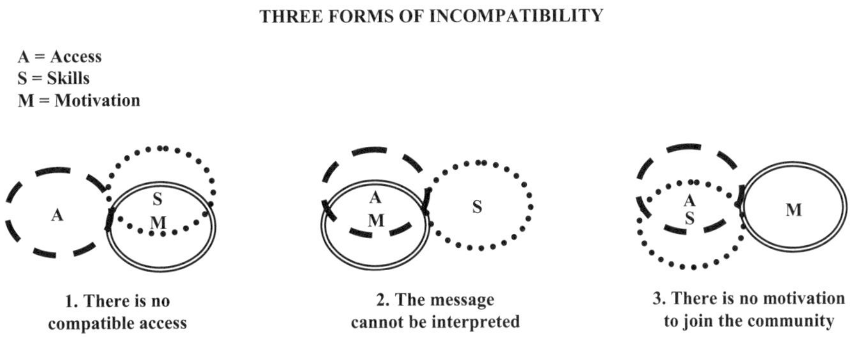

Figure 8.2 Communication problems (based on data at Viherä, 1999)

lack of access to a digital network (e.g. no internet connection) or to technical incompatibilities between hardware and software. Existing trends towards openness, interoperability and the general process of technological convergence provide important steps towards the reduction of this form of incompatibility because they enable software- and device-independent communication based on converging networks.

Another form of incompatibility concerns the lack of adequate competences (technical, social or cultural) that prevents the interpretation of a message despite having technological access and the motivation to interact. A common example is a person receiving a message from another person in an unknown language. Educational initiatives, at all levels and in all knowledge domains, typically aim at minimising such gaps in learners' skills.

The third and last form of incompatibility is the most challenging because it deals with the lack of motivation to participate as an active member of the community. This goes beyond personal access to digital networks and a number of personal competences because it encompasses the level of community interaction. There are various forms of communities, which entail different types of obligations, norms and practices. For instance, digital communities (Lugano, 2010) are fluid, rapidly evolving and geographically distributed social structures grounded on digital sharing. Unlike traditional forms of community, entering a digital community does not require any commitment towards a long-lasting relationship or mutual solidarity. Nevertheless, between prospective members, even in digital communities, there must be a compatible motivation, which may be based on a common interest, objective or experience. For instance, the first documented 'smartmob' (Rheingold, 2002) was possible not only because of widespread access to the SMS and its simplicity, but because the Filipino population shared the desire to protest against President Estrada.

Lack of access, competences or motivation when using ICTs in daily life represents a serious obstacle to the realisation of an inclusive society because it prevents users from participating in and benefiting from the opportunities associated with an information society. From the perspective of communication capabilities, minimising those three forms of incompatibility can be regarded as the objective of an inclusive information society. Although motivation is an essential driver in human action, it has seldom been included in the declaration of principles (WSIS, 2003) or strategies aiming to reduce the gap between users and non-users. Similarly, the debate on digital natives and digital immigrants has not paid much attention to motivational factors and their implications for attitudes towards and experience of ICTs. Without empirical studies analysing the multiple facets of inner motives by answering questions like 'why do you like/dislike, use/not use ICTs', important arguments about generational differences could be simply accepted without much, if any, critical reflection. Hence, our study provides a first concrete step towards the construction of intergenerational bridges between digital natives and digital immigrants and offers an insight into their motivational differences in the use of 'old' and 'new' communication media.

Data and Methods

Communication Camps

The dataset was collected during the Communication Camp 2005 that took place in Heinola (Finland) from 7th to 14th of June 2005. Communication Camps are a Finnish social innovation that have been organised since 1987 by the Viekas ry association. Over the years, the organisers have received support from various international and Finnish institutions, and from ICT companies. This cooperation has contributed to the grassroots development of the Finnish information society (Viherä, 1999; Lugano et al., 2006).

Communication Camps are a highly immersive informal learning experience that are organised once a year. Each summer, a number of campers, typically from fifty to eighty, of all ages, come together. In 2005, the youngest participant was aged 9 and the oldest 65. Therefore, both digital natives and digital immigrants were represented. Young and old participate as a one group in all activities without any distinction as regards their gender, age or level of digital literacy. Communication Camps apply the principle of peer mentoring, which means that there are no strict roles and learning from others is encouraged. Each group includes one or two 'resources', i.e. more experienced campers who have participated in at least three camps in the past. Their role is to facilitate the process of 'learning by doing' through tutoring. Finally, 'core' campers are the most experienced participants and supervise camp activities and develop the community spirit.

Once settled in, camp participants are divided into five groups that, on a daily rotation, take care of the five camp activities: production of a daily newspaper, management of the camp radio station, creation of digital videos, management of the information point and preparation of camp meals in the restaurant. On the last day, the groups are dissolved, so that the campers can freely practise the activity they enjoy the most.

Questionnaire

A structured questionnaire with basic instructions and a description of the study was distributed to the camp participants. The questionnaire was made available in two languages (Finnish and English) and could be filled in either online or on paper. Although the questionnaire included multiple questions, our analysis is limited only to the last question, which was an open-ended one asking those participating in the study to state briefly the advantages or disadvantages, reasons for use or non-use, and likes or dislikes related to letters, postcards, phone-calls, short messaging service (SMS), instant messaging (IM), emails, mailing-lists, internet forums, blogs and online social networking sites (SNS). It is worth noting that the data was collected in 2005 when blogs and especially SNS were not as popular as today. Although the number of non-users of such applications was quite high, we include them in our analysis because of their interest.

Digital Native – Digital Immigrant Classification

A total of 52 questionnaires were returned by the participants in the study (referred to below by the letter 'P'): 25 of them were filled in by digital natives, the remaining 27 by digital immigrants. Within the group of digital natives, 17 respondents were male and 8 were female. Gender ratio was more balanced in the group of digital immigrants, which included 12 males and 15 females. Considering campers' roles (Figure 8.3), 30 respondents were regular campers, of which the majority were digital natives. All 11 resource campers were digital immigrants, who also outnumbered digital natives among core campers.

We classified all campers that were born after 1990 as digital natives, and as digital immigrants the campers that were older than fifteen at the time of the study. Despite its critical importance (Jones et al., 2010), the choice of the landmark year is an issue of general controversy (Table 8.1). On this topic, Prensky (2001) remains vague, even where he suggests the year 1974, when the Pong videogame was invented, to mark the beginning of the era of digital natives. Jones et al. (2010) acknowledge that it is difficult to demarcate clearly the appropriate historical period and added that digital natives are the young people born sometime in the 1980s. In their study, Jones et al. (2010) choose 1983 as the landmark year. Along the same lines, Palfrey and Gasser (2008) mark the 1980s as the beginning of this new generation. Oblinger (2003, 2008), who speaks of digital natives using the related terms of 'Millennials' and 'Net generation', is instead very accurate in indicating 1982 as the year in which the generational change took place. She also mentions 1991 as the year during which a new generational step took place. Tapscott (2009), who marks January 1977 as the beginning of the new 'digital' generation, referred to this newest generation of digital natives as 'Generation

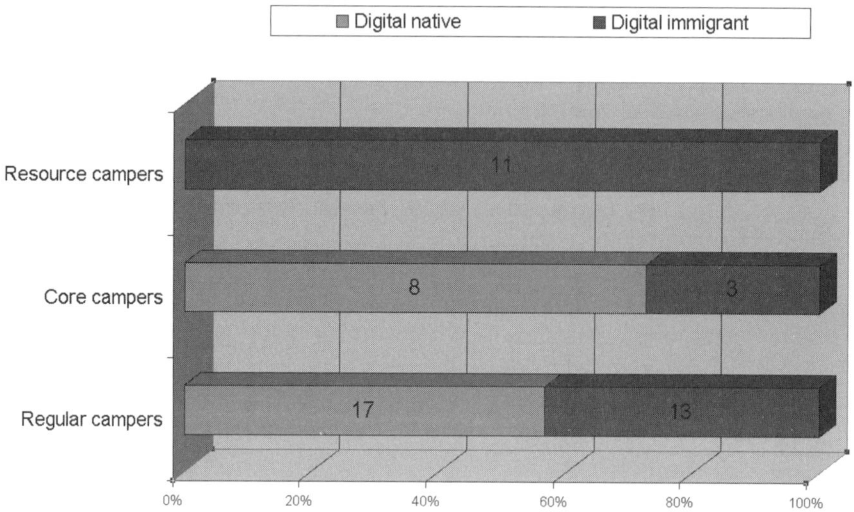

Figure 8.3 Distribution of respondents according to their roles at the Communication Camp

next'. Unlike Oblinger, according to Tapscott the first generation of digital natives ended in 1997.[4]

Table 8.1 Year selected by various authors to indicate the beginning of the era of digital natives

Scholar	Landmark year
Prensky (2001)	1974
Tapscott (2008)	1st generation: 1977–1997; 2nd generation: 1998–
Palfrey and Gasser (2008)	1980s
Oblinger (2003; 2008)	1st generation: 1982–1991; 2nd generation: 1992–
Jones et al. (2010)	1983

In our opinion, each choice can be easily criticised. As regards 1974, most individuals born in that year probably purchased their first mobile phone and became internet users in the late nineties, when they were in their twenties. Similarly, those who were born in 1982 accessed computer and mobile networks in their late teens. In both cases, both groups of users cannot be considered to be digital natives, because they migrated first from letters to emails and then to instant messaging, and from wired telephones to cordless and then to mobile phones. On the other hand, those who were born after 1990 have probably always had access to an internet connection, both at

4 See also Table I.1 in the introduction of this volume.

home and at school. For this reason, they are probably more used to writing with a keyboard than with a pen. In addition, they cannot imagine life without mobile communication because, for them, this has always existed.

The choice of the year 1990 is far from being definitive, but it is arguably the most appropriate date for Finland, a country that witnessed an early development of its information society (Nurmela and Ylitalo, 2003). Finnish statistics indicate that access to an internet connection, both at home and at school, was already widespread when children of that age were young, and mobile communications also took off early in this country. The pace of information society development should be taken into account in the choice of the landmark year, as it is not possible to speak of digital natives and digital immigrants in countries that have not yet become information societies. For them, the most suitable year for marking the transition might still be in the future.

Open-Ended Question: Analysis and Visualisation

For each answer to the open-ended question, we extracted and ranked the most significant keywords by using a vector space model for the analysis (Salton et al., 1975) and tag-clouds for the visualisation process (Kaser and Lamire, 2007).

As ten different media and two generations were considered, a total of twenty vectors were used. Each vector was filled by keywords extracted manually from the answers. In some cases, the term was taken from the text without any modification: for instance, the sentence *it is a fine way, but a little slow* produced two keywords: 'fine' and 'slow'. In other cases, a longer phrase was converted into a single or compound term with the closest meaning. In the sentence *it requires one to work for a long time to write a letter*, the keyword 'demanding' would have been chosen instead of 'long'. The latter procedure would have been more difficult if we had attempted the automatic extraction of keywords; therefore the manual approach was chosen to obtain higher reliability.

Tag-clouds, which are tools to visualise and to navigate information and which have become popular with the Web2.0 (O'Reilly, 2005), are created through Wordle[5], a free online tag-cloud generator. In a tag-cloud, the size of a keyword is proportional to its importance. In our case, it corresponds to the number of occurrences. Only the keywords that occur at least twice are visualised in this way.

Findings

Non-Digital Applications: Letters and Postcards

Letters and postcards were included in the open-ended question in order to see how differently they are perceived from digital applications. It was assumed that

5 http://www.wordle.net

substantial differences would be found when comparing digital natives and digital immigrants. The assumption was confirmed for letters but not for postcards, suggesting that none of the digital applications, such as multimedia messages (MMS), can be regarded as the digital equivalent of the postcard. In contrast, email is perceived as having evolved from letters.

Prensky (2001) wrote that 'digital natives are used to receiving information really fast. (…) they thrive on instant gratification and frequent rewards'. Letters and postcards do not fit in well with these expectations; one of the respondents summed it up well: *a letter is terribly slow, boring and old fashioned.* (P10, male, 13 years old) Digital immigrants showed an opposite attitude, actually appreciating the value of 'slow time' (Eriksen, 2001): *I'm too lazy to write, but it's nice to receive a letter: when I write, I always need to reflect more on what I say.* (P48, female, 54)

Another key difference concerns digital immigrants' appreciation of the tangible and long-lasting nature of letters: *the benefit of the letter is that one does not need to print it, and it lasts. Emails can be destroyed too easily.* (P46, f, 47). This quality was also appreciated by the younger generation of digital immigrants: *it's very nice to find a physical object in your mailbox*. (R39, f, 24). For digital natives these characteristics seemed less important, as they were not mentioned by any respondent from that group. However, some digital natives enjoyed the personal feeling that letters give, mainly by the presence of handwriting. This was also one of the features most appreciated by digital immigrants, who defined letters as a *warm and human way to be in touch with someone who is far.* (R36, m, 19)

Figure 8.4 A tag-cloud representing digital natives' and digital immigrants' view on letters

The characterisations of postcards and letters were quite similar (Figure 8.4), with digital immigrants providing slightly more positive descriptions than digital natives, who often complained about their high cost and slowness. Compared to letter, postcards were not really regarded as a real personal communication medium for several reasons: they could not be 'too personal' because *everyone can read a postcard.* (P19, f, 14) In addition, they were also 'uninformative' because *there is very little space for text.* (P9, m, 13). Despite the above restrictions, many digital natives still sent postcards, especially when travelling abroad, because postcards are *part of the holiday*. (P17, m, 14) In addition digital immigrants considered postcards as being holiday-memories, despite agreeing about their uninformative nature and high costs. However, they tended to like them: *I like sending postcards. I always carry stamps with me.* (P50, f, 57)

Traditional Mobile Applications: Phone Calls and SMS

Digital natives and digital immigrants regarded phone calls and SMS as their favourite media because they are both 'quick' and 'easy' (Figures 8.5 and 8.6). Phone calls are more expensive than SMS, but they provide an opportunity to *hear the other person's voice.* (P21, m, 15), to *discuss in real time* (P25, f, 15), to *change things quickly'* (P3, m, 11) and to feel connected to somebody when *I feel a bit lonely* (P39, f, 24). Being expensive, phone calls were not used by digital natives for frequent interaction: *I call only when I have something important to say.* (P14, f, 13)

The analysis of phone calls also revealed an important difference: while digital natives characterised phone calls with an exceptionally low number of adjectives, digital immigrants' descriptions were much richer and more differentiated, including, for instance, the social contexts of use (work, friends, and family).

Figure 8.5 A tag-cloud representing digital natives' and digital immigrants' view of phone calls

Digital natives preferred SMS texts not only because *they are not as expensive as the calls* (P2, m, 11), but also because *it is fun to send SMS.* (P3, m, 11) Some digital natives also complained that the composition of SMS is demanding and the writing process is too slow. The limited space for writing was regarded by some respondents as being a disadvantage because *it's easy to have misunderstandings* (P16, m, 14), and by others as an advantage because *it's handy to tell things shortly and briefly.* (P11, m, 13) Although digital immigrants were also avid SMS users, they also listed the negative implications of text messaging, stating that *they are modifying the traditional language* (P41, m, 28) and they are *getting teenagers addicted.* (P40, m, 25) Digital immigrants also highlighted two positive sides of SMS that were not evident in the younger generation of users, namely its discreet and unobtrusive nature as the primary alternative to the call: *if you do not dare to call, text.* (P37, f, 20) and *you can send an SMS when you don't have the courage to call.'* (P35, f, 18) On the other hand, *if the other person does not answer a call, you have to take a big step to leave a message on the answering machine.* (P34, m, 18)

Figure 8.6 A tag-cloud representing digital natives' and digital immigrants' view for SMS

1st Generation of Internet Applications: Email, Mailing Lists and Forums

Being invented in the seventies, email and mailing-lists can be regarded as the first generation of internet applications.

As expected, digital natives are more enthusiastic about and used Web2.0 applications more frequently than digital immigrants: indeed, one-fifth of the respondents in the former group answered *I do not use email* (Figure 8.7). Digital natives enjoyed email being free, but regard it as *boring and somewhat gloomy.* (P25, f, 15) Not all of them considered email to be a quick medium; for the youngest respondent *email is not quick.* (P1, m, 9) Instead, digital immigrants regarded email as being *too quick, you do not always remember to be polite.* (P45, m, 34) Email also has various social functions: while digital natives used email *only with the contacts that are not met regularly.* (P23, f, 15), digital immigrants used email for interpersonal communication, group conversations and doing business.

Digital natives complained about email being text-only and not interactive. They enjoyed being able to *send very long messages* (P50, f, 57), but also underlined the fact that email is less personal when compared to letters. In addition, digital immigrants also regarded spam messages being as a serious limitation of the email, which was not mentioned by any digital native.

Figure 8.7 A tag-cloud representing digital natives' and digital immigrants' view for email

Mailing-lists were relatively unknown to digital natives, of whom 40% did not use them and 24% had never heard of them. Mailing-lists were described as being difficult, annoying, boring and useless. The only positive comment made by digital natives as regards mailing-lists was about them being quick for spreading information to a group. Mailing-lists received a better assessment from digital immigrants, who underlined both their positive and negative aspects: 42% of the respondents in this group observed that mailing-lists are about group communication and 24% of them regarded mailing-lists as being quick and interest-related. However, a significant number of digital immigrants (28%) also complained about information overload. For P48 (f, 54), *users who disturb make most mailing-lists unusable.*

Internet forums were slightly better known than mailing-lists, but 48% of digital natives either did not yet know about them or did not use them. Although *it is easy and fine to browse many topics* (P16, m, 14), they were perceived as being risky places, full of paedophiles (P12, f, 13) and *tasteless comments.* (P9, m, 13) The public and communitarian nature of forums was not perceived as being a strength by some digital natives: *disadvantage: others can see what you write.* (P20, m, 15). Internet forums did not seem to be the preferred tool by digital immigrants either, as one-fifth of them were not using these forums. Respondents in this group agreed with digital natives, considering forums to be risky and useless: *Total anonymity makes some people go wild. However, when you have a good community, it is a good way to find information and support.* (P31, m, 17). For digital immigrants, forums were useful in providing quick answers to questions, especially to those related to work and hobbies: *I usually read the technical forums, where there are most of the answers to my questions.* (P40, m, 25) Like mailing-lists, forums suffered from information overload: *there are so many messages that I have the feeling of getting lost very easily* (P38, f, 24).

2nd Generation of Internet Applications: Instant Messaging, Blogs and Social Networking Sites

Digital natives identified the internet with its 2nd generation of internet applications, those referred to as the Web2.0 (O'Reilly, 2005). Digital natives enjoyed IM because it has all the characteristics they expect, such as speed, interactivity and multimedia (Figure 8.8). IM was perceived as being *handy, easy and cheap, even if you need to sit in front of the computer all the time* (P8, m, 12), and the fun it generates was also due to *the possibility to hear and see other persons* (P22, m, 15).

Digital immigrants agreed that IM is a quick and cheap way to chat with friends, but they also pointed to a number of negative aspects: IM can *lead to tiredness and it is not very personal* (P33, f, 17) and it *is not suitable for deep communication* (P36, m, 19). Furthermore, *you need at least one hour there to say hi to all the connected friends* (P41, m, 28). Finally, *questions and answers are not linear; sometimes it's difficult to follow the discussion if there are simultaneous*

Figure 8.8 A tag-cloud representing digital natives' and digital immigrants' view for IM

chats (P45, m, 34). In contrast to digital natives, none of the digital immigrants characterised IM as being easy to use.

Blogs and SNS were not yet very popular in 2005. A quarter of the digital natives did not know about blogs, while 32% did not use them. A third of digital immigrants reported not using blogs. Regarding SNS, 56% of digital natives did not use them, but almost all respondents (92%) knew what they were about. Among digital immigrants, 26% did not use SNS, while 11% had never heard of them before.

For both digital natives and digital immigrants, blogs were personal public diaries; it is *fun to read about other people's lives* (P14, f, 13), and it is a good way to *let other people to know about your day, your thoughts and opinions.* (P12, f, 13) For some, the public nature of blogs provided a motivation to write, to others, it did not: for P23 (f, 15) *it is a relief when other people read your stories*, but for P25 (f, 15) *it is not good to describe one's private life to everybody.* A blog *fits well for people like members of the Parliament who have to explain their life and work to everybody.* (P36, m, 15) In comparison to other media, blogs were not characterised by their speed, cost or easiness, but rather in terms of the consequences of being personal and public.

Online social networks were regarded by both digital natives and digital immigrants as being tools for group communication that are mostly oriented towards entertainment and fun through digital sharing. As in the case of other media, digital immigrants provided a richer characterisation of SNS, also considering their negative implications, which had not been stressed by digital natives: *SNS are a handy way to seek new friends/company of people thinking the same way, but you have to be quite critical in judging if other people are really who they say they are and do what they say they do.* (P28, f, 16) Another respondent highlighted the risks of digital sharing: *your material might end up in wrong hands.* (P33, f, 17)

Discussion

The analysis of the Communication Camp dataset indicates that digital natives and digital immigrants perceive and experience both old and new media in a different manner. This finding is in line with the original claim by Prensky

(2001). Although the dataset focused on motivations, it also offered an insight into the incompatibilities that exist in relation to the other two dimensions of communication capability (Viherä, 1999), namely access and skills (Table 8.2).

Table 8.2 Key differences between digital natives and digital immigrants

Dimension	Digital Natives	Digital Immigrants
Access	Cost barrier (higher impact on making phone calls, sending postcards) Compatibility in the use of media ecology (preference for phone calls, SMS and IM)	Cost barrier (limited impact on the use of communication media) Compatibility in the use of media ecology (preference for email, phone calls and SMS)
Skills	Technical skills (forum, mailing-lists are too difficult) Information processing modality (immediate feedback, multi-tasking) Critical thinking (less developed à homogeneous group)	Technical skills (management of spam, information overload) Information processing modality (need for reflection, limited multi-tasking skills) Critical thinking (more developed à highly diversified group)
Motivations	Personal values (informal interaction-style, fun-oriented) Perception of reality (appreciating 'bits' more than 'atoms')	Personal values (formal interaction style, work/family-oriented) Perception of reality (appreciating 'atoms' more than 'bits')

As expected, both digital natives and digital immigrants in Finland have convenient access to information and communication networks. However, service costs have a relatively different impact for the two generations: being economically dependent from their parents, digital natives prefer SMS to phone calls because the former is less expensive. Despite this difference, digital natives and immigrants agree that phone calls and SMS satisfy their everyday communication needs; as far as the internet is concerned, IM is the digital natives' favourite choice, while email is the most popular application among digital immigrants. Although not related to our dataset, both generations also use Facebook, currently the most popular SNS[6].

In regard to skills, little can be concluded about digital literacy from the dataset. On the basis of what has been labelled as 'difficult' or 'demanding', digital natives perceived letters and mailing-lists as not being straightforward. While the complexity of letters is due to the handwriting requirement, the difficultly of mailing-lists lies perhaps in the registration process and management through the combination of email and web interface. The fact that letters, emails, and mailing-lists are perceived as 'useless' or 'boring' does not indicate, in itself, that digital natives do not possess the required knowledge. However, it shows that they have low motivation for acquiring and using them.

On the other hand, the answers of digital immigrants highlight their difficulty in managing spam and information overload, problems that can be overcome with the support of adequate technological tools. The different nature of skill-related problems hints that the major gaps separating the two generations are represented by their different information processing modalities and by the maturity of their critical thinking.

In relation to information processing, digital natives show a clear 'need for speed': they appreciate the immediate feedback of phone calls, SMS and IM while perceiving letters and postcards as being slow services. In this respect, digital natives emerged as a homogeneous group because none of them characterised phone calls, SMS and IM as slow. Interestingly, email was considered by some digital natives as quick and by some others as slow, whereas, for digital immigrants, email was definitely a quick medium. The association of digital natives with the 'instant' and 'quick' labels is understandable, as that has also emerged in other existing studies. Jones et al. (2010: 722) observes that 'the new generation requires rapid access and quick rewards', although in their study this dimension was not empirically investigated. Additionally, Oblinger (2008: 12) argues, again without empirical backing, that 'the Net generation demands immediate response, expecting answers at the click of a mouse.') Digital immigrants, on the other hand, appreciate 'slow time' (Eriksen, 2001), which offers moments for reflection. It remains also to be verified whether digital immigrants have truly different information processing skills than digital natives, who, it is claimed, 'think and process information fundamentally differently from their predecessors.' (Prensky, 2001: 1).

Digital natives and digital immigrants also differed in the maturity of their critical thinking skills. Digital immigrants took a very critical attitude towards all types of communication media, and particularly towards new media, by underlining both positive and negative aspects. This produced, among other things, a large diversity of opinions and richness of characterisations. By contrast, the views of digital natives were more homogeneous. Although the judgment of digital immigrants may seem in some cases negatively biased, their position was more moderate than that of digital natives, who had more radical opinions: indeed,

6 http://www.onlineschools.org/blog/facebook-obsession

they either loved or hated a tool for social communication, perhaps overestimating either its positive or negative qualities. Such position may be either a characteristic of their generation, or simply due to their young age and lack of experience. Oblinger (2008: 19) supports the former view, arguing that:

> in a multi-tasking, fast-forward world, learners may not be stopping to reflect on what they know, how they behave, and the values they hold. In fact, the tendency of young people to not be reflective – to pause, think, and ponder – may simply be a characteristic of youth.

On the other hand, if the latter case were true, digital natives' radical positions would become more moderate with age. Assuming that the ability to think critically is linked with traditional educational methods, digital natives' development could be significantly constrained if future education systems were only be tailored to their demands and characteristics as originally suggested by Prensky (2001).

Concerning motivations, incompatibilities between digital natives and digital immigrants could be minimised in relation to two main, interrelated areas, namely personal values and perception of reality.

Spontaneous and informal interactions with friends provide a major reason for media use by digital natives, who find in IM an application that meets their expectations about multi-tasking and leisure-oriented lifestyles. Unlike letters or postcards, IM and SNS offer, through digital sharing, an opportunity to obtain immediate multimedia rewards. Even if these are typically ephemeral, photos, status updates and 'likes' represent a quick and effective means to maintain a status of perpetual contact with one's social entourage. Digital natives are used to continuously renegotiating the boundaries of their relationships, while committing little to most of them. These requirements are not satisfied by letters, which do not support multi-tasking and immediacy but require some commitment. Digital natives' 'need for speed' is also reflected in their appreciation for conciseness: SMSs are fun because they require finding creative ways to express much meaning in only a few characters. On the one hand, this may cause misunderstandings, but, on the other, it also represents a shared communication code that is part of a community culture.

For digital immigrants, old and new media are not only a means for interacting with friends, but also for managing work and family life. The diversity in the kinds of relationships they have also implies multiple interaction modalities and goals: in particular, digital immigrants often adopt a formal interaction style that privileges quality over quantity, and reflection over action. Since IM is often light, immediate, multi-tasking and multimedia, digital immigrants often describe it as superficial, cold and useless.

Digital immigrants also seem to perceive reality in a different manner, for instance by appreciating the tangible nature of printed letters and postcards, which are regarded as warm and full of meanings. Non-digital media are slow media: they cannot be exchanged with the frequency of SMS or with the frequency of status updates in IM and SNS. This is not necessarily a disadvantage, as in digital media each new message renders the previous ones rapidly obsolete, Although not so numerous, letters have more text than digital messages, are handwritten and long-lasting. These characteristics make them warm and valuable in the eyes of digital immigrants because they are a sign of a deep relationship.

Toward an Inclusive Society: Building Intergenerational Bridges Between Digital Natives and Digital Immigrants

None of the generational differences that have been discussed are truly new. Indeed, similar observations have also been made in previous studies (Prensky, 2001; Oblinger, 2008), which, however, lacked empirical backing. Certainly, further research is needed to understand more fully the existing generation gaps. Once such gaps have been identified, the next step consists in turning generational differences from risks into concrete opportunities for realising a more inclusive society. This requires having all citizens come 'on board' (Reding, 2006). To achieve this goal it is neither sufficient just to provide access to information and ensure widespread digital literacy, nor to understand the peculiar motivations of each single generation of ICT users and non-users. Indeed, the true challenge is to build *intergenerational bridges* by enabling a fruitful cooperation and dialogue between generations. If digital natives and digital immigrants were simply regarded as two distinct groups of users with different needs, expectations and lifestyles, there would be a risk of creating a balkanised information society rather than an inclusive one.

The Finnish experience of Communication Camps suggests that it is at least possible to create a cooperative environment in which personal or generational differences are not obstacles but resources for both individual and community development. This process may not be easily realised within formal education structures (e.g. school classrooms, adult education centres), which consist of a quite homogeneous learning communities in respect of age, needs and experiences. Unlike these formal structures, Communication Camps offer to heterogeneous social groups a unifying activity framework where they can contribute with unique views and experiences. Communication Camps strengthen participants' communication capabilities by granting free and convenient access to all of them and by offering a structure in which different generations of users develop personal skills, mutual understanding and group collaboration. The concept of the Communication Camp is flexible and can be successfully applied in any learning context, including organisations (Lugano et al., 2006).

In conclusion, Communication Camps are complementary to traditional learning settings because they enable the creation of intergenerational bridges. Through dialogue, the differences in perceiving and experiencing communication media will naturally blend and promote digital melting pot (Stoerger, 2009). Future research should carefully consider how to overcome the considerable challenges that exist to realising this vision on a wider scale, and in particular how to develop arguments and strategies to commit governments and other stakeholders to taking them seriously.

References

Bennett, S., Maton, K., and Kervin, L. (2008), 'The 'digital natives' debate: A critical review of the evidence', *British Journal of Educational Technology*, 39 (5), 775–786.

Bennett, S. and Maton, K. (2010), 'Beyond the 'digital natives' debate: Towards a more nuanced understanding of students' technology experiences', *Journal of Computer Assisted Learning,* 26, 321–331.

Eriksen, T.H. (2001), *Tyranny of the Moment: Fast and Slow Time in the Information Age* (London: Pluto Press).

Gilster, P. (1997), *Digital Literacy* (Hoboken, New Jersey: Wiley).

Howe, N. and Strauss, W. (2000), *Millennials Rising: The Next Great Generation* (New York: Vintage books).

Jones, C., Ramanau, R., Cross, S. and Healing, G. (2010), 'Net generation or digital natives: is there a distinct new generation entering university?', *Computers & Education,* 54 (3), 722–732.

Kaser, O. and Lemire, D. (2007), 'Tag-cloud drawing: algorithms for cloud visualization', Proceedings of the WWW 2007 Workshop on tagging and metadata for social information organization.

Loos, E.F. (2010), *De oudere: een digitale immigrant in eigen land? Een terreinverkenning naar toegankelijke informatievoorziening.* [Senior citizens: Digital immigrants in their own country? An exploration of accessible information delivery]. Inaugural lecture. (The Hague: Boom/Lemma).

Lorenzo, G. and Dziuban, C. (2006), 'Ensuring the Net Generation is net savvy', in Oblinger, D.G. (ed.), *ELI White Papers, Educause Learning Initiative.* Available at: <http://www.educause.edu/ir/library/pdf/ELI3006.pdf> (accessed 21.01.2011).

Lugano, G. (2003), *Finnish and Italian technology in the global environment of the European Community: a comparison of ICT strategies in education* [Master's thesis] (Bologna: University of Bologna).

Lugano, G. (2009) 'Towards an inclusive broadband society: An empirical study on digital natives and digital immigrants in Finland, research paper presented at the COST Action 298 conference *The Good, the Bad and the Challenging*, Copenhagen, 13–15 May 2009.

Lugano, G. (2010), *Digital Community Design: Exploring the Role of Mobile Social Software in the Process of Digital Convergence* [Doctoral thesis] Jyväskylä Studies in Computing 114. (University of Jyväskylä Press: University of Jyväskylä, Finland).

Lugano, G., Viherä, M.-L. and Viukari, L. (2006), 'Towards a network-based civil society: the communications camp paradigm', Proceedings of the International Conference on Advanced Learning Technologies (ICALT*)*, Kerkrade (Holland), 1012-1013.

Nurmela, J. and Ylitalo, M. (2003), *The Evolution of the Information Society: How Information Society Skills and Attitudes have Changed in Finland in 1996-2002* (Statistics Finland).

O'Reilly, T. (2005), 'What is Web2.0*'*, Oreillynet.com entry on 30.09.005. Available at: <http://oreilly.com/web2/archive/what-is-web-20.html> (accesssed 30.03.2011).

Oblinger, D.G. (2003), 'Boomers, Gen-Xers, and Millennials: Understanding the 'New Students', *Educause Review,* 38 (4), 36-47.

Oblinger, D.G. (2008), 'Growing up with Google. What it means to education', *Emerging Technologies for Learning* 3, 11–22.

Oblinger, D.G. and Oblinger, J.L. (2005), *Educating the Net generation* (Boulder, Washington D.C.: Educause).

Palfrey, J. and Gasser, U. (2008), *Born Digital: Understanding the First Generation of Digital Natives* (New York: Perseus Books).

Prensky, M. (2001), 'Digital natives, digital immigrants', *On the Horizon*, 9 (5), 1-6.

Prensky, M. (2009), *H. Sapiens Digital: From Digital Immigrants and Digital Natives to Digital Wisdom* (Innovate).

Reding, V. (2006), Strengthening the European Information Society: From talk to action, Keynote speech at i2010 conference Towards a ubiquitous European Information Society, Helsinki, 28.9.2006.

Rheingold, H. (2002), *Smartmobs: The Next Social Revolution* (New York: Basic Books).

Salton, G., Wong., A. Yang, C.S. (1975), 'A vector space model for automatic indexing', *Communications of the ACM* , 18 (11), 613–620.

Schulmeister, R. (2008), *Gibt es eine »Net Generation«?* [Work in Progress] (Universität Hamburg, Zentrum für Hochschul- und Weiterbildung).

Stoerger, S. (2009), 'The digital melting pot: bridging the digital native-immigrant divide', *FirstMonday online Journal,* 14 (7), July 2009 issue.

Tapscott, D. (1998), *Growing up Digital: The Rise of the Net Generation* (New York McGraw-Hill).

Tapscott, D. (2009), *Grown up Digital: How the Net Generation is changing your World* (New York: McGraw-Hill).

Viherä, M.-L. (1999), *People and Information Society: The Citizens' Communication Skills and the Opening of New Prospects for the Civil Society* [Doctoral thesis] Turku School of Economics, Series A-1:1999, (English summary 337–354).

Viherä, M.-L. and Nurmela, J. (2001), 'Communication capability as an intrinsic determinant for information age', *Futures,* 33, 245–265.

WSIS (2003), '*Declaration of Principles. Building the Information Society: A Global Challenge in the New Millennium*', Technical report WSIS-03/Geneva/Doc/4-E.

Chapter 9

Age and Internet Skills: Rethinking the Obvious

Alexander van Deursen

Introduction

Throughout history, technology has frequently played a dominant role in defining what skills have been considered important. For full participation in contemporary information based society, additional skills on top of reading, writing and using audiovisual media are required. This can be explained by applying seven communication capacities related to the internet (Van Dijk, 1999):

- *Speed.* The internet allows instantaneous worldwide communication. The amount of available information in a specific period of time is very large compared to traditional media.
- *Reach.* The potential social and geographic reach of the internet is worldwide. Although only a small part of the world's population has internet connectivity, the internet allows access to innumerable addresses and contacts.
- *Storage capacity.* The massive amount and variety of online information, very different in quality, puts new demands on people who have to use it.
- *Selectivity.* Users have to choose between Web addresses, menu options, online applications, and information to find the material they seek.
- *Stimuli richness.* The internet combines text, sound, speech, images, and video. Although this richness supports mental access, it also requires more mental capabilities to process the various stimuli.
- *Interactivity.* Interactivity makes internet use more attractive, stimulating, immediate, involving, and participatory. However, internet use is more demanding, since it requires many cognitive resources (Bucy and Newhagen, 2004).
- *Complexity.* Compared to the more traditional media, the use of the internet is more complex. Websites allow for information in which illustrations, graphs, images, and video can be used. Unfortunately, not all websites achieve this in a usable manner.

All these communication capacities increase the necessary skills required to use the internet, especially when compared to the more traditional print and audiovisual media. The characteristics of traditional media (e.g., low potential of selectivity and accuracy of information) create relative passivity in those using these media. In this respect, traditional media usage is different from digital media use. While traditional media enable active mental processing, digital media require users to do more in terms of interacting with interfaces. A minimum level of active engagement with the medium is required, and the possibility of interactions, transactions, and interpersonal communication is offered. Furthermore, older media do not provide such a large amount of information and range of non-linear choices. The internet's information features are used in ways similar to those in which print and audio-visual media are employed. The acts of searching, selecting, processing, and evaluating information from online video, images, sounds, texts, and numbers largely correspond to the skills used with traditional media and computers. However, the information provided by the internet is infinite and linked in a non-linear manner.

Younger and Older Generations Ability to Use the Internet

Unfortunately, in current educational programmes, the additional skills required to use the internet have not yet fully gotten to the heart of the debate. While compulsory education obliged all children to go to school and learn to read and write, learning to use the internet is not a standard component of the current curriculum. On the contrary, it is generally believed that while technologies such as the internet empower learners, they are additions to learning itself (Buckingham, 2007).

A general assumption concerning internet skills is that younger generations[1] are frequent, confident, and unproblematic internet users that can easily keep up with advances in communication technologies (see also Chapter 4 by Herold in this volume who challenges this assumption). Young people get to know the internet at an early age and thus are considered more skilful than seniors (De Haan and Huysmans, 2002). People who spend more time online – whether at work or any other location – will acquire more knowledge about the internet and thus develop better online skills (Hargittai, 2005). There is also evidence, though, that specific internet skills are insufficient among students (Klein et al., 2001; O'Hanlon, 2002; Davis, 2003; Harrison and Comber, 2003; Metzger et al., 2003; Volman et al., 2005 and Chapter 4 by Harold in this volume). And Loos (2010: 7, 15–16) criticises the popular (and unpleasant) assumption that with the passing away of the oldest age groups the internet skill problem will solve itself.

The older generations are considered problematic and lacking confidence as internet users, and could be regarded as 'laggards' in the process of innovation diffusion (Rogers, 1995). Reasons for this assumed troublesome internet use can be found in the fact that they never had the opportunity to acquaint themselves

1 Referred to as the 'digital generation', the 'net generation', etc. See also Table I.1 in the introduction and Chapter 4 in this volume.

with the internet at school. Furthermore, they lag behind in terms of ownership, skills, and use of computers and the internet (De Haan and Huysmans, 2002). Other reasons include problems with learning internet skills due to decreased working memory, reaction times (Boyd and Bee, 2009), and resistance to change (Castells, 2001). An important reason should also be sought in the social settings in which people operate. The initial uptake and further usage of the internet may be significantly affected by the amount of social support to which a user has access. New users need to be able to draw on social contacts to increase their skill levels and help gain confidence, and they need to be able to have access to emotional support and encouragement when they encounter problems. Seniors often operate in a social environment in which little help with computers and the internet is available. This is the opposite for younger people and people who use computers and the internet at work.

The question remains as to whether empirical evidence can be found that older internet users – compared to younger ones – are simply less skilled, or whether the picture is more complex. This chapter will therefore provide more insight into this whole issue by presenting the results of empirical research in the Netherlands.

Four Types of Internet Skills

To understand more fully the relation between age and the level of internet skills, it is necessary to have a clear understanding of what the concept of internet skills exactly entails. The literature concerning internet skills is not consistent either in the terms used or in the underlying concepts applied. There are many different terminologies (for an extensive overview see Bawden, 2001) and converging views, with no agreement on the exact definition of such skills. The development of tools to assess skills is particularly hampered by the lack of consensus on what constitutes measurable dimensions (Ba et al., 2002). I choose to associate the term 'internet skills' with the term 'digital skills' that is commonly used in digital divide research (e.g. Steyeart, 2002; Van Dijk and Hacker, 2003; De Haan, 2004; Eshet-Alkalai, 2004; Mason and Hacker, 2003; Van Dijk, 2005; Kvasny, 2006; Fuchs and Horak, 2008). Internet skills can be considered to be a specification; there are different skills, for example, in using mobile telephones or computers. Thus, the internet-adjective with the concept internet skills refers to the medium of interest here. The concept 'skills', however, requires further clarification. Several related terms are used interchangeably (e.g., 'literacy', 'competence', 'ability', 'capacity', 'expertise', 'fluency', or 'know-how'). Most common are 'literacy', 'competence', and 'skill', or combinations like 'literacy skills' or 'literacy competence'. Literacy[2] seems to be the most general concept, often considered as a set of skills or competencies. Since the goal is to identify measurable dimensions,

2 For more information about literacy see also Chapters 2, 3, 4, 7, 8 and the conclusion of this volume.

the terms skills and competences seem more appropriate than the more general word literacy. The concept of competence itself has different meanings, and it is not always clear whether competence refers to identifiable indices or is related to patterns of behaviour (Anttiroiko et al., 2001; Virkus, 2003). Anttiroiko et al. (2001) concluded that there are two dimensions to competence: knowledge and skills. They found knowledge to be the understanding of how our everyday world is constituted and works, while skills involve the ability to apply pragmatically, consciously or even unconsciously, our knowledge in practical settings. They conceived skills as being the technical aspects of competence, or the more technical "how to do" component. This confined technical notion of skills appears to be the convention, but it should nevertheless be used with caution. The New Oxford Dictionary of English describes skill more broadly as 'a person's ability to do something well; an expertise'. This ability is therefore not limited to technical aspects. In fact, the term skills seems to suggest a more (inter)active performance for media use than, for example, the term literacy suggests for reading and writing texts. For instance, using the internet does not only mean reading and writing on keyboards and screens but it also entails interaction with programs and with other people, transactions in goods and services, and making decisions. This requires more action than the more passive use of visual media like television or books, which mainly require knowledge and cognitive skills. Thus, on top of the more tool-related skills, specific skills are also needed to use the information provided.

I will draw on previous work that distinguishes between four types of internet skills (Van Deursen and Van Dijk, 2009a, 2010). The four types of internet skills can be divided into both medium- and content-related skills, hereby avoiding a technologically deterministic viewpoint.

The first type of medium-related internet skills are the 'operational internet skills', derived from concepts such as 'instrumental skills' (Steyaert, 2002), 'technical competence' (Mossberger et al., 2003), 'technological literacy' (Carvin, 2000), and 'technical proficiency' (Søby, 2003). All these concepts indicate a set of basic skills in using internet technology.

The second medium-related internet skills are the formal internet skills that relate to the hypermedia structure on which the internet is built. This structure requires the skills of navigating and orientating.

The first content-related internet skills are the information internet skills, derived from studies that adopt a staged approach in order to explain the strategies users adopt when trying to fulfil their information needs.

Finally, strategic internet skills constitute the second content-related internet skills. These relate to people's capacity to use the internet as a means to reach particular goals and achieve the more general goal of improving one's position in society. The proposed definition of strategic skills is based on the classical approach to decision-making whose emphasis lies on procedures through which decision-makers can reach an optimal solution as efficiently as possible (Miller, 2006).

The four internet skills together contain some gradients of difficulty. They illustrate that the provision of operational and formal skills alone is not sufficient when using the internet. The four internet skills have a sequential and conditional nature (Van Deursen et al., 2011). Content-related skills somehow depend on the medium-related skills because the absence of medium-related skills means that one will never reach the stage to perform the content-related skills. The internet, in comparison with the more traditional media, for example, makes information-seeking more difficult because it assumes a number of new operational and formal skills to begin with. They are listed in Table 9.1.

Table 9.1 Medium- and content-related internet skills (Based on data at Van Deursen and Van Dijk, 2009a, 2010)

Medium-related Internet skills	
Operational Internet skills	Operating an Internet browser: Opening websites by entering the URL in the browser's location bar; Navigating forward and backward between pages using the browser buttons; Saving files on the hard disk; Opening various common file formats (e.g., PDFs); Bookmarking websites. Operating Internet-based search engines: Entering keywords in the proper field; Executing the search operation; Opening search results in the search result lists. Operating Internet-based forms: Using the different types of fields and buttons; Submitting a form.
Formal Internet Skills	Navigating on the Internet, by: Using hyperlinks embedded in different formats such as texts, images, or menu's. Maintaining a sense of location while navigating on the Internet, meaning: Not becoming disoriented when navigating within a website; Not becoming disoriented when navigating between websites; Not becoming disoriented when opening and browsing through search results.
Content-related Internet skills	
Information Internet Skills	Locating required information by: Choosing a website or a search system to seek information; Defining search options or queries; Selecting information (on websites or in search results); Evaluating information sources.
Strategic Internet skills	Taking advantage of the Internet by: Developing an orientation toward a particular goal; Taking the right action to reach this goal; Making the right decision to reach this goal; Gaining the benefits resulting from this goal.

For the purposes of this chapter, I will base my conclusions on three series of performance tests conducted among the Dutch population where more than 300 subjects were tested for their current level of internet skills (Van Deursen and Van Dijk, 2011a/b). In all three studies, subjects had to complete 17 assignments on the internet. Eight assignments were used for measuring operational internet skills, four for measuring formal internet skills, three for measuring information internet skills, and two for measuring strategic internet skills. The three studies differed in terms of the context in which the skills were applied: government, general-leisure, and health information services, respectively. The assignments related to situations that are closely linked to types of real-life questions that people face. In all three studies, subjects were recruited by applying a stratified random sampling method over gender, age, and education. For a detailed overview of the method applied and a description of the assignments charged to the subjects, see Van Deursen and Van Dijk (2010, 2011a/b). In this chapter, I will focus on the results of these tests, with a strong emphasis on the impact of age.

Age and the Levels of Internet Skills

The average level of assignments completed (in percentages) for the four age categories over the three studies is shown in Figure 9.1. In the first two figures, the average completion rates of the medium-rated skill assignments are presented. We can observe a clear decrease in the level of internet skills as age increases. Subjects aged between 55 and 80 were only able to complete around 50% of the relatively basic assignments. Regarding the content-related internet skills, however, the decrease in skills levels is less obvious. Also, the low average completion rate reveals that there is much room for improvement in all age categories.

Yet, the overview provided in Figure 9.1 one does not tell the whole story. Solely focussing on these charts might lead to the conclusion that younger people perform best when using the internet. Such conclusions are often based on the basic technical skills. However, the situation is more complex. When Van Deursen et al. (2011) examined the relationship between age and the four internet skills in more detail the findings have some major implications. First of all, they concluded that the level of content-related internet skills is strongly influenced by the level of medium-related internet skills. This fits the assumed conditional nature of the medium- and content-related internet skills. Content-related skills somehow depend on the medium-related skills because the absence of medium-related skills means that one will never be in a position to perform the content-related skills. Also, there is a direct significant positive effect of internet experience on the medium-related skills. The number of hours spent online weekly did not reveal any significant effects. Education has a direct significant effect both on the medium-related skills and on content-related skills. The effect of education on the content-related internet skills is also indirect, via the medium-related internet skills. The most important finding concerns age. Van Deursen

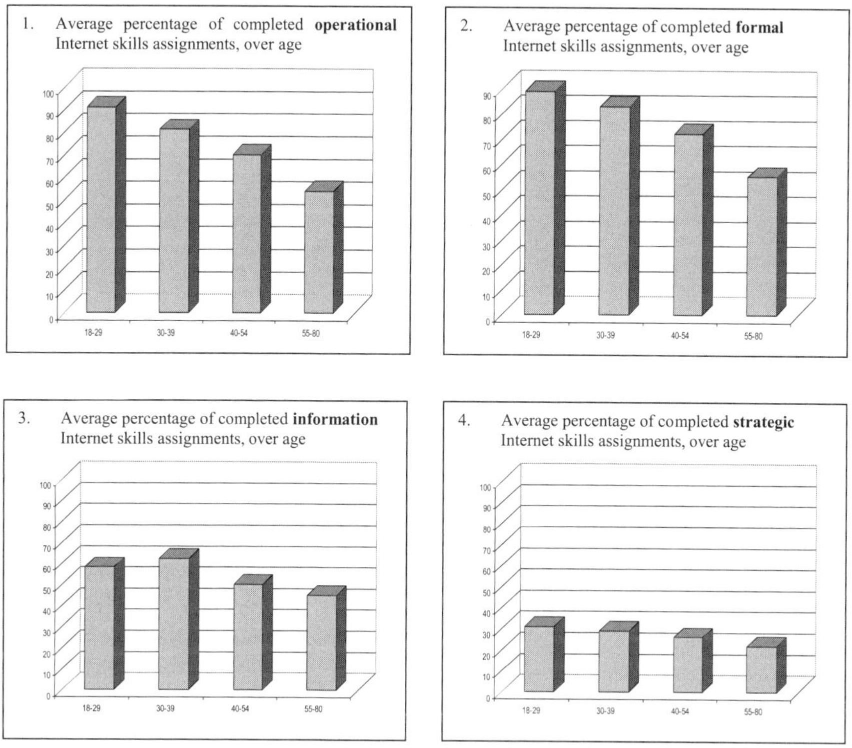

Figure 9.1 Average assignment completion, over age (based on three performance tests, see Van Deursen and Van Dijk, 2011a, 2011b)

et al. (2011) concluded that higher age appears as a negative contributor to the medium-related skills (i.e., operational and formal internet skills); the younger generations perform better as regards these skills. However, the results regarding content-related skills are different. *In fact, there is a direct and positive significant effect linking age to the content-related skills.* This implies that as age increases, the level of content-related internet skills also increases. However, there is also an indirect effect of age on the content-related internet skills, via the medium-related internet skills. Overall, these medium-related skills have such a major influence on the performance of content-related-skills that older people still score slightly lower on the performance of content-related internet skills than younger people.

Differences in Online Behaviour

In this section, I will focus on the specific internet skills that cause people to have problems when using the internet, and how these problems differ by age.

The findings are based on the analysis conducted by Van Deursen and Van Dijk (2009a) and cover the first performance test, in which 109 subjects participated.

Operational Internet Skill Related Problems

Some of the basics of using an internet browser appeared problematic for people aged over 65. A substantial proportion seem to have problems with recognising the address bar (i.e. they had no clue on where to enter a Web site's URL), which makes initiating the internet session difficult. Problems with starting also occurred amongst seniors who, without the immediate appearance of Google, were unable to recognise the internet browser at all. Other basic problems that seniors ran into were not removing the 'about:blank' part in the address bar and only opening websites using the 'Open' option in the file-menu of Internet Explorer.

Over a third of the subjects – mainly the senior and lower educated participants – were not able to save an online file to the hard disk. Seniors often did not have a clue as to how to start the save process, or they saved the whole webpage instead of the file, or they assumed that the file was automatically saved after opening the save dialog, or they made website shortcuts to the desktop or added the website to the favourites instead of saving a file. Others closed the save dialog instead of clicking 'save'.

Other problems that mainly seniors experienced related to filling out web-based forms and to the use of search engines. In online forms, some fields were overlooked, making it impossible to complete the form. Although most senior internet users knew how to use a search engine, some of them experienced problems identifying search engines on websites (when they were clearly present), or with entering search queries that were typed without spaces, preceded by 'www', or entered into the address bar.

Finally, mouse and scrollbar related problems mainly occurred among seniors. They often only used the scrollbar's tiny arrow buttons for traversing long distances on a page, and were not aware that it was possible to drag the easier-to-use middle part of the scrollbar. Using the mouse only resulted in minor delays, caused by clicking multiple times on search buttons or clicking the wrong button.

Formal Internet Skill Related Problems

Concerning the formal internet skills, again the seniors group of users experienced the most problems. The problems they encountered included overlooking website menus or using the menu itself (especially roll-over menus where seniors did not understand they could move the mouse cursor to the menu items that appeared). How to return to the homepage of a website from a deep-link was also not self-evident. In some instances, seniors tried to find the homepage using the internet browser's help function, believing they were already on the homepage of a website when this was not the case, or they clicked 'Up' when they were already at the top of a page or else they clicked on a link to the current page. Another common problem occurred when new browser windows were opened. In these cases, seniors did not understand why the back button was suddenly deactivated. They overlooked the website in the original window, even when it is still visible in the background. Furthermore, after choosing a search result from the search result list, seniors often did not return to the original search result list. Instead, they turned to Google again and retyped the same search query.

Information Internet Skill Related Problems

Regarding the content-related information and strategic internet skills, problems occurred over all age groups. Many subjects performed search operations with search queries that did not fit the information problem or were far too general (e.g., typing the keyword 'money' when searching for 'minimum wages'). Furthermore, almost nobody limited the number of search results by using Booleans or advanced search methods (e.g., exact word combinations or entering dates). Since in most cases search engines return a vast number of unsuitable search results, intensive selection is required before the results become useful. The problems that subjects experienced included opening sponsored or commercial results (which in most cases did not suit the information problem), not going beyond the first three search results, not going beyond the first page of search results, selecting one or more irrelevant search results, and selecting irrelevant information pages within websites. The findings revealed that age had a negative influence on the selection of irrelevant search results, meaning that as age increases less irrelevant results were chosen. A striking observation was that nobody seemed to pay attention to the source of the information found. Finding the answer seemed to be the primary objective; it did not seem to matter where the information came from.

Strategic Internet Skill Related Problems

The use of websites that support users in making informed decisions were often found, but they did not always suit the assignment. In one of the assignments, for example, subjects had to choose one of three political parties that best matched three given standpoints. Websites that support the political party's decision were often confused with other websites that supported decisions, even for positions on retirement (which had nothing to do with the assignment). Of the subjects that used these websites, almost nobody was able to generate useful outcomes. Furthermore, many subjects across all age groups had trouble staying focussed on the original goal of the internet session. The same accounts for combining information sources. In most cases, information from only one website was used, when in fact this was not enough to resolve the strategic assignment (e.g., choosing a hospital with the shortest waiting list).

Conclusion

In contemporary society, the younger generations are associated with frequent and confident use of the internet. They are considered to be unproblematic internet users that can easily keep up with advancements in communication technologies. Conversely, older generations are considered problematic and lacking confidence as internet users. In this chapter, I have argued that these assumptions should be carefully reconsidered.[3]

Higher age does indeed contribute negatively to the level of the more basic medium-related operational and formal internet skills. The result is that seniors are seriously limited in their basic internet use. They have problems when saving files or when using search engines (e.g., entering keywords in the address bar or typing keywords attached to each other). Furthermore, while websites may seem to be easy to navigate to their designers, older users may find them disorientating and confusing. Although young people perform far better as regards these medium-related internet skills, they still show a strikingly low level of information and strategic internet skills (people of all ages have trouble with the formulation of suitable or specific search queries, with selecting relevant search results, or with the evaluation of information). In fact, as age increases, the content-related internet skills actually improve. Unfortunately, increasing age also leads to considerable problems with the operational and formal internet skills that strongly influence the performance on the information and strategic internet skills.

After reading this chapter it should be clear that the popular (and unpleasant) assumption that with the passing away of the oldest age groups the internet skill problem will solve itself is false.[4] This assumption seems to be primarily based on the level of operational and formal internet skills. Unfortunately, this assumption is further strengthened by the seniors themselves. When they are asked to assess their own level of internet skills, older people score lower than younger people do. People who have little confidence in their ability to use the internet, who are dissatisfied with their internet skills, or who are uncomfortable using the internet may be said to have weak self-efficacy beliefs (Eastin and Larose, 2000; see also Chapter 7 by Schreder et al. in this volume). Those with low levels of self-efficacy are less likely to adopt and use the internet in the future than those with high degrees of self-efficacy (Eastin and Larose, 2000). Society also contributes to the offensive view that older people are awkward users of technology. Take, for example, commercials in which seniors are presented as clumsy. It seems necessary that this stereotype be carefully reconsidered in order to encourage older people to take up new technologies. Additionally, in most cases, younger people seem unable to benefit from communication technologies such as the internet. In fact, younger people could learn valuable lessons from older people instead of vice versa. Fortunately, in educational settings, the results regarding age are

3 See also Chapter 4 by Herold.

4 See also Loos (2010: 7, 15–16).

slowly becoming recognised. Research conducted within this field found that while students use the internet at a relatively young age they nevertheless lack the skills of reflection in regard to assessing search results and critically evaluating web sites (e.g., Lorenzen, 2001; Metzger et al., 2003; Pritchard and Cartwright, 2004; Kuiper, 2007).[5]

Another explanation for the fact that seniors experience operational and formal internet skill problems could be sought in their use of the more traditional media such as television. If they have no or only little experience with computers and the internet, they might compare the use of these media with watching a television screen.[6] On a television screen, all information is visible in a 'box' that they observe. The use of computers and the internet is fundamentally different: what is seen on the screen can be moved by scroll bars, and only reveals a miniscule part of the whole information presence. If you are so used to watching television, why would you think of moving a window unless someone showed you? Of the operational and formal skills that seniors experience, many can be explained simply by the fact that they have not formally been taught to take certain steps (why move your mouse to appearing menu items, how can you save something from a screen?). Van Deursen and Van Dijk (2009b) provided several clues on how new media developers should account for people with low skill levels of operational and formal internet skills. It is not always age that is the problem, but the wrong assumptions that designers make about the knowledge that users have.[7]

Regarding the effects of age, it must be emphasised that the results obtained account for the current era and current generations. It is not known whether the same differences will persevere in the future. Although operational and formal skills are easiest to account for, they might well persist, since technology changes, and with these changes, new specific operational and formal skill-related problems will come into existence. Information and strategic internet skills are more likely to be determined by educational levels in the future. When younger people are trained at school, they might become better at these skills.

When searching for an explanation for the finding that age is a negative contributor to the medium-related skills and a positive contributor to the levels of content-related internet skills, it seems that this is because additional intellectual abilities are needed to master information and strategic internet skills. The high levels of operational and formal internet skills observed among young people do not guarantee the development of these additional abilities.

The most important factor – determining all types of internet skills – is the level of educational attainment. The higher educated the subject, the better they perform on operational, formal, information, and strategic internet skills. Research within the digital divide discourse is often marked by differences in educational attainment, especially concerning internet access. Katz and Rice (2002) argue that

5 See also Chapter 4 by Herold.

6 See also Chapter 10 by Loos and Mante-Meijer on 'technology generations'.

7 See also Chapter 6 by Chisnell and Redish.

lower educated groups are unable to apply the content provided by the internet to their functional needs.

Although low general literacy levels are often related to digital inequality, regarding internet skills, another assumption is very common. It is often argued that people learn internet skills more through practice, by trial and error, than in formal educational settings (De Haan and Huysmans, 2002; Van Dijk, 2006). Arguably this mainly applies to operational and formal internet skills, but not for information and strategic skills. It appears that information and strategic internet skills do not grow with years of internet experience or amount of time spent online weekly. The fact that the benefits of sheer practice only counts for operational internet skills furthermore challenges the assumption that with the passing away of seniors, the internet skill problem will solve itself. The finding that information and strategic internet skills do not actually increase with years of internet experience or with the amount of time spent online can be explained by the possession of general intellectual abilities that strongly relate to information and strategic internet skills. These abilities do not necessarily improve from longer-term or heavy internet use.

The relatively weak relation of internet experience and time spent online to operational and formal skills can also be explained. People often keep repeating similar mistakes when using the internet. Computer users tend to rely on acquired skills, even when they are aware that they could learn more efficient procedures for achieving the same results (Cahoon, 1998). This probably also accounts for internet use. People learn by trial and error, but when they more or less achieve the goals they had in mind, people will persist in making the same mistakes online. This certainly is the case when there is no one around to point out mistakes.

References

Anttiroiko, A.V., Lintilä, L. and Savolainen, R. (2001), 'Information society competencies of managers: conceptual considerations', in Pantzar, E., Savolainen, R. and Tynjälä, P. (eds), *In Search for a Human-Centered Information Society* (Tampere: Tampere University Press).

Ba, H., Tally, W. and Tsikalas, K. (2002), 'Investigating children's emerging digital literacies', *Journal of Technology, Learning and Assessment,* 1 (4), 1–48.

Bawden, D. (2001), 'Information and digital literacies: A review of concepts', *Journal of Documentation,* 57 (2), 218–259.

Boyd, D.A. and Bee, H. (2009), *Lifespan development* (Boston: Pearson).

Buckingham, D. (2007), *Beyond Technology: Children's Learning in the Age of Digital Culture* (Cambridge: Polity).

Bucy, E. and Newhagen, J. (2004), *Media Access: Social and Psychological Dimensions of New Technology Use* (London: LEA).

Cahoon, B. (1998), 'Teaching and learning Internet skills', *New Directions for Adult and Continuing Education*, 78, 5–13.

Carvin, A. (2000), More than just access: Fitting literacy and content into the digital divide equation. Available at: <http://www.educause.edu/ > (accessed January 2009).

Castells, M. (2001), *The Internet Galaxy: Reflections on the Internet, Business and Society* (Oxford: Blackwell).

Davis, P.M. (2003), 'Effects of the web on undergraduate citation behavior: Guiding student scholarship in a networked age', *Libraries and the Academy*, 3 (1), 41–51.

De Haan, J. and Huysmans, F. (2002). *Van huis uit digitaal; Verwerving van digitale vaardigheden tussen thuismilieu en school* (The Hague: Sociaal Cultureel Planbureau).

De Haan, J. (2004), 'A multifaceted dynamic model of the digital divide', *IT & Society*, 1 (7), 66–88.

Eastin, M.S. and LaRose, R. (2000), 'Internet self-efficacy and the psychology of the digital divide', *Journal of Computer-Mediated Communication*, 6 (1).

Eshet-Alkalai, Y. (2004), 'Digital literacy: A conceptual framework for survival skills in the digital era', *Journal of Educational Multimedia and Hypermedia*, 13 (1), 93–106.

Fuchs, C. and Horak, E. (2008), 'Africa and the digital divide', *Telematics and Informatics*, 25 (2), 99–116.

Hargittai, E. (2005), 'Survey measures of web-oriented digital literacy', *Social Science Computer Review*, 23 (3), 371–379.

Harrison, C. and Comber, C. (2003), 'The impact of information and communication technologies on pupil learning and attainment', ICT in Schools. Coventry, GB: Research and Evaluation Series No. 7, Becta.

Katz, J. and Rice, R. (2002), *Social Consequences of Internet Use: Access, Involvement, and Interaction* (Cambridge, MA: MIT Press).

Klein, D.C.D. and Yarnall, L. and Glaubke, C. (2001), *Using Technology to assess Students' Web Expertise* (Los Angeles, CA: CRESST).

Kuiper, E. (2007), *Teaching Web Literacy in Primary Education* (Amsterdam: Vrije Universiteit).

Kvasny, L. (2006), 'Cultural (re)production of digital inequality in a US community technology initiative', *Information, Communication & Society*, 9 (21), 160–181.

Loos, E.F. (2010), *De oudere: een digitale immigrant in eigen land? Een terreinverkenning naar toegankelijke informatievoorziening. [Senior citizens: Digital immigrants in their own country? An exploration of accessible information delivery].* Inaugural lecture. (The Hague: Boom/Lemma).

Lorenzen, M. (2001), 'The land of confusion? High school students and their use of the World Wide Web for research', *Research Strategies,* 18, 151–163.

Mason, S.M. and Hacker, K.L. (2003), 'Applying communication theory to digital divide research', *IT & Society*, 1 (5), 40–55.

Metzger, M.J., Flanagin, A.J. and Zwarun L. (2003), 'College student web use, perceptions of information credibility, and verification behavior', *Computers & Education*, 41 (3), 271–290.

Miller, K. (2006), *Organizational Communication, Approaches and Processes* (Belmont, CA: Thomson Wadsworth).
Mossberger, K., Tolbert, C.J. and Stansbury, M. (2003), *Virtual Inequality: Beyond the Digital Divide* (Washington, DC: Georgetown University Press).
O'Hanlon, N.O. (2002), 'Net knowledge: Performance of new college students on an Internet skills proficiency test', *The Internet and Higher Education*, 5 (1), 55–66.
Pritchard, A. and Cartwright, V. (2004), 'Transforming that they read: Helping eleven-year-olds engage with Internet information', *Literacy*, 38 (1), 26-31.
Rogers, E.M. (1995), *Diffusion of Innovations* (New York, NY: Free Press).
Søby, M. (2003), *Digital Competences: From ICT Skills to Digital Bildung* (Oslo: University of Oslo).
Steyaert, J. (2002), 'Inequality and the digital divide: myths and realities', in Hick, S. and McNutt, J. (eds), *Advocacy, Activism and the Internet* (Chicago: Lyceum Press).
Van Deursen, A.J.A.M. and Van Van Dijk, J.A.G.M. (2009a), 'Using the Internet: Skill related problems in users' online behavior', *Interacting with Computers*, 21, 393–402.
Van Deursen, A.J.A.M. and Van Dijk, J.A.G.M. (2009b), 'Improving digital skills for the use of online public information and services', *Government Information Quarterly*, 26, 333–340.
Van Deursen, A.J.A.M. and Van Dijk, J.A.G.M. (2010), 'Measuring Internet skills'. *International Journal of Human Computer Interaction*, 26 (10), 891–916.
Van Deursen, A.J.A.M. and Van Dijk, J.A.G.M. (2011a), 'Internet skills and the digital divide', *New Media & Society*, 13 (6), 893–911.
Van Deursen, A.J.A.M. and Van Dijk, J.A.G.M (2011b), 'Internet skills performance tests: Are people ready for eHealth?', *Journal of Medical Internet Research*, 13 (2), e35.
Van Deursen, A.J.A.M., Van Dijk, J.A.G.M. and Peters, O. (2011), 'Rethinking internet skills: The Contribution of gender, age, education, internet experience, and hours online to medium- and content-related internet skills', *Poetics*, 39, 125–144.
Van Dijk, J. (1999), *The Network Society: Social Aspects of New Media.* (London etc.: Sage).
Van Dijk, J. and Hacker, K. (2003), 'The Digital Divide as a complex and dynamic phenomenon', *The Information Society*, 19(4), 315–327.
Van Dijk, J. (2005), *The Deepening Divide: Inequality in the Information Society* (London etc.: Sage).
Van Dijk, J. (2006), 'Digital divide research, achievements and shortcomings', *Poetics*, 34 (4–5), 221–235.
Volman, M., Van Eck, E., Heemskerk, I. and Kuiper, E. (2005), 'New technologies, new differences: Gender and ethnic differences in pupils' use of ICT in primary and secondary education', *Computers & Education*, 45 (1), 35–55.

Chapter 10
Getting Access to Website Health Information: Does Age Really Matter?

Eugène Loos and Enid Mante-Meijer

Introduction[1]

Digital Gap or Digital Spectrum?

In the majority of the western countries the population is aging at a rapid pace. At the same time, society is increasingly becoming more digitalised. Information is supplied to a growing extent, and frequently solely, in digital form. It is obvious, that this trend poses dangers for people, like senior citizens, who have problems using such new media. They risk being excluded from crucial information (Duimel, 2007: 7). A complicating factor is that the landscape in which older people currently reside[2] is largely shaped by what De Lange (2007: 23) calls the 'decollectivisation of the life course':

> The late modern life course becomes a series of *individual* passages; leaving the parental home, finding a job, becoming unemployed, marrying or not marrying, divorce, having children, retiring, growing (very) old – individuals must find their own way, without these transitions being embedded in any traditional institutional frameworks or accompanied by collective rituals. Constructing continuity and coherency in the life course is up to the individual. (translation)

What does this 'decollectivisation of the life course' entail for senior citizens living in an ever more digitised society? Schnabel (1999: 18) pointed out the vital part ICT could play in this respect over a decade ago:

> If this development continues, in a few years every single individual will have a virtual connection with all the members of his social network, will be able to build virtual new social networks and will have access to an inconceivable amount of information. (translation)

1 This chapter is based on an unpublished paper of Loos and Mante-Meijer (2009a) and also uses parts of Loos (2010, 2011a/b).

2 See also Hagberg (2004: 163) who argues that we all live, literally and metaphorically, in a technological landscape. See also Chapter 5 by Hagberg in this volume.

This prediction has largely been fulfilled. According to Wellman et al. (2003) there has been a move to 'networked individualism'[3], in which the person has become a 'portal'.

In our information society, more and more information about products and services is provided by new media, such as the internet. This development risks excluding those citizens who cannot or do not wish to use the medium. Duimel (2007: 24–57, 104–105) argues that this could be explained by the fact that these citizens (so-called 'non-liners'[4]) are afraid of trying something new and making mistakes. The costs, unfamiliarity with the possibilities of this new medium and emotional factors, such as shame, performance anxiety and loss of face may well also play a role. The size of this group should not be underestimated. According to figures for the Netherland issued by CBS (Statistics Netherlands), in 2010 some 40% of the 65 to 75 year-olds had never used the internet, compared to 14% of the group aged 55 to 65 and 5% of the 45 to 55 year-olds.[5] CBS publishes no figures for the age group 75 and over, but their non-use of the PC and the internet is probably even higher. If senior citizens are non-liners, their access to information is limited, which can endanger their participation in our society.

Some researchers even argue that there is a widening generational 'digital gap' between those people who are able to use new media and those who are not. It was Prensky (2001) who coined the notions of 'digital natives' and 'digital immigrants'. From an educational point of view, he considers students to be 'digital natives' who

> are all native speakers of the digital language of computers, video games and the Internet. So what does that make the rest of us? Those of us who were not born into the digital world but have, at some point later in our lives become fascinated by and adopted many or most aspects of the new technology are and always will be compared to them, *Digital Immigrants*. (Prensky, 2001: 1, 2)

Do they really exist, these 'digital natives', the generations who grew up with new media and are able to use them without any problem? And is there really an older generation of 'digital immigrants' playing catch-up by trying to learn how to use new media? Other researchers, e.g. Lenhart and Horrigan (2003), take a different perspective. They introduced the notion of a 'digital spectrum', in which people use the new media to varying degrees, depending not only on age but also on factors such as sex, education and frequency of internet use.

Senior citizens can learn to work with the new media up to a certain point, although the question remains as to what extent people continue to master new

---

3 See Wellman et al. (2002, 2003) for a further discussion of the role of the internet for networked individualism and the implications for social cohesion.

4 See also Table I.1 in the Introduction of this volume.

5 http://statline.cbs.nl

media with which they have not grown up.[6] Becker (1992a/b) and Becker and Hermkens (1993) point out how important the formative period in the life of humans (between the 15th and 25th year of life[7]): people born in a certain year and who form a cohort all 'have experienced certain life events'.[8] Obviously, the introduction of a new technology counts as such an event, which can lead to the rise of a new 'technology generation' (Sackman and Weymann, 1994: 41–43; Weymann and Sackman, 1998).[9] Huysmans et al. (2004: 20) argue:

> Successive cohorts grow up, each with their own specific constellation of available media, media competency and media preferences. These early experiences with media could later lead to shared behaviour patterns. (translation)

Socialisation theory states that people are formed by the period in which they grow up. Socio-economic and political circumstances and the technology available during their formative years shape their behaviour.

It is also plausible, though, to assume that differences will be visible within a technology generation regarding the degree to which each is able to master a new medium. The fact that individual differences increase as people age, is termed aged heterogeneity by Dannefer (1988: 360):

> Thus, members of a cohort are sometimes described as "fanning out" as they age, becoming more unlike each other on any characteristic (e.g. Baltes, 1979).

Health Information as a Primary Good

If we wish to ensure that senior citizens can continue to participate in our society, then accessible information is of prime importance. Especially health information is vital for senior citizens, in view of their age (Coombs, 2008; Loos and Mante-Meijer, 2009a: 11–12). Van den Hoven (1994: 369)[10], referring to Rawls (1971, 1993), goes so far as to refer to 'primary goods', which have

> a "use" in every rational plan of life in the sense of being normally necessary means to formulating, pursuing, and executing a rational plan incorporating any final ends whatsoever (…).

---

6 See also the concept of 'structural lag' proposed by Riley & Riley (1994) that can be used to show how the 'dynamism of structural change' and the 'dynamism of changing lives' are inextricably bound together. Lawton (1998) also discusses this subject.

7 Becker (1992b: 21) relies here on Mannheim (1928/1929). Also see Peiser (1999) and Bouma (2000: 68, 76) on the role of the formative years in media usage.

8 Becker (1992b: 25) refers to Ryder (1965) for his definition of the concept of 'cohort'.

9 See also Chapter 7.

10 See also Bovens (2003: 96-97).

As more and more health information is provided by websites nowadays, it is important that these digital information resources remain available to senior citizens. This will allow them to ensure their access to the information related to the product and services they need, provided by public and private organisations. In handbooks, such as *Older Adults, Health Information, World Wide Web*, edited by Morrell (2002), guidelines for website design for senior citizens are presented.[11] Literature reviews (e.g. Chisnell and Redish, 2004; Arch, 2008; Loos and Mante-Meijer, 2009b), show how international studies of digital information accessible for senior citizens are based on interviews that were conducted with website users or else their navigation behaviour was observed (e.g. Pernice and Nielsen, 2002). Research by Van Deursen (2010) (see also Chapter 9 in this volume) provides insights into the various internet skills of different generations. What is lacking, however, is insight into the similarities as well as the differences in the actual navigation behaviour of older and younger people. This chapter therefore presents the results of an explorative Dutch eye-tracking study[12] that focuses on the following question: to what extent do people from younger and older generations navigate websites in different ways when searching for health information?

Eye-Movement Characteristics of Navigating Older Users

There are a limited number of *eye-tracking* studies furnishing insight into the way younger and older generations *navigate* websites. The article 'Older adults and the Web: Lessons learned from eye-tracking', by Tullis (2009) reported empirical research results about differences between younger and older U.S. users in the way they use web pages:

> An eye-tracking study of a prototype website was conducted with 10 younger adults (ages 20–39) and 10 older adults (ages 50–69) to determine if there are differences in how they scan web pages. They performed the same task on the website. On the average, the older adults spent 42% more time looking at the content of the pages then did the younger adults. They also spent 51% more time looking at the navigation areas. The pattern of fixations on almost all pages showed that the older adults looked at more parts of the page then did the younger adults. (…) One thing we did not see was any difference in the likelihood of older and younger users to view page content "below the fold" (i.e., that they had to scroll the view). (Tullis 2007: 1030, 1038)

11 See also Becker (2004) who evaluated web usability for older adults seeking online health resources.

12 See McElhal (2007) for a further explanation of eye-tracking and the purposes for which this eye-tracking can be used.

This study shows interesting patterns that may be validated by future comparable empirical research. Another example of such research is that of Houtepen who in 2007 conducted an explorative eye-tracking study in the Netherlands with 13 younger users (18–25 years) and 7 older users (older than 50). Like in Tullis' study, they were requested to perform search tasks to find health information (in this case at the websites of the five largest Dutch health insurance companies). The results showed that:

- the older users needed more time to fulfil the task (almost 6 minutes compared to the 2.5 minutes the younger users spent to fulfil their task);
- older people read more and make less use of the website's search box facility.

Like Tullis' study, Houtepen's research shows that older users need more time to conduct a search task[13] and that they follow a different navigation pattern.[14] Hill et al. (2011: 1152) refer to studies by Fukada and Bubb (2003), Tullis (2007), Capozzo et al. (2008) and Zaphiris and Savitch (2008), which conclude, with one exception (Josephson and Holmes, 2004), that older users are slower than younger ones. A measurement study, using three websites and a Web-wide task, with 20 older users and a control group of 20 users between the ages of 21 and 55 conducted by Pernice and Nielsen (2002) also confirms the differences in time spent on the task: 12:33 minutes for the older users versus 7:14 minutes for the younger control group. Pernice and Nielsen (2002: 4) also offer an explanation for this difference:

> Websites tend to be produced by young designers, who often assume that all users have perfect vision and motor control, and know everything about the Web.[15] These assumptions are rarely upheld, even when the users are not seniors. However, as indicated by our usability metrics, seniors are hurt more by usability problems than younger users. Among the obvious physical attributes often affected by human aging process are eyesight, precision of movement, and memory.

The studies conducted by Tullis (2007), Houtepen (2007), and Pernice and Nielsen (2002), as well as studies cited in the reviews by Chisnell and Redish (2004, 2005), Arch (2008) and Loos and Mante-Meijer (2009b), offer insights into differences

13 Docampo Rama et al. (2001) and Romano (2010: 1362) also reported that older users needed more time to conduct search tasks at websites.

14 The eye-tracking study of Josephson and Holmes (2004) also compared patterns of fixations of different generations of users (6 users age 8-11, 6 users age 15–25, 6 users age 35–45 and 6 users age 55–65) and found no differences. This is probably due to the very low number of participants and the relatively young age of the older age group.

15 See also Chisnell and Redish in Chapter 6.

related to spent on time on tasks and navigation patterns between younger and older users. However, a few critical comments would seem in order:

- The number of participants in the studies was very low, which means that research with more users is necessary.
- These studies focused only on age, failing to take into account the role of factors such as sex, education and frequency of internet use[16]. It is therefore unclear whether differences within an age group are larger than the differences between younger and older people.

Explorative Eye-Tracking Study: Research Questions and Methodology

What is needed is research with larger groups of older and younger users, in order to take into account the role of factors like sex, education and frequency of internet use, and hence look beyond mere age. Now the question is, of course, how to set up and conduct such research. In this chapter we use the data of our eye-tracking study carried out among younger and older users (respectively about 21 years old and 65 years and older) in the Netherlands over the course of 6 days in April 2009 (Loos and Mante-Meijer, 2009b). Compared to the above mentioned earlier eye-tracking research, our eye-tracking study boasted a relatively large number of participants: 29 young people and 29 older people (of whom 18 were daily internet users), that also amply fulfils the minimum of eight participants required for this type of usability study.[17]

For all users we examined the role of age. Attention was also paid to the role that sex, level of education (higher or lower) and the frequency of internet use (daily or not daily) played for navigation behaviour. We focused on effectiveness (i.e. the task was successfully accomplished within a 5 minute time limit), efficiency (i.e. the time needed to accomplish the search task) and navigation behaviour (i.e. patterns of eye fixations[18] and the use of the search box[19]). This instrument uses infrared to measure eye movements in navigation patterns in a non-invasive manner as the equipment is built into the rim of the monitor. Heatmaps are

16 Hill et al. (2011) did examine the role of age and the internet experience of senior citizens. This eye-tracking study (among 12 novice older computer users and 6 more experienced), though, did not take into account the role of sex and education, and did not include young participants into their research design. Djamasbi et al. (2010) conducted an eye-tracking-study to examine the role of images for the visual appeal of web pages. They focused on younger users (age 18–31), but did not include older participants in their research design, nor did they take into account the role of sex, education and internet experience.

17 See Wichansky (2000), referred to by Goldberg and Wichansky (2003: 512).

18 By using an eye-tracker, based on heatmaps described below.

19 See Loos and Mante-Meijer (2009b) for a complete overview of all navigational aspects and the gazeplots of individual younger and older users which were also analysed in this eye-tracking study.

Table 10.1 Different user groups

User group	N
All users	58
All older users	29
All younger users	29
All female users	28
All male users	30
All younger female users	14
All younger male users	15
All older female users	14
All older male users	15
All older users with higher education	19
All older users without higher education	10
All older users using internet daily	18
All older user not using internet daily	11

generated, with the different colours showing what the participants looked at on a webpage and how often navigation areas are visited by using different colours (red, yellow and green: respectively very intense, moderate and low intensity), based on the number of fixations of different groups of users.

The users performed a search task at the website of ANBO (a Dutch organisation for senior citizens)[20] and the website of Univé (a Dutch (health) insurance company). At each website they had to find information about discounts related to health insurance that was located on a specific web page of both organisations (see Loos and Mante-Meijer (2009b) for more information). The results of a search task at a third website (a Dutch municipality) that the participants visited are not presented here because the search task was not related to health information. In order to avoid a learning effect, we presented the search tasks to the participants in a random order.

It appeared that sex and education did not have a major impact on the navigation behaviour. For this reason we will present – beside the impact of age – the effects of the frequency of internet use, which, as we will see, influences the way people navigate the website while conducting a search task.

20 For this website we asked the older users to perform the search task for themselves and younger users were asked to perform the search for their grandparents.

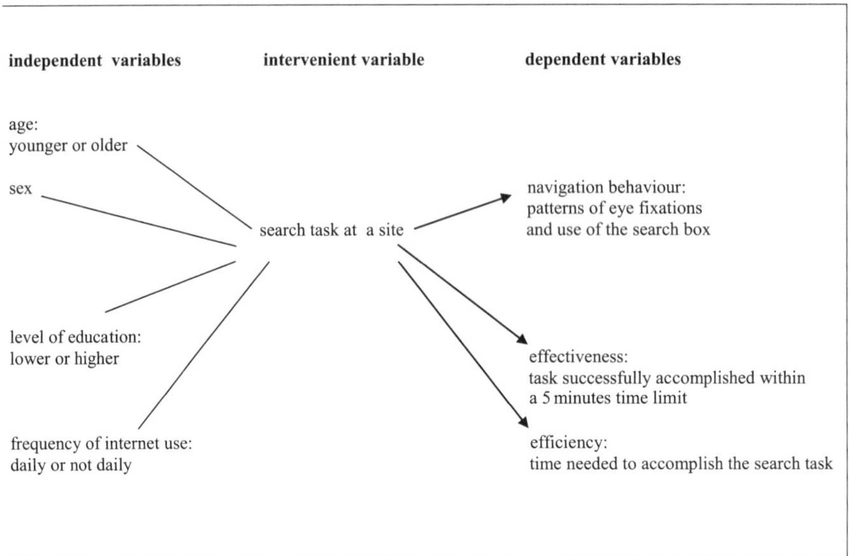

Figure 10.1 Research design

Results Search Task Performed at the ANBO website

Effectiveness (task successfully accomplished within the 5 minute time limit)

Most users (87.9%) accomplished the search task within the 5 minutes time limit, although some differences were apparent between user groups. 82.8 % of all older users accomplished the search task successfully versus 93.1% of all younger users. Older people who used the internet daily were more successful than older people who did not: 88.9% versus 72.7%.

Efficiency (time needed to accomplish search task)

On average, users needed 86 seconds to accomplish their search task. Younger users were almost twice as fast as older users, averaging 64 seconds versus 111 seconds. Older users making daily use of the internet were faster than those who did not, averaging 99 versus 135 seconds.

Use of the Search Box

The heatmaps that are presented in the next subsection will show us that the majority of users did not make use of the search box during the search task. The following data confirm this result: Only 13.8% in both the older and the younger age group used the search box. This result is not in line with the findings of Houtepen's study, which showed that older people used the search box less frequently than did younger users. A possible explanation is that the search task at the ANBO website in our eye-tracking study was rather easy to perform (see subsection effectiveness), so most users apparently did not need to use the search box. Older people making daily use of the internet used the search box in 22.2 % of the cases; of the group who did not use the internet daily, not a single person made use of the search box.

Navigation Areas

The patterns of fixations of older and younger users seem to be different. Most of the younger users looked at the right place where they were supposed to click (the upper part of the green column) in order to arrive at the web page containing the information they were looking for, but more older users than younger ones looked longer at the wrong place to click: the pink column. This is shown by the red zone appearing in that navigation area on heatmap Plate 1 (see Plates), which is absent on heatmap Plate 2 (see Plates). So, at first sight the patterns of fixations of older people compared to those of younger people seem to be different. However, if we compare the patterns of fixations of older people *using the internet daily* (heatmap Plate 3, see Plates) with those of the younger age group (heatmap Plate 2, see Plates), these patterns are in fact not as dissimilar as first thought. Like the younger users, the older people using the internet daily looked less intensily (no red zones in this navigation area) in the pink column, in contrast to the patterns of fixations of the older people *not using the internet daily* where a clear red zone is visible in that column (heatmap Plate 4, see Plates). In other words, the frequency of internet use impacts more heavily on our patterns of fixations than does age.

Results Search Task Performed at the Univé website

Effectiveness (task successfully accomplished within 5 minutes time limit)

Most users (89.7%) accomplished the search task within the 5 minute time limit, although some differences were apparent between user groups. 79.3 % of the older users accomplished the search task successfully versus 100% of the younger users. There appeared to be almost no difference between older people who used the internet daily and older people who did not.

Efficiency (time needed to accomplish search task)

On the average, users needed 91 seconds to accomplish their search task. Younger users were faster than older users, averaging 81 seconds versus 104 seconds. Older users who made daily use of the internet were faster than those who did not, averaging 98 versus 113 seconds.

Use of the Search Box

The heatmaps presented in the next subsection will show us that many users made use of the search box (at the right top of the red navigation bar) and the other parts of the navigation bar during the search task. The following data confirm this result: 67.2% of all participants used the search box. The percentage of younger users making use of the search box is higher than that of the older users: 75.9% versus 58.6%. This result confirms the findings of Houtepen's study, which showed that older people used the search box less frequently than the younger people did. In particular, those older people who did not make daily use of the internet daily did not use the search box very often (only 27.3%); 77.8 % of the group who used the internet daily made use of the search box.

Navigation Areas

The patterns of fixations of older and younger users seem to be different (Plates heatmap 5 and 6, see Plates). First of all the large red-yellow-green zones show that older users looked in a more intense way at more navigation areas on the home page than did younger users. This confirms the findings of Tullis' study. Another notable fact is that the older users more often look at and click on *links* that lead to the information they are looking for while the younger users used the *navigation bar* more often. In Plate heatmap 6 (see Plates) of the younger users the large red zones with a small yellow-green part and the red-white clicking demarcations in the navigation bar show this clearly. Older users used the navigation bar less often, which appears clearly in Plate heatmap 5 (see Plates) as the large yellow-green zones and the limited number of red-white clicking demarcations in the red navigation bar. So, at first glance, the patterns of fixations of older people appear to differ from those of younger people. However, if we compare the patterns of fixations of *older people who use the internet daily* with those of the younger age group, these patterns are, in fact, not as dissimilar as first thought. In particular, the use of the navigation bar by older *people using the internet daily* is interesting in this regard: Plate heatmap 7 (see Plates) clearly shows a red zone that is comparable to the one of the younger age group in Plate heatmap 6 (see Plates). This red zone is absent in heatmap 8 (see Plates) which shows the patterns of fixation of the older people *not using the internet daily.* Hence, as regards the use of the navigation bar on this website, the frequency of internet use impacts more heavily on our patterns of fixations than does age.

Evaluation: Navigation Behaviour and the (Ir)relevance of Age

On the one hand our eye-tracking study confirms the conclusions from previous studies noted earlier: older people tend to take more time looking at the content of the website page. This was true for the search tasks on both websites. It appeared that older people, compared to younger people, looked longer at the navigation area and at the ANBO home page they directed their focus more often at the wrong area. They were also slightly less successful than their younger counterparts.

On the other hand, these generational differences became smaller when the older user was more experienced i.e. used the internet more frequently. This result was also found by the eye-tracking study carried out by Hill et al. (2011: 1159) among 12 novice older computer users and 6 more experienced[21] older computer users (2011:

> In conclusion, on three web-viewing tasks, marginally experienced older adults displayed eye-movement behaviors consistent with "typical" behaviors, as measured by mean fixation durations. By contrast, less experienced users of similar ages displayed eye-movement behaviors that have generally be regarded as characteristics of older people. This study suggests that behaviors previously identified as characteristics of ageing might be related instead to other factors, such as experience, and challenges assumptions about the effects of age as opposed to other aspects that divide the older age group. Age and personal experience remain highly correlated properties, which questions the merit of any over-simplified approach to improving the user experience of the older demographic.

So, the heatmaps from the ANBO and Univé homepages clearly confirm that age is only to a certain extent responsible for the navigation behaviour of younger and older generations. Internet experience also plays a role. We agree with Kronjee et al. (2003: 4) who are critical about the use of age as the ultimate explanatory variable in much social scientific research:

> Not only is it open to question whether age is the most appropriate variable for the topics that these researcher wish to investigate, it is also questionable whether the reported differences actually yield the insight claimed. Even if age should be an explanatory variable, simply reporting differences according to age is not enough. After analysing the effect in age differences, they should examine which theory should best be used to interpret the age effect. (translation)

Our eye-tracking study carried out shows that in the case of patterns of fixations for search tasks on websites, age is not the explanatory variable for navigation behaviour. The frequency of internet use plays a more important role.

Interesting results were also found as regards the use of the search box. On the ANBO website the search box was seldom used, whilst on the Univé website the search box was used by a majority of the participants. There was no generational difference when we look at how often the search box was used for the search

21 12 novice older computer users (mean age 77, range 71–93) and 6 more experienced older computer users (mean age 78.5; range 70–90). The experience was related to the use of Email, word processing or the access of the internet (Hill et al., 2011: 1154).

task at the ANBO website. At the Univé website the percentage of younger users making use of the search box was clearly higher than that of the older users, which result confirms the findings of Houtepen's study. It appeared that for both websites that the frequency of internet use also played a role: Those who used the internet frequently also used of the search box more often.

So, although differences in navigation behaviour related to a health information search task are to some extent age-related, differences are also seen within the group of older people, a good example of 'intra-age variability' (Dannefer, 1988; see also Chapter 6 by Chisnell and Redish and Chapter 7 by Schreder et al. in this volume) due to frequency of internet use. Older people are often more diverse than younger persons. Bouma (2000: 68), for example, explains that:

> Education and job specialization have been rising all through the 20th century, and the new generations of older citizens have learned to be both assertive and active. It is certain that they will be a heterogeneous group, since cumulative life experiences vary so much more than among young adults.

In this eye-tracking study, the black-and-white distinction between Prensky's 'digital natives' and 'digital immigrants' was absent.[22] Instead, what emerged was far more a digital spectrum rather than a digital divide (Lenhart and Horrigan, 2003). This means that in this case socialisation theory, which states that people are formed by the period in which they grow up (as socio-economic and political circumstances and the technology available during their formative years shape their behaviour), does not apply to all senior citizens. The main differences are visible *within* this group, which could be considered as a 'technology generation' regarding the degree to which each is able to master a new medium. So, we agree with Hill et al. (2011: 1157) that 'inexperience is likely to be an important factor, possibly as important as age itself'.

Implications for Designers

If future empirical research confirms our findings, the implication for website designers (who often belong to a younger generation – see also Chapter 6 by Chisnell and Redish) might be that they should take into account diversity between and *within generations* by 'designing for dynamic diversity' (Gregor et al., 2002), '(…) the premise of which is that older people are much more diverse in terms of life experience and levels of capability and disability than their younger counterparts (…)' (Chisnell and Redish, 2004: 48).

22 See also Schulmeister (2008) and Bennett et al. (2010) for a critical review of Prensky's rigid division and his lack of empirical evidence to support this.

In particular, older users who use the internet less frequently and have a broader reading pattern on websites[23], and the very old who are confronted with age-related limitations owing to declining visual, hearing, cognitive and motor functions[24], so called 'age-restricted users'[25], have to receive more attention. Bouma (2000: 71–72), for example, comments that age-related functional limitations occur with a certain regularity from the age of 75 onwards, and are common from the age of 85 and over. So, as people grow older, there is no escaping the fact that age can start to play a certain role regarding the accessibility of the digital information, and that it then may be regarded as an explanatory variable. 'Age-restricted users' are at considerable risk from age-related functional limitations, making it difficult and more time-consuming for them to search information on websites.[26] Wright (2000: 86) notes that in such a case, 'multi-modal redundancy', for example, using both visual and auditory signs, could help. Zajicek and Morissey (2003), referring to 'multimodality', also advocate the use of text and sound. Moreover, White et al. (2001) discuss special software that facilitates the access of groups with age-related functional limitations to our information society.

Researchers and designers working on new 'interface architecture' would be wise to make a note of such insights where older people are concerned.[27] The fear that this might irritate younger and more experienced users is unfounded. A study carried out by Johnson and Kent (2007) showed that, rather than having an adverse effect on a site's user friendliness, it tended to enhance it for all users (see also Chapter 6 by Chisnell and Redish in this volume).

References

Arch, A. (2008), *Web Accessibility for Older Users: A Literature Review.* W3C working draft 14 May 2008. Available at: <http://www.w3.org/TR/wai-age-literature>.

Baltes, P.B. (1979), 'Life-span developmental psychology: Some converging observations on history and theory', in Baltes, P.B. and Brim jr., O.G. (eds), *Life-Span Development and Behaviour*, Vol. II. (New York: Academic Press).

23 See also Houtepen (2009) and Tullis (2009: 1030, 1038).

24 See also Bouma (2000), Czaja and Lee (2009) and Loos and Mante-Meijer (2009a: 38–39) for an overview of the studies on age-related functional limitations in these areas.

25 Hawthorn (2003) referred to by Chisnell and Redish (2004: 50). See also Hanson (2001) on age-related disabilities and the Web.

26 Economists refer in this connection to 'obsolescence'. Also see Thijssen (2006: 15–25) and Van Loo (2005).

27 See also Chadwick-Dias et al. (2003).

Becker, H.E. (ed.) (1992a), *Dynamics of Cohort and Generation Research: Proceedings of a Symposium held on 12, 13 and 14 December 1991 at the University of Utrecht, the Netherlands* (Amsterdam: Thesis publishers).

Becker, H.E. (1992b), *Generaties en hun Kansen* (Amsterdam: Meulenhoff).

Becker, H.E. and Hermkens, P.L.J. (eds) (1993), *Solidarity of Generations: Demographic, Economic and Social Change and its Consequences* Vol. II. (Amsterdam: Thesis publishers).

Becker, S.A. (2004), 'A study of web usability for older adults seeking online health resources, ACM Transactions on Computer-Human Interaction (TOCHI), 11 (4), 387–406. Available at: <http://doi.acm.org.ezproxy.auckland.ac.nz/10.1145/1035575.1035578>.

Bennett, S., Maton, K., and Kervin, L. (2008), 'The 'digital natives' debate: A critical review of the evidence', *British Journal of Educational Technology*, 39 (5), 775–786.

Bouma, H. (2000), 'Document and interface design for older citizens', in Westendorp, P., Jansen, C. and Punselie, R. (eds), *Interface Design & Document Design* (Amsterdam: Rodopi).

Bovens, M.A.P. (2002), Information rights. Citizenship in the information society, *The Journal of Political Philosophy*, 10, 317–341.

Capozzo, D., Groezinger, R.L., Ng, K.-F.F. and Siegel, M.J. (2008), *Appeal of Web Page Layout and Characteristics based on Age: Usability Research through Eye-tracking at Fidelity Investments Inc.* (Worcester USA: Worcester Polytechnic Institute).

Chadwick-Dias, A., McNulty, M., Tullis, T.S. (2003), 'Web usability and age: How design changes can improve performance', CUU'03, November 10–11, 2003, Vancover, British Columbia, Canada. Available at: <http://www.bentley.edu/events/agingbydesign 2004/presentations/tedesco_chadwickdias_tullis_webusabilityandage.pdf>

Chisnell, D. and Redish, J. (2004), *Designing Websites for Older Adults: A Review of recent research.* AARP. Available at: <http://www.aarp.org/ olderwiserwired>.

Chisnell, D. and Redish, J.C. (2005), 'Designing web sites for older adults: Expert review of usability for older adults at 50 web Sites', report to AARP, February 2005. Available at: <http://www.aarp.org/olderwiserwired>.

Coombs, T.T. (2008), 'Internet use across the life-span', in Donsbach, W. (ed.), *The International Encyclopedia of Communication* (Malden, MA: Blackwell).

Czaja, S.J. and Lee, C. (2003), 'Designing computer systems for older adults', in Jacko, J.A. and Sears, A. (eds), *The Human-Computer Interaction Handbook: Fundamentals, Evolving Technologies and Emerging Applications* (Mahwah, NJ: Lawrence Erlbaum).

Dannefer, D. (1988), 'What's in a name? An account of the neglect of variability in the study of aging', in Birren, J.E. and Bengtson, V.L. (eds), *Emergent Theories of Aging* (New York: Springer).

Djamasbi, S., Siegel, M. and Tullis, T. (2010), 'Generation Y, web design, and eye tracking', *Journal of Human-Computer Studies*, 68, 306–323.

Docampo Rama, M., Ridder, H. and Bouma, H. (2001), 'Technology generation and age in using layered user interfaces', *Gerontechjournal*, September 2001, 1 (1), 25–39.

Duimel, M. (2007), *Verbinding maken: Senioren en Internet* (The Hague: Sociaal en Cultureel Planbureau).

Fukada, R. and Bubb, H. (2003), 'Eye tracking study on Web-use: Comparison between younger and elderly users in case of search task with electronic timetable service', *PsychNology Journal*, 1 (3), 202–228.

Goldberg, J.H. and Wichansky, A.M. (2003), 'Eye tracking in usability evaluation: A practitioner's guide, in Hyönä, J. Radach, R. and H. Deubel, H. (eds), *The Mind's Eye: Cognitive and Applied Aspects of Eye Movement Research* (Amsterdam: Elsevier).

Gregor, P., Newell, A.F. and Zajicek, M. (2002), 'Designing for dynamic diversity: Interfaces for older people', *ASSETS* 2002, 151–156.

Hagberg, J.-E. (2004), 'Old people, new and old artefacts: Technology for later life', in Öberg, B.-M., Närvänen, A.-L., Näsman, E. and Olson, E. (eds), *Changing Worlds and the Ageing Subject: Dimensions in the Study of Ageing and Later Life* (Aldershot: Ashgate).

Hanson, V.L. (2001), 'Web access for elderly citizens', *WUAUC'*01, May 22–25, 2001. Alcácer do Sal, Portugal.

Hawthorn, D. (2003), 'How Universal is good design for older users?', conference paper, ACM SIGCAPH Computers and the Physically Handicapped, Proceedings of the 2003 Conference on Universal Usability Issue, 73–74.

Hill, R., Dickinson, A., Arnott, J., Gregor, P. and McIver, L. (2011), 'Older users' eye movements: Experience counts', *CHI 2011*, May 7–12, Vancouver, BC, Canada.

Houtepen, L. (2007), *Op zoek naar Informatie. Onderzoek naar het vinden en beoordelen van informatie op de websites van de vijf grootste zorgverzekeraars* [Unpublished Master thesis] (Utrecht: Utrecht University / Utrecht School of Governance).

Hoven, M.J. van den (1994), 'Towards ethical principles for designing politico-administrative information systems', *Informatization and the Public Sector*, 3 (3/4), 353–373.

Huysmans, F., Haan, J. de and Broek, A. van den (2004), *Achter de schermen: Een kwart eeuw lezen, luisteren, kijken en internetten* (The Hague: Sociaal en Cultureel Planbureau).

Johnson, R. and Kent, S. (2007), 'Designing universal access: web application for the elderly and disabled', *Cognition, Technology and Work*, 9, 209–218.

Josephson, S. and Holmes, M.E. (2004), 'Age differences in visual search for information on web pages', *Eye Tracking Research & Application: Proceedings of the 2004 Symposium on Eye tracking research and applications* (San Antonio Tx).

Kronjee, G. (2003) 'Voorwoord', in Wagemakers, A. and Quispel, Y., *Verkenning van het gebruik van leeftijd in onderzoek* (Utrecht: Landelijk Bureau Leeftijdsdiscriminatie).

Lange, F. de (2007), *De mythe van het voltooide leven: Over de oude dag van morgen* (Zoetermeer: Meinema).

Lawton, M.P. (1998), 'Future society and technology', in Graafmans, J., V. Taipale, V. and Charness, N. (eds), *Gerontology: A Sustainable Investment in the Future* (Amsterdam: IOS Press).

Lenhart, A. and Horrigan, J.B. (2003), 'Re-visualizing the digital divide as a digital spectrum', *IT & Society*, 5, 23–39.

Loo, J. van (2005), *Training, Labor Market Outcomes, and Self-management* (Maastricht: ROA).

Loos, E.F. (2010), *De oudere: een digitale immigrant in eigen land?Een terreinverkenning naar toegankelijke informatievoorziening* [Senior citizens: Digital immigrants in their own country? An exploration of accessible information delivery]. [Inaugural lecture] (The Hague: Boom/Lemma).

Loos, E.F. (2011a), 'Generational use of new media and the (ir)relevance of age', in Colombo, F. and Fortunati, L. (eds), *Broadband Society and Generational Changes* (Frankfurt am Main etc.: Peter Lang).

Loos, E.F. (2011b), 'In search of information on websites: A question of age?', in Stephanidis, C. (ed.), *Universal Access in Human-Computer Interaction. Users Diversity,* HCI International 2011, LNCS 6766 (Berlin, Heidelberg, New York: Springer).

Loos, E.F. and Mante-Meijer, E.A. (2009a), 'Getting access to website health information: Does age really matter?', research paper presented at the conference Digital Media Technologies Revisited, University of the Arts, Berlin, 20–21 november 2009.

Loos, E.F. and Mante-Meijer, E.A. (2009b), *Navigatie van ouderen en jongeren in beeld: Explorerend onderzoek naar de rol van leeftijd voor het informatiezoekgedrag van website-gebruikers [Navigation of older and younger people: Explorative study into the role of age on website users' information search behaviour]* (The Hague: Lemma).

Mannheim, K. (1928/1929), 'Das Problem der Generationen', *Kölner Vierteljahreshefte für Soziologie*, 7 (1928), 157–185 and (1929), 309–330.

Mares, M.L. and Woodard, E. (2006) 'In search of the older audience: Adult differences in television viewing', *Journal of Broadcasting & Electronic Media*, 50, 595–614.

McElhal, M. (2007), Eye-tracking: Eye candy vs I can do. Available at: <http://www.webcredible.co.uk/user-friendly-resources/web-usability/eye-tracking> (accessed 20.07.2011).

Morrell, R.W. (2002), *Older Adults, Health Information, and the World Wide Web* (Mahwah, NJ: Lawrence Erlbaum).

Peiser, W. (1999). 'The television generation's relation to the mass media in Germany: Accounting for the impact of private television', *Journal of Broadcasting & Electronic Media*, 43, 364–385.

Pernice, K. and Nielsen, J. (2002), *Web Usability for Senior Citizens. Design Guidelines Based on Usability Studies with People Age 65 and Older* (Fremont: Nielsen Norman Group).

Prensky, M. (2001), 'Digital natives, digital immigrants', *On the Horizon*, 9 (5), 1–6.

Rawls, J. (1971), *A Theory of Justice* (Cambridge, Massachusetts, London: Belknap Press of Harvard University Press).

Rawls, J. (1993), *Political Liberalism* (New York: Columbian University Press).

Riley, M.W. and Riley, J.W. (1994), 'Structural lag: past and future', in Riley, M.W., Kahn, R.L. and Foner, A. (eds), *Age and Structural Lag* (New York: Wiley-Interscience).

Romano, J.C. (2010), 'Using eye-tracking to examine age-related differences in web site performance', *Proceedings of the Human Factors and Ergonomics Society 54th Annual Meeting*, 1360–1364.

Ryder, N.B. (1965), 'The cohort as a concept in the study of social change', *American Sociological Review*, 30, 843–861.

Sackmann, R. and Weymann, A. (1994), *Die Technisierung des Alltags. Generationen und Technische Innovationen* (Frankfurt: Campus Verlag).

Schnabel, P. (1999), 'Individualisering in wisselend perspectief', in Schnabel, P: (ed.), *Individualisering en sociale integratie* (Nijmegen: Sun).

Schulmeister, R. (2008), *Gibt es eine »Net Generation«?* Work in Progress. Hamburg, (Universität Hamburg: Zentrum für Hochschul- und Weiterbildung). Available at: <http://www.zhw.uni-hamburg.de/uploads/schulmeister-net-generation_v2.pdf> (accessed 20.07.2011).

Thijssen, J.G.L. (2006), *De tweede loopbaanhelft. Ontwikkelen en perspectieven in een vergrijzende samenleving.* Rede in verkorte vorm uitgesproken bij het afscheid als gewoon hoogleraar Strategisch Human Resource Management aan de Universiteit Utrecht, departement Bestuurs- en Organisatiewetenschap, op donderdag 16 november 2006 (Utrecht: Utrecht University / Utrecht School of Governance).

Tullis, T.S. (2007), 'Older adults and the Web: Lessons learned from eye-tracking', in Stephanidis, C. (ed.), *Universal Access in Human-Computer Interaction. Coping with diversity*, HCI, LNCS 4554, (Berlin, Heidelberg, New York: Springer).

Van Deursen, A.J.A.M. (2010), *Internet Skills: Vital Assets in an Information Society* [Dissertation] (Enschede: University of Twente).

Wellman, B., Boase, J. and Chen, W. (2002), 'The network nature of community: Online and offline', *IT & Society*, 1 (1), September 2002, 151–165.

Wellman, B., Quan-Haase, A., Boase, J., Chen, W., Hampton, K., Isla de Diaz, I. and Miyata, K. (2003),'The social affordances of the internet for networked individualism', *JCMC*, 8 (3), April 2003.

Weymann, A. and Sackmann, R. (1998), 'Technikgenerationen', *Literatur- und Forschungsreport Weiterbildung*, 42, 23–35.

White, K., Jerrams-Smith, J and Heathcote, D. (2001), 'Improving access for elderly and severely disabled persons: a hybrid adaptive and generic interface', in Stephanidis, C. (ed.), *Universal Access in HCI: Towards an Information Society for All,* Vol. III, 1025–1028 (Mahwah, NJ: Lawrence Erlbaum).

Wichansky, A.M. (2000), 'Usability testing in 2000 and beyond', *Ergonomics*, 43 (7), 998–1006.

Wright, P. (2000), 'Supportive documentation for older people', in Westendorp, P., Jansen, C. and Punselie, R. (eds), *Interface Design & Document Design* (Amsterdam: Rodopi).

Zajicek, M. and Morissey, W. (2003), 'Multimodality and interactional differences in older adults', in Carbonell, N. (ed.), *Multimodality: A Step Towards Universal Access. Special Issue of Universal Access in the Information Society*, 2 (2), 125–133.

Zaphiris, P. and Savitch, N. (2008), 'Age-related differences in browsing the Web', SPARC Workshop on "Promoting Independence through New Technology", Reading, New England.

Conclusion

Eugène Loos, Leslie Haddon and Enid Mante-Meijer

In *Generational Use of New Media* we presented the everyday new media practices of the younger and older generations inhabiting our multimedia landscape. They are all increasingly being confronted with new digital roadways intended to lead them to information about products and services that are relevant for them. One key question addressed in this volume is how we can help to guarantee the digital world is presented through new media in such a way that this remains accessible to and usable by these generations. But this has also required us consider more broadly and critically how both younger and older users engage with this new technological landscape. This has meant questioning some of the stereotypes about both an autonomous younger internet generation and technologically incapable older one, appreciating some of the social considerations as well as design ones that have a bearing upon the way that they interact with this multimedia landscape.

As we mentioned in the introduction of this volume, generations are only too often regarded as being homogenous entities. So, in *Generational Use of New Media* we also questioned the assumption that younger people are all capable of using new media without any problem and that older people are all 'non-liners' (Duimel, 2007)[1] who are therefore cut off from the positive societal effects of new media use. We presented studies that provided insight into to the differences and the similarities between younger and older people using new media, such as websites, in their *everyday life*[2]. And as individual differences increase as people age ('aged heterogeneity' – Dannefer, 1988: 360)[3] we also paid attention to the various sub-populations by presenting studies focusing on different groups of senior citizens.

In other words can we conclude that the multimedia landscape in which the younger and older generations live is characterised rather by a digital spectrum (Lenhart and Horrigan, 2003) than by a digital divide separating digital natives and digital immigrants (Prensky, 2001). To provide insight into the ways in which younger and older generations access and use digital information this three part volume presented the results of research projects from different countries.

1 See also Table I.1 in the introduction of this volume.

2 See also Schutz and Luckman (1983), De Certeau et al. (1984), Highmore (2002), Bakardjieva (2005), Haddon et al. (2005), Sheringham (2006) and Hartman (2008) for a discussion of the relevance of this notion.

3 See also Chapters 6, 7 and 10.

In part I we presented studies conducted in the EU and Hong Kong to gain insight into the ways that younger people look at and use new media and what this means for the relationships between parents and children (the first three chapters) and students' information literacy (chapter 4).

Haddon's chapter 'Parental Mediation of Internet Use: Evaluating Family Relationships' used EU Kids Online's survey data and concluded:

> The questions developed in this survey may not have been developed specifically to measure parent-child relations per se, but when combing different data, measuring a variety of dimensions, it is possible to build up some picture of those family relationships, at least a regards parental mediation of ICTs. Generally relationships appear to be positive, the interventions are regarded as helpful, they are often heeded (at least far more than would be anticipated in some accounts of rebellious teenagers) and appreciated.

In 'Teenagers, the Internet and Morality' – this volume's second chapter – Bauwens who used and triangulated a multitude of data from the Belgian research project 'Teens and ICT: Risks and Opportunities' (TIRO) came to the following conclusion:

> When it came to moral literacy, and especially when confronted with ethical questions that sharply impinged upon their personal identity, young people turned to lessons learned from adults in composing a toolkit for dealing with the social and cultural meaning of the internet, even if they imagined themselves among peers.

Then, in Chapter 3, entitled 'Family Dynamics and Mediation: Children, Autonomy and Control' Cardoso, Espanha and Lapa paid attention to the parental-child relationship in Portugal. They draw on data from a nationwide face-to-face survey and an online survey which indicate a diversification of parental control on various fronts: from the TV to the mobile phone and from computer games to the internet. Their main conclusion was:

> The family in the early 21st century is undergoing a process of reconfiguration and negotiated democratisation between parents and children. (…) The question that remains is whether the family as an institution will adopt these characteristics or fight against them because they erode traditional patriarchal power. Our analysis suggests that, in families where we find a shared appropriation of networked communication, we will witness less conflict and also a more balanced management of autonomy between parents and children. Looked at the other way, in households where mass communication prevails as the communicational model shared by parents and networked communication as the one shared by children, we will witness more conflict and fewer medium used in the shared construction of autonomy.

We ended the first part with the contribution 'Digital Natives: Discourses of Exclusion in an Inclusive Society' by Herold who focused not on children in families like the authors in the first three chapters but on the information literacy of students in Hong Kong belonging to the 'digital generation'[4]. He suggested that their attitudes and skill levels ill-equip them for everyday life in our information society – they are not real digital natives:

> The lack of skills and their inability and unwillingness to acquire necessary skills is masked by an increased use of ever more powerful, but also ever more easy to use, tools that allow students to produce superficially acceptable results with a minimum of effort or expertise. (…) Ironically, both sides in the debates around the abilities of the 'digital generation' are less concerned with the creation or emergence of an 'inclusive' society, and focus more on discourses of 'exclusivity'. While the advocates of the high levels of technical skills among the 'digital generation' emphasise the exclusion of older people from crucial new developments in society, critics of the notion – me included – talk more about the (self)exclusion of young people from an increasingly digital society through their lack of knowledge and skills.

In this quotation Herold refers critically to the attention paid to the exclusion of older people and their lack of technical skills (see also chapter 9 by Van Deursen).

In the second part of our volume we presented studies from Sweden, the USA and Austria focusing on the way(s) in which new media can offer barrier free information to older people, bringing an inclusive society within reach. Here the focus is on the barriers that older people experience when they want to be active inhabitants of the multimedia landscape. The studies discussed how possibilities can be employed to use new media to facilitate their inclusion and to enhance their 'self-efficacy'.

In Chapter 5 'Being the Oldest Old in a Shifting Technology Landscape' Hagberg discussed how older people in Sweden age differently depending on the technological nature of the areas in which they live. Using data of qualitative interviews in a city and a rural community he argues that in dynamic areas where there are many early adopters of new technology or services older people can be included, but in stagnating areas where the infrastructure tends to be eroded they are excluded. He also discusses two moral questions:

> The first moral question is whether the oldest old should have the right to be outside, to keep their habits and routines, and not have to learn new practices. And if so, how should the individual's independence be upheld? The second moral question is how the oldest old who want, but are unable to use, new technology, can be supported. I would argue that an individual who has lived a long life and

4 See also Table I.1 in the introduction of this volume for this and other labels applied to the younger people using new media.

> gone through all the phases of the life course but the very last, has a special right to have access to technology that is crucial for her participation, independence and mobility in society. Obviously ICTs and how that conglomerate of agencies and applications will develop are of critical importance.

He concluded:

> Many that debate the problems of the coming ageing society tone down the ways in which old people are excluded from new technology in the belief that the exclusion is a consequence of the generation to which they belong. The next generation of old people, one supposes, will see things differently. In one regard, this is right. Many more in the coming generations will use ICTs in the form we know it today. However, the digital divide will then run through other parts of the technology landscape. Other systems will be spreading, from which old people at that time will be estranged.[5] The ageing turn, which is inscribed in the biological and social logic of ageing and in the understanding of that life will soon be over, will also be a reality for the coming oldest old. The Janus face of technology is that it takes and it gives. It creates the new and destroys and undermines the old. It redistributes between generations. It can enforce the antagonism between young and old. It can be a part of the discrimination against old people. It can bridge age differences and abolish the consequences of age. One face of the God Janus looks in the direction of the future. His other face looks back, into the past.

Chisnell and Redish presented in Chapter 6 'Modelling Older Adults for Website Design' factors that are facilitating access to and use of websites. Based on their own empirical research in the USA they also pleaded for the adoption of a specific perspective that would take into account older adults when designing websites:

> Just thinking about old age as a collection of disabilities is old business. The new world of designing for older adults is about creating websites and other technology that are useful and desirable as well as accessible to the broadest range of users. Older adults are a large and growing market, increasingly online, increasingly using social media, and with money to spend. You can design with older adults in mind and still meet the needs of younger people – in fact, helping older adults makes products better for younger people, too.

We ended the second part of the volume with chapter 7 'The Ticket Machine Challenge: Social Inclusion by Barrier-free Ticket Vending Machines'. The results of their own empirical research in Austria and comparable studies in other countries helped Schreder, Siebenhandl, Mayr and Smuc to understand the importance of self-efficacy for barrier free information for older people:

5 See also the introduction of this volume.

> When developing the new layout, it will be important to ensure that people who are nervous of the ticket machines or are characterised by low technological self-efficacy are given the feeling that they can master the task easily and without the help of others. As initial steps, the choice of options could be better structured and a clearer visual demarcation introduced between higher level menu elements. Another relative easy and intuitive step is to avoid computer terminology and to use everyday language instead (e.g., yes/no instead of ok/cancel).

In the third and final part of *Generational Use of New Media* we contrasted the ways younger and older people use new media by presenting empirical research from Finland and the Netherlands.

Lugano and Peltonen presented in Chapter 8 'Building Intergenerational Bridges between Digital Natives and Digital Immigrants: Attitudes, Motivations and Appreciation for Old and New Media' the results of an empirical research they conducted in one of the Finnish Communication Camps, a highly immersive informal learning experience, organised once a year when campers, of all ages, come together.

> As expected, both digital natives and digital immigrants in Finland have convenient access to information and communication networks. However, service costs have a relatively different impact for the two generations: being economically dependent from their parents, digital natives prefer SMS to phone calls because the former is less expensive. Despite this difference, digital natives and immigrants agree that phone calls and SMS satisfy their everyday communication needs; as far as the internet is concerned, IM is the digital natives' favourite choice, while email is the most popular application among digital immigrants. (…) In conclusion, Communication Camps are complementary to traditional learning settings because they enable the creation of intergenerational bridges. Through dialogue, the differences in perceiving and experiencing communication media will naturally blend and promote digital melting pot (…).

In Chapter 9 'Age and Internet Skills: Rethinking the Obvious' Van Deursen challenged the general assumption concerning internet skills that younger generations are frequent, confident, and unproblematic internet users that can easily keep up with advances in communication technologies and that the older generations are considered problematic and lacking confidence as internet users. Based on the results of Dutch performance tests related to four types of internet skills (operational, formal, information and strategic skills), he concluded:

> Higher age does indeed contribute negatively to the level of the more basic medium-related operational and formal internet skills. The result is that seniors are seriously limited in their basic internet use. They have problems when saving files or when using search engines (e.g., entering keywords in the address bar or typing keywords attached to each other). Furthermore, while websites

> may seem to be easy to navigate to their designers, older users may find them disorientating and confusing. Although young people perform far better as regards these medium-related internet skills, they still show a strikingly low level of information and strategic internet skills (people of all ages have trouble with the formulation of suitable or specific search queries, with selecting relevant search results, or with the evaluation of information). In fact, as age increases, the content-related internet skills actually improve. Unfortunately, increasing age also leads to considerable problems with the operational and formal internet skills that strongly influence the performance on the information and strategic internet skills.

Van Deursen argued that the older users' experience operational and formal internet skill problems could be explained by their use of television, a medium with which they grew up[6]:

If they have no or only little experience with computers and the internet, they might compare the use of these media with watching a television screen. On a television screen, all information is visible in a 'box' that they observe. The use of computers and the internet is fundamentally different: what is seen on the screen can be moved by scroll bars, and only reveals a miniscule part of the whole information presence. If you are so used to watching television, why would you think of moving a window unless someone showed you? Of the operational and formal skills that seniors experience, many can be explained simply by the fact that they have not formally been taught to take certain steps (why move your mouse to appearing menu items, how can you save something from a screen?).

Finally, Chapter 10 'Getting Access to Website Health Information: Does Age Really Matter?' was based on the results of an eye-tracking study focused on the similarities and differences in navigation patterns between younger and older users and conducted in the Netherlands. Loos and Mante-Meijer concluded that age does matter only to a certain degree:

> On the one hand our eye-tracking study confirms the conclusions from the previous studies noted earlier: older people tend to take more time looking at the content of the website page. This was true for the search tasks on both websites. It appeared that older people, compared to younger people, looked longer at the navigation area and at the ANBO home page they directed their focus more often at the wrong area. They were also slightly less successful than their younger counterparts. On the other hand, these generational differences became smaller when the older user was more experienced i.e. used the internet for a longer period.

6 See also 'technology generations': Sackman and Weymann (1994: 41–43), Weymann and Sackman (1998), Chapter 7 by Schreder et al. and Chapter 10 by Loos and Mante-Meijer.

Towards Media Literate Younger and Older Generations

The different chapters of this volume present an overview of the varied population of the multimedia landscape. New media present not only advantages of inclusion but also dangers of exclusion for the everyday life of both younger and older generations.

After having looked back at each chapter specifically, we will finally draw some general conclusions. What can we learn from the studies presented in *Generational Use of New Media*?

Let us first present and discuss the various ways the younger and older generations use new media:

- Despite all the labels for younger people portraying them as experienced users of new media (see Table I.2 in the introduction), there is no empirical evidence that all younger people are able to use these media without any problem in their everyday life. The results of the studies in Chapter 4 by Herold and Chapter 9 by Van Deursen show clearly that it is a myth that younger people are all well-equipped to deal with new media.
- We also need to appreciate children's use of the internet specifically in the social context of family life, and here the first three chapters by Haddon, Bauwens and Cardoso et al. provide us with insights into the dynamics of the parental-child relationship. Rather than seeing young people as a autonomous 'internet generation' operating in a world distinct from and unfamiliar to parents, we find parents actively engaging with children's online experiencing in various ways, and apart from some conflicts and scepticism about adults' concerns, in general most children appreciate that mediation, including drawing upon the moral guidance of their parents.
- As in the case of the young, several authors have drawn attention to the ways in which the social dimensions of being older has a bearing on their relationship to the internet as much as physical capabilities. For example, Chisnell and Redish (Chapter 6) draw attention to their attitudes, Schreder et al. (Chapter 7) to their self-efficacy, while Lugano and Peltonen (Chapter 8) highlighted how their motivations and appreciation of technologies differed from younger users and Hagberg (Chapter 5) puts this into the wider context of how both previous generational experiences and older people's evaluation of their future options can affect their orientations to the internet. All these factors may be as important in understanding their engagement with technologies, or lack of it, as design considerations.
- However, various authors (e.g. Chisnell and Redish (Chapter 6), Schreder et al. (Chapter 7)) have indicated how the physical aging process remains on important consideration when understanding the internet use of older people. Loos and Mante-Meijer (Chapter 10) also argue that 'age-restricted users' are at considerable risk from age-related functional limitations, making it difficult and more time-consuming for them to search for information on websites. In such a case, 'multi-modal redundancy', for

example, using text, images, sound and special software that facilitates the access of groups with age-related functional limitations to our information society could be a solution. That said, sometimes the aging process can be less influential than stereotypes would have us believe.

Loos and Mante-Meijer also found that the navigation behaviour of older people with internet experience is actually more comparable to that of younger people than to the navigation behaviour of older people without internet experience. In other words, frequency of internet use impacts more heavily, in this case on our patterns of eye fixation, than does age.

- Finally, the literature reviews and empirical studies in different countries presented in *Generational Use of New Media* (see Table I.3 in the introduction) show that we should take into account diversity not only between and but also within generations. This could be done by 'designing for dynamic diversity' (see Chisnell and Redish in Chapter 6; Loos and Mante-Meijer in Chapter 10).

Keeping in mind these points can help us to present digital information about services and products through new media in such a way that this remains accessible to and usable by various generations. We can conclude that the multimedia landscape in which these generations live is characterised rather by a digital spectrum (Lenhart and Horrigan, 2003) than by a digital divide separating digital natives and digital immigrants (Prensky, 2001). The concept of media literacy[7], defined by (Livingstone, 2004: 18) as 'the ability to access, analyse, evaluate and create messages across a variety of contexts' could be leading future empirical research in order to get insight into the everyday new media practices of all generations. Proceeding in that way would enable us as a society 'not only to identify but also to facilitate the acquisition of those skills and abilities required by the population at large to use today's information and communication technologies effectively and safely' (ibid).

References

Bakardjieva (2005), Internet Society. The Internet in Everyday Life (London etc.: Sage).

Dannefer, D. (1988), 'What's in a name? An account of the neglect of variability in the study of aging', in Birren, J.E. and Bengtson, V.L. (eds), Emergent Theories of Aging (New York: Springer).

De Certeau, M., Giard, L. and Mayol, P. (1984), The Practice of Everyday Life, Vol. 2 (Minneapolis, MN: University of Minnesota Press).

7 For more information about 'literacy' see also Chapters 2, 3, 4, 7 and 9.

Duimel, M. (ed.) (2007), Verbinding maken: Senioren en internet (The Hague: Sociaal en Cultureel Planbureau).

Haddon, L., Mante, E., Sapio, B. Kommonen, Fortunati, L. and Kant, A. (2005), Everyday Innovators: Researching the Role of Users in Shaping ICTs (Dordrecht: Springer).

Hartman, M. (2008), 'Everyday life: Domesticating the invisible', in Pierson, J., Mante-Meijer, E., Loos, E. and Sapio, B. Innovating for and by Users. (Luxembourg: Office for Official Publications of the European Communities).

Highmore, B. (2002), Everyday Life and Cultural Theory: An Introduction (London, New York: Routledge).

Livingstone, S. (2004), 'What is media literacy?', Intermedia, 32 (3), 18–20.

Lenhart, A. and Horrigan, J.B. (2003), 'Re-visualizing the digital divide as a digital spectrum', IT & Society, 5, 23–39.

Prensky, M. (2001), Digital natives, digital immigrants, On the Horizon, 9 (5), 1–6.

Schutz, A. and Luckman, T. (1973), The Structures of the Life-World (Evanston, IL: North-Western University Press).

Sheringham, M. (2006), Everyday Life: Theories and Practices from Surrealism to the Present (New York, Oxford: Oxford University Press).

Weymann, A. and Sackmann, R. (1998), 'Technikgenerationen', Literatur- und Forschungsreport Weiterbildung, 42, 23–35.

Index